John. P. Mackintosh
on Parliament and social democracy

25

John P. Mackintosh
on
Parliament and
social democracy

Edited and introduced by David Marquand

Longman
London and New York

Longman Group Limited
Longman House
Burnt Mill, Harlow, Essex, UK

*Published in the United States of America
by Longman Inc., New York*

First published 1982

British Library Cataloguing in Publication Data

Mackintosh, John P.
  John P. Mackintosh on parliament and social democracy.
  1. Political science
  I. Title II. Marquand, David
  320 JA66
  ISBN 0-582-29587-4

Library of Congress Cataloguing in Publication Data

Mackintosh, John Pitcairn, 1929–1978
  John P. Mackintosh on Parliament and social
democracy.

  "Bibliography of the writings of John P.
  Mackintosh, by Bernard Crick and Anne
  Daltrop": p.
  Includes index.
  1. Great Britain. Parliament–Addresses,
  essays, lectures. 2. Cabinet system–Great
  Britain–Addresses, essays, lectures.
  3.Socialism–Great Britain–Addresses, essays,
  lectures. I. Marquand, David. II. Title.
  III. Title: On Parliament and social democracy.

Printed in Great Britain at The Pitman Press, Bath

Contents

Contents

Preface

This book is an edited selection of some of John P. Mackintosh's most important and representative writings, other than those specifically concerning Scotland, which appear in a companion volume edited by H. M. Drucker of the University of Edinburgh. Professor Bernard Crick has acted as general editor for both these books in his dual capacity as adviser on Politics books to Longman and as literary adviser to Dr Una Maclean in relation to her late husband's publications and papers. I am grateful to them both for having asked me to undertake this task and must make clear that the opinions expressed in the introduction and the selection are entirely my own.

It should be noted that Henry Drucker's book also contains a chronology of John Mackintosh's life and that his papers have recently been deposited with the National Library of Scotland.

My selection is taken from articles or lectures, except that I have included a long passage from one of his books, *The Government and Politics of Britain* (by kind permission of the publishers, Messrs Hutchinson) in order to give a more complete presentation of his thought.

David Marquand

Introduction

John Pitcairn Mackintosh was born in India on 24 August 1929. He died in Edinburgh on 30 July 1978, of a malignant tumour of the heart. A growth had appeared in one of the chambers of his heart in the summer of 1977, and he had almost died then. But the growth was removed in open-heart surgery, and was at first diagnosed as benign. Later tests showed that it had elements of malignancy in it, but after he had recovered from the operation John seemed in good health, and he threw himself into his work with his usual ebullient energy. In January 1978, an X–ray suggested that another growth had appeared, but a second X–ray shortly afterward contradicted the impression given by the first. John lived at an even more hectic pace than usual for the next five months, and in the early summer he and his wife were planning a holiday. Then he fell ill again. This time the doctors could do nothing; the end came within weeks.

By the time he died, he and I had been friends for twelve years and colleagues for eleven. We had got to know each other soon after the 1966 election, in which we had both been returned to Parliament for the first time. Between then and my resignation from the House of Commons in 1977, we must have spent hundreds of hours in each other's company. We were on the same side in the battles that divided the Labour Party in those years; though we did not always agree about details, our attitudes to the fundamentals of national and party politics were close and became closer as time went on. He influenced me enormously – more than any other colleague and more, I now realize, than I knew at the time. For months after his death, I found myself wondering how he would react to a new development or what reply he would give to a new argument; sometimes I still do. But I mourned more than an intellectual or political mentor. I admired his intelligence, his courage, his integrity, his marvellous lucidity and his astonishing energy and drive. I loved him for his warmth, his openness, his generosity, his

1

wild, irreverent wit, and his unquenchable gaiety and good humour. What follows must be read against this background. This book consists of a selection of John's political essays and speeches. I have tried to choose the examples which best illustrate the development of his thought, particularly in the last few years of his life. In the rest of this introduction I shall try to explain, as fully as I can in the space available, why I think he came to hold the views expressed and where I believe their significance lies. But I am uneasily aware that I lack the detachment which some might consider necessary for such an exercise. I am not exhuming the ideas of a long-dead worthy, known to me only through his writings and actions. I write as a partisan, to some extent as a disciple; and it would be dishonest to pretend otherwise.

Why such a book at all? The answer is two-fold. For some years, John occupied a unique position in British public and academic life. His family had returned from India to Scotland when he was about ten years old. He was educated at Melville College, Edinburgh, and then at Edinburgh University, where he was awarded a first in history. After graduating from Edinburgh he read PPE at Balliol College, Oxford; then spent a further year as a post-graduate student at Princeton. In 1953 he came back to Scotland, as assistant lecturer at Glasgow University; in 1954, he was appointed to a lectureship in history at Edinburgh. He spent the next ten years as a university teacher – first at Edinburgh, then at Ibadan University in Nigeria, then at Glasgow again and finally at the new University of Strathclyde, where he was appointed to a Chair in Politics in 1965, at the age of thirty six. In 1962, he published *The British Cabinet*, which was quickly recognized as the definitive modern study of the subject and which still holds the field. In 1966, he followed this with *Nigerian Government and Politics*, making use of his experiences in West Africa. Thus by his late thirties, John had established himself as an important figure in his profession, and was well on the way to becoming one of its leading figures.

For him, however, the academic study of politics had always gone hand in hand with their practice. As he explained in the first essay in this book, his interest in politics was 'obsessive'; and the obsession could not be satisfied by contemplation from outside. He adored the gossip and bustle of political life – the endless speculation about who's up and who's down; the drama and tension of a big debate; the sense of being in on great events. He also adored the unpredictability – the sudden switches of focus from one topic to another; the swings of personal and party fortune; the tantalizing knowledge that 'while there's death there's hope'. He even adored – or at any rate flourished remarkably amid – the mundane chores of the prospective candidate or the constituency MP. Above all, he adored the argument. Arguing with him was like trying to dislodge an enthusiastic terrier which had somehow seized hold of one's trouser leg and refused to let go. He was impossible to beat. The most one could hope for was a draw; and he only conceded that when his position was hopelessly untenable. Argument – open, un-inhibited, uncompromising argument – was the element in which he moved. He could no more keep clear of it than he could keep clear of oxygen. His love of argument and his confidence in the power of argument lay at the heart of his political philosophy. They also determined his political style and his commitment to politics as an activity.

As he wrote in 'Forty Years On?' [1.2],* he became a socialist as a schoolboy, and joined the Labour Party as an undergraduate. At Edinburgh, he helped to set up the Labour Club and was one of the heroes of the debating society; his friends expected him to end up as Prime Minister. He reached the first rung of the ladder soon after his return from the United States. In the 1959 election he contested the safe Conservative seat of Edinburgh, Pentlands, losing by almost 9000 votes. When he came back from Nigeria, he was adopted as Labour candidate for Berwick and East Lothian, a sprawling slice of south-east Scotland, stretching from the Border to the outskirts of Edinburgh. This was a better prospect than Edinburgh, Pent-lands: in 1959 the Conservative majority was less than 3000. But it had never been a Labour seat, and the sitting Conservative MP, Sir William Anstruther-Gray, the Deputy Speaker, had a significant personal vote. However, in 1964, John managed to whittle the majority down to 600. In 1966, he was elected by 22,620 votes to 20,931, and gave up the Strathclyde Chair. Apart from an interval of ten months between the general elections of February and October 1974, he represented Berwick and East Lothian for the rest of his life.

He seemed to have a glittering future ahead of him. His maiden speech – a characteristically Mackintoshian bravura, in which he confessed that he had 'always regarded an Hon. Member of this House . . . much as a small boy tends to regard a new model car or a special jet plane', and proceeded to castigate the Chancellor of the

---

* Numerals in square brackets refer to documents at the end of each Part.

Exchequer, James Callaghan, for failing to pay sufficient attention to the needs of the Berwick and East Lothian farmers – was delivered with what seemed to me breathtaking self confidence and panache. Soon afterwards, I noted in a diary, which I kept intermittently in those days, that he was 'probably the ablest person in the new intake and ought (I suspect) to go furthest'. I still think it was a fair assessment. John was easily the most effective debater in the 1966 intake, both in Parliament and on the public platform. He had the quickest and clearest mind, and the most energy and drive. As he showed in his rapid mastery of the technicalities of agriculture – indispensable for the member for a farming constituency – he could grasp the essentials of an unfamiliar subject astonishingly quickly. He would undoubtedly have made a successful reforming minister and might have made a great one. In the right post, he would also have brought much-needed sparkle to the drab and unprepossessing Labour Governments of those years.

It was not to be. If Gaitskell had lived, John's talents would almost certainly have been recognised, probably at an early stage in his parliamentary career. Wilson and Callaghan viewed him with more jaundiced eyes. They knew where they were with left-wing rebels; Wilson, at any rate, probably had a soft spot for them. But John was not a left-winger, though he sometimes sided with the left on particular issues. He was, however, a rebel by nature – instinctively suspicious of authority; incapable of sucking up to people who were more important than he was; forever blurting out unwelcome truths. These traits have never been popular with the solid, unimaginative *apparatchiki*, who normally dominate the whips' offices of the two big parties. They were more than usually unpopular with the Wilson Kitchen Cabinet. From the point of view of the party leadership, he was a maverick: unclassifiable, and therefore suspect. He soon became worse than suspect. The attitudes which had brought him into politics in the first place also gave him a peculiarly demanding view of the nature of political leadership. To him, argument was the lifeblood of democracy. If the true arguments for and against a given course of action were twisted or fudged in public – or, worse, still, brushed under the carpet and left out of the public domain altogether – democracy would be undermined. It followed that the supreme duty of a democratic politician, and, still more, of a democratic leader, was to tell the truth – to explain, openly and unambiguously, what he was doing and why. In the early 1960s, before he came into the House of Commons, John seems to have imagined that Wilson would be a leader of this sort. He was disillusioned within a few months of his election. Wilson's leadership, he came to believe, was in fact cowardly, shabby and corrupting – dangerous to the Labour Party and dangerous to the health of British politics. Being John, he could not keep these opinions to himself. In any case, he did not want to. Having devoted a substantial section of *The British Cabinet* to showing that, in modern conditions, it is impossible to get rid of a Prime Minister who wants to stay, he set about organizing a backbench *putsch* to do precisely that. Not surprisingly, it was a failure. John must have been one of the worst conspirators in parliamentary history. Other plotters managed to reconcile themselves with Wilson; one or two rose quite high. John did not. He remained an open, uncompromising and occasionally savage critic of Wilson's leadership and entourage; and when Wilson retired, he was almost as critical of Callaghan. Both sometimes forgave less wounding critics; neither forgave John. In twelve years in the House of Commons he was given no office of any kind, not even a junior spokesmanship in Opposition.

His party's loss was mankind's gain. John achieved more from the back benches than most people achieve from the front bench. He was one of the handful of backbenchers – one of the only two in his own parliamentary generation – who could fill the Chamber when he rose to speak. He was listened to, not because of what he was, but because of who he was; not because of his position in some formal or informal hierarchy, but because what he said was intrinsically worth hearing and because it was irradiated with emotional energy and conviction. Outside Parliament, he achieved even more. John Mackintosh, the Member of Parliament, could no more abandon the academic study of politics than John Mackintosh, the Professor of Politics, had been able to resist the lure of political action. In his time in the House of Commons he published two more books and a formidable quantity of scholarly articles and contributions to symposia, as well as writing regular columns for *The Times* and *The Scotsman*, travelling widely, lecturing and broadcasting incessantly, chairing the Hansard Society and helping to edit the *Political Quarterly*. As though this were not enough, he was appointed in 1977 to a part-time professorship in politics at Edinburgh University, and the headship of the Politics Department. In his first year there, he wrote and delivered a course of seventy-five lectures in what was for him an almost new field. When the course was over, the students gave him a standing ovation.

This book is the product of his double life as academic and politician. A century ago, even a generation ago, such double lives –

though never common – were, at any rate, comparatively easy to lead. The pioneers of the academic study of politics in this country – Graham Welles, Harold Laski, G. D. H. Cole, the Webbs – were not usually members of Parliament, but they were political activists all the same. They took it for granted that study would atrophy if it were divorced from practice, and they did their best to make sure that the world of ideas and reflection stayed close to the world of action and decision. At the same time, practitioners – Bryce, Masterman, L. S. Amery – made important contributions to political studies. Even in the period immediately after the war, such practitioners as Strachey, Crosland, Crossman and Jay contributed far more to political thought, at any rate on the left, than any academic. In the last twenty years or so, however, this double tradition of the activist academic and the reflective practitioner has begun to peter out. Partly because of the swing of intellectual fashion, and partly because of the growth of the academic profession, academic students of politics are more and more prone to write for each other rather than for the educated, but non–specialist public, and to behave – at any rate in their professional lives – either as detached technicians or as an alienated clerisy, not as citizens sharing in a common venture with all the other members of the society in which they live. Political life has changed as well. Both the great parties have moved towards their respective ideological extremes, but in doing so they have also become more wary of ideas and of those who produce them – particularly, of course, if the ideas concerned are heretical, as worthwhile ideas are bound to be. Meanwhile, the House of Commons has become enormously more demanding in time, energy and, for that matter, sleep; and the load imposed by constituency casework has become far heavier. The old tradition is not quite dead, either in the academy or in Parliament, but its members belong to an endangered species. The first and most obvious reason for reprinting a selection of John's occasional writings on politics is simply that, by the time he died, he had become the most distinguished representative of this tradition.

There is a second reason as well for presenting these essays. John entered the House of Commons with a double commitment: first, to the 'revisionist' social democracy of Hugh Gaitskell and Tony Crosland and, secondly, to a particular view of parliamentary government, above all to a particular view of the House of Commons and of its proper relationship with the executive. As he explained in his autobiographical essay 'Forty Years On?', he had started his political life as a Bevanite, but because he admired Bevan's oratory and drive and shared his suspicion of American foreign policy, not because he was strongly attached to public ownership of the means of production. In Labour's internal battles over public ownership in the late 1950s and early 1960s, he sided, if perhaps a little reluctantly, with Gaitskell. For him as for the other Gaitskellites, public ownership was merely a means to an end, not an end in itself. The end was 'equality'. There is no evidence that John defined that notoriously slippery term at all precisely, and I doubt if he paid much attention to its nuances until a much later period in his life. But although it is not clear what kind of equality he was for, there is not much doubt about the kind of inequality he was against. He was against the Edinburgh of his childhood – the Edinburgh of his essay 'Forty Years On?', where:

Each station of society had its own accent, its own residential areas, and for each section there was an appropriate group of schools. There were the free corporation schools for the working class and two well-known corporation schools which charged small fees and were filled on a highly selective basis by the abler and more ambitious sections of the working class. Then came several grant-aided schools, which had ranges of fees and locations enabling them to cover the spread from lower-middle through middle-middle to the verges of the upper-middle class while the wealthier lawyers, medical consultants and professors sent their children to private and expensive boarding schools in the city. As children we knew exactly where anyone was placed in the social scale; once their accent, address and school were known, they were categorised.

In his last essay, 'Has Social Democracy Failed in Britain?', he wrote of Tony Crosland's revisionism that its 'main objective was to produce a situation where professors and plumbers, bankers and bakers, lived on the same street, could mix freely and unselfconsciously and enjoy the same holidays and sports, and have the same pensions while their children mixed freely in the same schools'. That sounds remarkably like the street in Princeton, New Jersey, he remembered in 'Forty Years On?', 'where the neighbours were plumbers and joiners [and] where playing the superior class trick did not pay off'. Whether or not this was true of Crosland – and some of his writings, at any rate suggest that his version of equality was 'stronger' than John implied – it was certainly true of John. I doubt if he was ever a strong economic egalitarian. He was too much the meritocratic Scot for that. He believed in working hard, worked prodigiously hard himself and saw no reason why hard work should not be rewarded. But he was a passionate social egalitarian, by instinct as well as by conviction. He loathed people who played the 'superior class trick', not only because they offended his moral or philosophical principles, but viscerally, in his guts.

He never pretended to be anything other than a successful member of the professional middle class and had a robust contempt for the growing number of his parliamentary colleagues who did. He enjoyed good food and wine, was much better dressed than most Labour MPs and found Tony Crosland's scruples about wearing evening clothes unnecessary and slightly absurd. But he also enjoyed going to wrestling matches in his constituency and telling bawdy jokes at a farmers' dinner. He hated the smooth, the smug, the self-important and the toadying. He was with the bottom dogs and against the top dogs: with the dissenters and against the Establishment: with the provincial and against the metropolitan. This side of him – the small boy proving himself against the big boys in the playground, the pugnacious Scot determined to beat the southern English smarties at their own game – was sometimes concealed by the assured university professor and public figure, but it was there to the end. Because of it, John was better equipped to see the world through the eyes of those against whom the 'superior class trick' is played than were many with a more obvious public commitment to equality. He went into politics to help create a society in which the trick would be unplayable.

By the time he reached the House of Commons, the revisionist right of the Labour Party thought it knew how to do this. Social expenditure had to be increased. The taxation system had to be made more progressive. Social policy, particularly education policy, had to be made more egalitarian. Above all, the rate of growth had to be raised. John shared these views, and shared the analysis underlying them. In one important respect, however, he was beginning to go beyond revisionism, or at any rate beyond revisionism as articulated by Gaitskell and Crosland. The Fabian tradition in British socialism, to which they both belonged, had never developed a distinctive theory of the state. The early Fabians had taken the existing structure of the British state for granted, and with one or two exceptions their revisionist heirs did the same. Their task, they assumed implicitly, was to win control of the existing structure, and then to use it to change society in accordance with their values. They paid only cursory and intermittent attention to the possibility that the structure might be based on, or permeated with, values opposed to theirs, and that attempts to put their values into practice by working through it might therefore be doomed or even self-contradictory. In *The Future of Socialism* – the Bible of the revision-ist generation – Tony Crosland argued that the power of the 'en-larged and bureaucratic state' and of the 'bureaucratic mass orga-nisation, whether public or private' was now more significant than the kind of economic power which had preoccupied socialists before the war. Later in the book, he suggested that bureaucratic power might buttress, or even promote, inequalities of status. Later still, he warned that the growth of the bureaucratic state might endanger liberty. But he did not examine the political, as opposed to the so-cial, implications of these insights or incorporate them into the rest of his argument. The message of *The Future of Socialism* was that socialists could and should achieve their objectives through redis-tributive taxation and public-expenditure policies, through egalita-rian social policies and through policies designed to improve the quality of life. There was no discussion of the political and adminis-trative machinery through which such policies would have to be im-plemented. The suggestion was that they would be implemented through the existing machinery of Parliament, Cabinet and the Whitehall departments. Yet, in the absence of indications to the contrary, this presumably meant implementing them through pre-cisely the bureaucratic state, whose power, on Crosland's own showing, buttressed status inequality and possibly endangered liberty.

John did not have a theory of the state either. But he did see the need for one; and he was not prepared to take the British state on trust. His research on the Cabinet convinced him that the so-called 'Westminster Model' of parliamentary government no longer work-ed in the way the old-fashioned text books said it worked. Gradual-ly, he also came to feel that its actual working was as serious an affront to the values which had brought him into politics, as the distribution of income or the survival of an antiquated class struc-ture. The picture still painted in many books on British government, he wrote in the final chapter of the first edition of *The British Cabinet*, was:

... based on a simplified version of what did take place in the last third of the nineteenth century. Britain was governed by 'the Cabinet System' and the central institution was Parliament. ...

Now the country is governed by a Prime Minister, his colleagues, junior ministers and civil servants, with the Cabinet acting as a clearing house and court of appeal. Despite the number of and strength of the various pressure groups, governments with a definite will to act and popular backing have a wide field open to them. Governments are restrained not so much by Parliament or by the opposition as by their own desire to keep in step with public opinion and to increase their strength.

That much emerged clearly enough from the evidence presented in the rest of the book; though John's interpretation was attacked by a number of commentators, he saw no reason to modify it. He sounded less confident about the wider, normative implications of his findings. Academic studies of modern British politics, he complained, concentrated on description. These showed that the system had changed fundamentally but there was a 'dearth of work by political theorists which would show how far these changes are desirable'. The 'anti-theories' of T. D. Weldon on the left and Michael Oakshott on the right were equally unhelpful. Weldon blurred the distinction between the state and voluntary associations. Oakshott's theory that men pursued the 'intimations' in their own traditions, provided no criteria for choosing between traditions.

Is the decline of Parliament to be regretted? Most of the proposals for alleviating the decay of the House of Commons are met with the rejoinder: 'Will it work?' By this what is usually meant is: 'Will it work without in any way altering the present dominance of the Executive?' Reports by Select Committees on Procedure or by academic pamphleteers are pointless until the primary question is decided. How much power should the Executive have and how far is it desirable that either the public or a representative chamber should know about or participate in the processes of Government? If there is a strong feeling that participation is necessary, there will be little difficulty in making the appropriate alterations in the standing orders of the House of Commons.

. . . British parliamentary democracy was built up by men who passionately (and, it would appear, wrongly) pursued an ideology which allowed them to emphasise some aspects of their tradition and to reject elements which they found undesirable. Our forms of government continue to change, perhaps not for the worse, but it is a pity that the thinkers and ideologues sit silent while some 'intimations' are allowed to decline in favour of others.[1]

'Perhaps not for the worse'; 'it would appear wrongly'. Genuine hesitation? Defensive camouflage to fend off a counter–attack? Or tongue-in-cheek mock modesty? Whichever they were, they suggest that John was not as sure of the answers to his own questions as the rest of the passage implies. As with equality, however, he knew what he was against even if he was not quite certain what he was for. Even in the absence of a theory to determine the right relationship between Parliament and the executive, he had no doubt that the existing relationship was wrong. Precisely how much Parliament should know about or participate in the processes of Government was a question for the future. What was clear was that it should know and participate far more than it was doing at present.

It should do so for a variety of overlapping reasons, summarised most clearly in the 1968 essay, 'What is wrong with British Parliamentary Democracy?' In the first place, legislation would work better if it were better understood: a stronger Parliament would be able to force Governments to explain what they were doing and why, in a way that existing Governments often failed to do. Secondly, the present system neglected the interests of the consumer and the taxpayer as against the interests of the organized producer groups. The producer groups were consulted in the pre-legislative stage; Parliament, the only possible representative of the consuming and tax-paying general public, was not. Thirdly, the civil service had grown so much in size and activity that it could no longer be supervised effectively by the sixty or seventy ministers in nominal charge of it. The only body available to supplement them was the House of Commons, which had to be equipped with a range of specialist committees empowered to investigate the operation of the Whitehall machine in the public interest. Fourthly, the supply of adequate talent for political leadership would dry up if the status of the House of Commons continued to decline and if men of ability continued to be dissatisfied with the life of a backbencher. Lastly, and most importantly, existing trends were sapping public confidence and undermining the foundations on which the whole democratic system was based.

At the time when British democracy was established, Gladstone had no hesitation about speaking for two hours to assembled villagers on the complexities of the Eastern Question. Now there is a sense, particularly among senior professional men, business executives and officials that it is hard to explain the actual facts of a situation to the public, that government by secrecy and slogans is the best way of proceeding. The opposite side of this coin is the popular belief that there is an inner elite who govern but who do not reveal all the facts. . . .

British Parliamentary democracy is in real danger because it is being ground away by these two pressures.

This double commitment – to revisionist social democracy, on the one hand, and to a more open, more participatory form of government, with a stronger and more independent-minded House of Commons, on the other – was central to John's politics throughout his time as a Member of Parliament. In the battles that divided the parliamentary Labour Party in the late 1960s he was for devaluation and against deflation; for abandoning British bases east of Suez and against the 'world role'; for a statutory incomes policy and against uncontrolled collective bargaining; and for Roy Jenkins's Race Relations Act and against James Callaghan's legislation to keep out the East African Asians. In his last Parliament, he helped to set up the Manifesto Group to stem the drift to the left on the back benches, spoke out for a return to statutory wage controls at a time when it was still heresy to question the social contract, tried to emasculate Michael Foot's proposals to legalize the closed shop in journalism, canvassed with desperate enthusiasm for Roy Jenkins in the Labour Party leadership election, and, together with Brian Walden, sabotaged the so-called Dock Labour Bill with a brilliantly-timed last-minute abstention.

From his entry to the House of Commons onwards, he was also one of the leading advocates of parliamentary reform, above all of an effective committee system. Soon after his election, he was appointed to the Select Committee on Procedure. He quickly became one of its most energetic and influential members, playing major parts in the enquiries which led to the creation of the Expenditure Committee early in 1971 and to the report on the process of legislation in 1971. Behind the scenes, he helped to persuade Richard Crossman during the latter's term of office as Leader of the House, to make the experiment of setting up a select committee to oversee the Ministry of Agriculture – an experiment which was brought to an untimely end not long afterwards because the committee, thanks partly to John's influence, insisted on examining contentious subjects in a way that embarrassed the Government. He returned to these themes again and again in the next ten years. As late as the summer of 1978, only a few weeks before his death, he broadcast a Radio 3 talk, patiently demolishing the parliamentary traditionalists' argument that a powerful committee system would weaken the floor of the House, and praying his agriculture committee experiences in aid. Except in incidentals, the case he argued then was the case he had argued at innumerable Procedure Committee meetings in the 1960s. For that matter, it was the case to which he had pointed implicitly in the concluding pages of *The British Cabinet*.

In one sense it is true to say that the John Mackintosh of 1978 stood where the John Mackintosh of 1966 had stood. He was still a revisionist social democrat, who loathed the British class system and wanted greater social equality. He was still a parliamentary reformer, suspicious of executive power and anxious to subject it to more effective scrutiny and control. But although he still wanted the same things, he was no longer sure that he should go on pursuing them in the same way. When he was elected to Parliament in 1966, revisionist social democracy appeared to be the wave of the future. The social-democratic parties of Scandinavia and Central Europe were firmly revisionist in outlook. In the countries where they were in power, their policies seemed to work; in the countries where they were not in power, their programmes seemed increasingly attractive to the electorate. Even the sluggish, unadventurous, rather anti-intellectual British Labour Party seemed to be taking the revisionist road, in fact, if not in form. Though Harold Wilson had resisted Gaitskell's attempt to take Clause Four out of the Labour Party constitution, he was not a dogmatic nationalizer for nationalization's sake. The platforms on which the Party had won its election victories in 1964 and 1966 had contained nothing to which a conscientious revisionist could object. Their central planks – indicative planning, rapid economic growth and higher social expenditure – had either been advocated in *The Future of Socialism* or were logically deducible from the analysis there set out. By 1966, the Cabinet which was supposed to implement these policies contained the ablest and most prominent representatives of the revisionist generation; even those who had taken the anti-revisionist side in the battles of the 1950s seemed predominantly revisionist in practice.

A decade later, no one could pretend that the hopes of 1966 had been realised. Even the central European and Scandinavian social-democratic parties were not always as solidly revisionist as they had been in the early 1960s. In the British Labour Party, revisionist social democracy was unmistakably on the defensive – as, for that matter, was the equivalent Conservative tendency, once exemplified by Harold Macmillan and Iain Macleod. In the election for the Labour Party leadership in 1976, Michael Foot, the old Bevanite and the chief candidate of the left, led in the first ballot and lost to

Callaghan in the final ballot by only 29 votes. Crosland came nowhere, and Roy Jenkins withdrew after the first ballot. In the mass party outside Parliament, the social democrats had lost battle after battle. The National Executive Committee had been under left-wing control since the early 1970s, as, with occasional remissions, had the Annual Conference. In a number of places, social-democratic Labour MPs were fighting off attacks from far-left factions, of the sort which had already driven Dick Taverne, one of the ablest and most outspoken of John's generation of social democrats, out of the Labour Party and eventually out of the House of Commons. Even in constituencies without organized far-left factions it seemed increasingly difficult to find an audience for the kind of social democracy to which John had been committed for twenty years.

For the social democrats were losing, or perhaps even failing to fight, the battle of ideas as well as the battle for power. Since 1975, at any rate, the Government's policies had been far from left-wing, but they were presented half-heartedly, almost apologetically, in a grey and leaden style that carried little conviction. In any case, they did not spring from a coherent social-democratic philosophy or form part of a coherent social-democratic strategy. Outside the Government, the running was increasingly being made by the somewhat inchoate, but firmly anti-revisionist, neo-Marxism that underlay the left's 'alternative strategy'. More alarmingly still, all this was accompanied by a defensive and inward-looking proletarianism, which made it easy to discredit the social democrats as 'elitists' or class traitors. Most alarmingly of all, revisionism had not produced the results which John had expected of it. Revisionist ministers had been in office for most of the time since 1964, and even their non-revisionist colleagues had mostly followed a revisionist course. Yet Britain did not seem to be significantly less class-divided than she had been fifteen years before, and the distribution of wealth and income was not significantly more egalitarian. As for the rate of growth, on which the whole revisionist case had been based, that was lower than it had been in the bad old days of the 1950s.

Revisionist social democracy moreover, was most obviously on the defensive in the battle over British membership of the European Community; and although John had not shown much interest in the European question when he was first elected, he had soon become one of the most enthusiastic and outspoken pro-marketeers in the Parliamentary Labour Party. He was a pro-marketeer first by instinct, just as he was a revisionist social democrat by instinct. The open-mindedness and sense of adventure which had led him to throw up his job and go to Ibadan in the early 1960s made him an enthusiastic participant in conferences and seminars on the continent, and enabled him to make warm friendships with a number of continental social democrats, particularly in Germany. He was a regular fixture at the annual Anglo-German Conference at Königswinter, and a close friend of the founder, Dame Lilo Milchsack. The German SPD became something of a spiritual home; and the fact that the German Social Democrats had become strong supporters of the Community, in spite of initial hesitations, influenced him a great deal. Besides, he liked the continent. He once suggested to me that the internal Labour Party division over Community membership was really a division between garlic-eaters and garlic-haters. John was emphatically a garlic eater. He saw nothing sacrosanct in British habits or British attitudes. He enjoyed travelling and meeting new people from new backgrounds. He was not only willing, but eager, to learn from continental experience.

Yet it would be wrong to explain his Europeanism in exclusively personal and emotional terms. He was a pro-marketeer by conviction as well. I doubt if the economic arguments for entry moved him much, not because he was sceptical of them, but because at this stage of his career, at any rate, he generally gave politics priority over economics. What persuaded him was the straightforward political argument that Britain, having lost her empire and the world role that went with it, had no worthwhile role at all outside Europe. The special relationship with the United States was not an alternative; still less was the moral leadership of the Third World. The choice lay between membership of the European Community and isolation. To John, the isolationist option seemed morally wrong as well as politically disastrous – not least because of its implications for the world outside Europe. In the 1966 Parliament, Southern Africa bulked at least as large in his political concerns as Europe did, and he was one of the leading members of a back-bench lobby for a tough line against the Smith regime in Rhodesia. But the notion that Britain could play an internationalist role in the Third World while standing aloof from her neighbours across the Channel, that it was possible to advocate world government in the remote and unforeseeable future, while insisting that Britain should not surrender any of her freedom of action to the European Community here and now, seemed to John not only inconsistent, but perverse. Some of his most effective polemics against the anti-marketeers were aimed at this chink in their armour.

In the mid 1960s, when John was first converted to Europeanism, he expected these attitudes to prevail, not only in the country at large, but in the Labour Party as well. He was probably laying it on a bit thick when he told his German audience in 1967 that 'a vast majority of the Labour Party [now] support the European idea'. All the same, he assumed that it would have majority support in the reasonably near future. In 1967, it is worth remembering, there was a good deal of evidence on his side. Harold Wilson's decision to apply for membership of the Common Market was approved by a comfortable majority of the Parliamentary Labour Party; and although there were hesitations in the constituency parties, it was not absurd to hope that vigorous leadership would slowly eradicate them. Indeed, if the Labour Party had won the 1970 election, and had secured entry on roughly the terms obtained by the Conservatives, entry probably would have been approved by most Labour MPs; even if constituency sentiment had been preponderantly against, most constituency activists would almost certainly have reconciled themselves to the fact of membership sooner or later. In the event, of course, the Labour Party lost the election. Then it swung into increasingly violent opposition, ostensibly only to the terms negotiated by the Conservatives, but in reality to membership itself. After 1974, it is true, the party leadership swung back. The rank and file, however, remained hostile and embittered; and, although John had the satisfaction of seeing his cause triumph in the 1975 Referendum, he knew only too well that its supporters were in a minority in his own party, and that the Referendum had made no difference to the attitudes of the majority.

Not only was revisionist social democracy on the defensive: parliamentary government, or at any rate John's conception of parliamentary government, seemed to him to be on the defensive too. On one level, it is true, some of his early hopes had been realized. Thanks partly to his advocacy, support for a strong committee system had become almost an orthodoxy among the younger generation of backbenchers, irrespective of party. Though the Agriculture Committee had perished in infancy, the Expenditure Committee had been set up, and at least some of its sub-committees had been much more troublesome to the executive than the old Estimates Committee had dreamed of being. Party discipline had relaxed as well. Backbenchers seemed more prepared to behave obstreperously in the chamber, and even in the division lobbies, as well as in committee rooms upstairs. But although Parliament had become slightly less subservient to the executive, and slightly more participatory in its internal organization, it had somehow become more drab and pedestrian. There were fewer eccentrics in Parliament, fewer jokes even. As John put it in one of his last book reviews, British politicians had been 'diminished'.

They long for preferment, and are not as colourful or individualistic. They speak on more trivial matters. The ambassadors' gallery is not crammed with representatives of foreign powers awaiting the word from Britain's leaders. Even the sense of humour has gone. Churchill's witticisms about Lady Astor ('I may be drunk but the Hon. Lady is ugly, and tomorrow I will be sober') or about Sir Clive Bossom ('What a name: it is neither one thing nor the other') would not go down well now. Indeed, even unconscious humour is not appreciated, as I recall when I was the only person to laugh when Mrs Thatcher pointed a finger at Jim Callaghan, then Chancellor of the Exchequer, and said: 'No wonder the Hon. Gentleman's policies are all wrong: he needs a woman under him at the Treasury'!

At the same time, Parliament's authority seemed to have waned. Powerful groups were more prone to defy it, and to get what they wanted by doing so. A majority of the Parliamentary Labour Party, John pointed out disgustedly in his essay on the 'Declining Respect For the Law', had voted, both in a party meeting and in the House itself, for the retrospective withdrawal of the proper legal disqualification imposed on the Clay Cross councillors who had refused to implement the 1972 Housing Finance Act. Two successive Governments, one Conservative and the other Labour, had had to abandon attempts to change the law dealing with industrial relations and to impose a statutory incomes policy because of the opposition of powerful producer groups. Partly as cause and partly as consequence, arguments which presupposed Parliament's inability properly to represent the electorate, seemed to be gaining ground, particularly on the left. The Labour Party had demanded a Referendum on entry into the Community, even though the House of Commons had already voted for entry by a majority of more than 100. The subsequent Labour Government actually held a Referendum on the terms it had 'renegotiated' with its Community partners, even though the House of Commons approved those terms by a majority of more than two to one. Pro-European MPs were denounced as 'elitists' because they voted in accordance with their own judgement of the issue, instead of deferring to their constituency parties. Governments were increasingly prone to rely upon, or at least to pay lip service to, the doctrine of the mandate, which implied that laws passed by Parliament were somehow illegitimate unless the substance had previously been approved by the electorate.

Most damagingly of all, the whole notion of democratic leadership was being undermined. John never worked out an explicit theory of leadership, but the concept was nevertheless central to his political philosophy. He told me once that the political leader he most admired was Gladstone. At first, I thought it an odd choice. Gladstone, the earnest, conscience-probing High Churchman, was not, at first sight, a likely model for the uninhibited, reckless John Mackintosh. But I gradually came to realise that there was a strong Gladstonian streak in him after all. He may not have shared Gladstone's religious faith. He did share Gladstone's belief in the capacity of ordinary people to understand complicated arguments if they were honestly put, and to respond to an altruistic appeal outside themselves. He also shared Gladstone's belief that it was the duty of a political leader to put the issues clearly to those whom he was seeking to lead, to say what he thought of the issues himself and to try to win the majority to his view. As he argued in his prescient essay of 1972, 'Anybody still for Democracy?', Gladstone would have thought it:

. . . quite immoral . . . for a politician to go looking for issues, to go constructing programmes. His task was to explain how the government should be conducted and if injustices become apparent, he should explain how they should be remedied. If the electorate agreed, they would support him. If not, there could be no question of altering his views to win votes. Time and the follies (or successes) of his opponents would reveal who was right. And, of course, the electorate could make a wrong decision – after all, had they not once given Disraeli a majority? – but, in the end, truth must triumph.

These assumptions, John believed, lay at the heart of British parliamentary democracy; and the view of politics and political man which they implied was as valid in the late twentieth century as it had been in the late nineteenth. Two corollaries followed. In the first place, democracy was as much a matter of leadership as of majority decision. The majority should prevail, but after the arguments had been put, not before. Leaders like Harold Wilson who did not put the arguments honestly eroded the foundations on which the whole democratic system was based. So, however, did the proponents of direct democracy, who assumed that the majority was always right and left no room for leadership at all. Secondly, leadership was a skill; and should be recognised as such. Here, too, 'Anybody Still for Democracy?' contains the best statement of the case.

The public are right to press politicians and officials to explain their policies. The answer that it is 'too complicated for the electorate to understand' is properly resented, but, on the other hand, it should be appreciated that to press for *accountability* and *open government* is not to suggest that ministers do not face problems as or more difficult than those encountered by, say, the managing directors of multi-national companies . . .

The idea current in certain political circles that an MP who has strong views and retains them when they are unpopular is guilty of 'arrogance . . . elitism . . . and undemocratic behaviour' would have been quite incomprehensible to the originators of the democratic doctrine in England. Democracy was based on the quest for truth by the leaders and the allocation of support by the electorate. After all, the opposite position – attributed to an American local politician who said: 'These are my views, ladies and gentlemen, and if you do not like them, I will change them' – would make parties and elections and debate unnecessary. A country's leaders could simply adapt their views to the results of the latest opinion polls.

As the tone of that last paragraph implies, it seemed to John that these attitudes were, if anything, even more suspect in the Labour Party of the middle and late 1970s than support for British membership of the European Community or an explicit commitment to Gaitskellite revisionism. Even in the 1960s, he had often been in a minority on particular issues – notably on the related issues of Scottish devolution and regional government, which are discussed in the companion volume to this book. But in the 1960s, he had had the exhilarating sense that, on fundamentals, opinion was moving in his direction. In the 1970s, it seemed to be moving further and further away from him – and to be doing so on almost all the questions about which he cared most. Something had gone wrong; and it seemed clear to John that part of the 'something' was that he and his friends had failed to achieve the aims which had seemed so easily achieved ten years before. It was not clear why they had failed; and still less clear what should be done instead. In the last few years of his life, the lion's share of John's intellectual energies was spent on a puzzled, troubled, and sometimes almost anguished search for the answers to these two questions. He died with the search unfinished. The full-scale reassessment of social-democratic political theory to which he was beginning to feel his way, and which he was better qualified to produce than anyone else in British political or academic life, remained unwritten. But he did at least erect some signposts. The second reason for reprinting the essays and speeches collected here is that they help to show why he had come to feel that such a reassessment was needed. In addition to this, they contain some revealing pointers to the kind of reassessment he was beginning to carry out.

****

Where the signposts led is a matter for speculation. John died nine months before Roy Jenkins's call for a realignment of the 'radical centre' and more than two years before Michael Foot's election as leader of the Labour Party. For years before he died he had been at odds, not merely with the Labour left, but with a large part of the Labour right. He was a close friend of David Steel's, and it is clear from some of the newspaper columns published later in this book that he hoped for a realignment of some kind. In the summer of 1977, when he was recovering from his operation, he toyed with the idea of telling his constituency party that he would not stand as a Labour candidate in the next election unless they were prepared explicitly to accept his right to vote against official party policy in the next Parliament. During a long week-end he spent with me a couple of months later, he told me that he expected – and even half-hoped – to lose Berwick and East Lothian at the next election, that he intended to stand for the Scottish Assembly which he still expected to come into existence before long, and that one of the reasons he wanted to belong to such an Assembly was that he could use it as a base from which to promote a realigment of Scottish politics. But no solid conclusions follow. John would have been appalled by the Labour Party's move to the left after the 1979 election, and would have fought hard to stop it. I think it more probable than not that he would have broken away from the party altogether, and that he would have taken the lead in setting up a new social-democratic grouping of some kind. I cannot be sure. All I am sure of is that he would have taken his own decisions in his own way, in his own time, and that they would have been brave decisions, bravely executed.

There is less room for doubt about what the signposts actually said. Inevitably, much of it was negative. John was fighting in a battle for political survival, in which the enemy seemed to be advancing on all sectors. He could not afford to wait until he was sure of his own position; he had to attack the enemy's position before he was forced to yield more ground. Much of what he wrote was the literary equivalent of a rearguard action, designed to discomfit the opposition and to buy time for him and his beleaguered friends to prepare a counter-attack. His speeches on Community membership clearly come into this category. So do his newspaper attacks on the 'populist Right' of Mrs Thatcher and Sir Keith Joseph, and his brutal demolition of the anti-liberal Conservative essays edited by Maurice Cowling. So, too, do his more considered attacks on the political and economic theories of the Labour left. But it is no disgrace for a polemicist to be negative; and John's polemics often drew blood. No one who heard them will easily forget his conference denunciations of the anti-marketeers as little Englanders and xenophobes. As far as I know, the radical, egalitarian case against what he called the 'populist/socialist' view of Labour politics – the view that the Labour Party's function is to support all working-class demands, irrespective of their effect on differentials within the working class – has never been better put than in his essay on the differences between socialism and social democracy. His later essay, 'Is the Labour Party Facing Catastrophe?', pointed with equal effect to the central weakness of the neo-Marxist view that Britain's economic ills spring from the monopoly power of the multi-nationals – the fact that it cannot explain why multinational domination of the British economy produces a poor economic performance whereas multinational domination of foreign economies produces good ones.

For John however, it was not enough to point to the weaknesses of the neo-Marxist left and the Tory-populist right. If social democracy were to recover, social democrats had to admit that they had made mistakes as well. John believed that they had made three mistakes above all. In the first place, they had relied too heavily on a form of social engineering beyond their means, and beyond the means of any democratic government. Crosland, John wrote in his remarkable, posthumously-published essay, 'Has Social Democracy Failed in Britain?', had hoped 'to alter social attitudes by means of economic and institutional changes when it is by no means clear that the latter will bring about the former'. Thus Croslandite revisionists had assumed both that comprehensive education would diminish class differences and that the taxation of inherited wealth would narrow social 'distances'. They had not reckoned with the possibility that, in a comprehensive school system, some comprehensives might confer more prestige than others, nor that, if inherited wealth were taxed out of existence, differences of earned income, which they did not want to abolish, might be as divisive socially as differences of wealth had been in the past. Secondly, they had taken it for granted that the values of liberty and equality would always be compatible. In fact, John argued in the unpublished manuscript 'Liberty and Equality', gains in equality often had to be purchased by losses in liberty. There was a trade-off to be made; and social democrats, who were committed to both, should not assume that one must always take precedence over the other. Thirdly, the revisionists had failed to understand the true implications of their own commitment to economic growth, and had therefore failed to deliver the increased growth they promised.

The last failure was the most serious one, or, at any rate, had the most serious consequences. Neo-Marxism and Tory populism were both the fruits of economic decline. Their adherents generalized from Britain to the rest of the world, but the failures which had given rise to them were, in reality, uniquely British. Had the British economy grown as fast as the German, no one would have paid attention to them. Revisionist social democracy would have been as firmly entrenched in the Labour Party as it was in the SPD; and the Labour Party would have been as firmly entrenched in Westminster as the SPD was in Bonn. Not only would social democracy have flourished: parliamentary government would have flourished too. John did not spell out his view of the connection between Parliament's loss of authority and Britain's economic decline, but it is not difficult to infer what it would have been from the rest of his argument. One of the reasons why Parliament had lost authority was that the great producer groups had successfully defied it. One of the reasons for their defiance was that their members considered themselves entitled to the higher living standards which they had been unable to obtain in any other way. Their success was in part due to the fact that Government's failure to deliver higher living standards had eroded public confidence in it. The more successful their defiance, moreover, the more difficult governments found it to run the economy, and the poorer Britain's economic performance became.

So far, most of the broad band of opinion between the neo-Marxist left and the Tory-populist right would probably have agreed. To John, however, most of the conclusions offered by his fellow occupants of that band seemed unconvincing. What might be called the 'green' conclusion was always anathema to him: the conclusion that low, or even zero, growth might have to be accepted as a fact of life, and that it might be necessary to reduce expectations to fit the economy instead of trying to expand the economy to fit expectations. Indeed, some of our fiercest arguments consisted of my denouncing him as an economic Dr Pangloss because he refused to admit that that conclusion might be valid, even if unpalatable, while he denounced me as a fashionable pessimist, willing to consign the Edinburgh poor to continued poverty because I lacked the perseverance to go on looking for solutions to problems which could be solved if only we had the will to solve them. As he made clear in his *Times* column replying to Lord Hailsham's call for limited government, he was no more attracted by 'overload' theories, which suggested that governments had failed because they had attempted too much and (by implication) that the best way to enjoy a higher rate of growth was to stop trying to achieve it. He had become more and more sceptical about the actions actually undertaken by British governments in the 1960s and 1970s, but he remained an activist by nature. Social ills were inherently curable: though they sometimes had to be cured by society itself rather than by governments, governments had to give the lead to society.

He had more sympathy for the view most persuasively propounded by Professor Finer, and echoed by many centrist commentators in the press, that the rest of the evil lay in Britain's adversarial party system and in the electoral system underpinning it. But that also failed to satisfy him: as he put it in the long essay on 'Britain's Malaise', it was hard to see why a political system which had permitted Britain's industrialisation in the nineteenth century 'should now suddenly have become a disastrous handicap'. On the other hand, the kind of 'interventionism' which had been fashionable in the 1960s and to which most of the centre and right of the Labour Party still clung in default of anything better, seemed to him to be based on a fallacy. It assumed that the problem lay in a shortage of funds for investment. The real problem was that there were too few projects in which to invest, and too few industrialists who wanted to do any investing.

What was left? Part of the answer was institutional. Government had repeatedly been defeated by the great producer groups because it had had to fight them in a series of separate duels, in which the producer-group leaders were under enormous pressure from their members not to give way, while the general public, whose interests Government was trying to uphold, watched indifferently from the sidelines. The solution was to take a leaf out of the book of the medieval Crown, struggling to impose its authority on recalcitrant barons. Like modern producer-group leaders, John pointed out in his chapter in PEP broadsheet *Reshaping Britain* [2.5], 'medieval barons'

> ... often had all the attributes of monarchs in their own areas. Indeed, as with the modern pressure group, some barons could obtain the prior allegiance of their tenants in any dispute with the Crown. If there was a dispute between the Crown and some power-full baron, the Crown would not wish to take on such an overmighty subject single-handed while the barons watched to see if it would be worth their while to engage in similar confrontations. So it was in the Crown's interest to draw these tenants-in-chief into a constant consultation on national policy. If this was achieved, the barons went on record in front of their peers and any subsequent refusals to observe laws that had been agreed were defiance not merely of the Crown but also of the other tenants-in-chief ... It was this desire to legitimise policies and laws by getting the prior consent of the most powerful men in the country that led to the creation of Houses of Lords which were, in practice, the most important chambers in medieval parliaments.

In the same way, the modern producer-group leaders should be brought to a reconstituted Upper House, where they would confront each other as well as the Government and where they would be under pressure from the public as well as from their own members.

Institutional change, however, was only part of the answer; and not the most important part. The most important part was cultural, perhaps even moral. Not only had the revisionists of the 1950s lacked a theory of the state. but also they had lacked a theory of the mixed economy. Continued economic growth was fundamental to their whole programme, but they had failed to realise that the springs of growth were social and cultural rather than narrowly economic. So far from underestimating the strength and vitality of the private sector, as the neo-Marxists implicity assumed, they had grossly overestimated them. They had taken it for granted that the old engines of capitalism – individual acquisitiveness, the profit motive, the drive for technological innovation – would go on operating in the old way, irrespective of the social and cultural environment. As it turned out, in an environment in which the profit motive was regarded as sordid or immoral, in which civil servants or medical consultants had a higher status than managers or entrepreneurs and in which the material incentives to risk-taking were eroded by taxation, they would not work, or at any rate would not work properly. Individual acquisitiveness continued to exist in such an environment, of course. Unfortunately, it hindered economic growth by sucking talent out of the market sector and into the non-market sector, instead of fostering it. But the solution did not lie in rolling back the frontiers of the state, or even in lowering marginal tax rates, as the Tory populists imagined. What was needed was a much more fundamental change of values; and that required a theory of the mixed economy, above all of the private sector, around which a new social consensus could form.

What was true of the economy was also true of the polity. Parliament's loss of authority, John believed, was due, at bottom, to a confusion of values, leading to confusion of purpose and confusion of expectations. The participatory system of the late nineteenth century had been twisted out of shape by the plebiscitary pressures of the twentieth century, but the new system which these pressures had produced kept to the forms of the old one, and was justified in terms appropriate to the old one. The result was that no one knew what to expect or, in an important sense, what to do. MPs were still supposed to represent their constituents, but they were also supposed to represent their party activists and to do the bidding of their party leaders. Parliament was supposed to legislate, but the Government, which actually introduced the legislation and could normally expect to carry it through to the statute book, was also supposed to consult affected interest groups before the legislation was brought in. In these circumstances, it was not surprising that Might became Right, that Governments were pushed aside by overmighty subjects or that Britain's political institutions were trapped in a downward spiral of declining legitimacy and declining effectiveness. These evils could be put right only by clearing up the confusion of values which lay behind them. The British had to choose whether they wanted plebiscitary democracy or parliamentary democracy; once they made that fundamental choice, the necessary institutional changes would follow without much difficulty. John's attitude to these matters was expressed at its clearest in the discussion of the 'Westminster Model' which I have taken from his Hutchinson University Library textbook, *The Government and Politics of Britain*. In its final pages, he wrote sadly that Britain:

. . . has not gone through dramatic experiences (of rapid industrialisation, defeat in war, or class or race conflict) which would produce a powerful political philosophy, a philosophy which would then provide the answers to the major problems of political organisation. There are remnants of old beliefs, a new hedonism, an interest largely in the outcome of government, an impatience with authority, a dislike of elite assumptions, all mixed together. As a result it is likely that the solutions adopted will be mixed but will, on the whole, confirm the present drift towards centralised executive power, towards a weakening of the system of representative government in favour of plebiscitary government while the major decisions are taken by the centralised executive relying on the Civil Service and in conclave with the powerful external pressure groups which represent the public as producers. The public as citizen, taxpayer and consumer will probably continue to feel bemused, neglected and somewhat alienated.

It sounds like a prediction, but I do not think it was meant to be a prediction, any more than Orwell's *Nineteen-Eighty-Four* was meant to be a prediction. It was a warning of what would happen if – if things were allowed to go on as they were; if political leaders lacked the courage to lead in a better direction; and if society lacked the courage to follow. Time has done nothing to make it less pertinent.

In the end, then, it all came back to Gladstone and the Scottish sages of 'Forty Years On?'. Men and women had the capacity, and therefore the duty, to make moral choices; and the moral choices they made determined their social and political arrangements, not the other way round. John died before he had had time to work out all the choices which needed to be made in this country now. What he said was incomplete, and there was much he did not say. It is not difficult to point to loose ends, even to inconsistencies. But at least he had made a start. He had addressed himself to many of the thorniest issues with which a revised and libertarian social democracy will have to deal. It still seems to me a political as well as a personal tragedy that he is not here to tie up the ends himself.

David Marquand

Reference

1 John P. Mackintosh, *The British Cabinet* (1st edn), 1962, pp. 524–7.

Part 1

The life of politics

1.1 'A passion for politics' (From *The Twentieth Century*, second quarter, 1967, pp. 10–11)

It would be true to say that I have an obsessive interest in politics. When *Who's Who* sent me a form to fill in, the section on education included the fact that I had studied politics, 'career' was answered by a list of posts held as a teacher of politics, in 'publications' I put the two books and many articles I have written on politics, then came my ten years as a candidate through three general elections before election to the House of Commons. Finally under the heading 'hobbies' I mentioned some side interests but felt the picture would be misleading if I excluded my main pastime, 'talking politics'.

Considering this obsession, I am tempted to argue that those caught up by it are more deeply involved, more utterly absorbed than those fascinated by other occupations. But this is probably unfair and arises from a tendency to generalise on my experience of two professions, my own thirteen years in academic life and contacts through my wife with the medical profession. In all walks of life there are those who lose sight of anything but their work and who become bores about their own immediate concerns. Certainly many at the top of all callings take themselves, and this includes their work, too seriously.

But in university life, most men rest on their oars once they become Professors. They continue to write, they may sit on more important committees, but they have proved that they can handle the basic tasks of teaching, research and a little administration. Once they have learned to cope, the nature of the challenge does not change. It is much the same type of problem that will come up year after year to be tackled in much the same way. And there are not many occasions when they will have to jostle with rivals, to compete, show their paces and take decisions which could lead to serious failures, to a new questioning of their capacity to perform. The same is true of medicine. Once secure in a sizeable practice or a hospital consultantship, a doctor's work may be very heavy but the pace slackens, the cases may require great expertise but the framework in which decisions have to be taken is constant and provides considerable protection.

For businessmen in certain types of firms, for senior civil servants and for trade union leaders, the situation is more like politics in that the problems do alter, new factors may emerge, errors of judgement are apparent in that plans may not work out and, if this happens, a carefully-acquired reputation may collapse. I think some businessmen, particularly if they are at the head of considerable firms, may get as totally absorbed as politicians. It is evident that some trade union leaders have found a post as General Secretary of a major union more colourful and rewarding than membership of the House of Commons and there is no doubt that the top men in Whitehall are exhilerated and absorbed by their very positive feeling that they govern the country.

So the passion for politics may not have a quality different from the enthusiasms developed in other challenging, decision-taking, occupations, but I still think there are differences. Politics deals with the class of decisions which has the most far-reaching effects, which sets the context for all other forms of activity. While architects may not have to consider the views of surgeons, while journalists may not feel it is necessary to know about the theatre or the City, all of these men must be interested in some aspects of public affairs: will the Buchanan Report be adopted; how much money is there for the Health Service; will the Monopolies Commission be asked to investigate newspaper mergers; can there be a theatre subsidy or will Britain apply to enter the Common Market?

Also politics draws wider groups into its band of devotees, the circle extends far beyond those actually engaged in the occupation. There are the students of politics, the academic commentators, the Lobby, the party stalwarts in the constituencies, each section contributing a number of those who become fascinated by the working of the machine, by the issues and personalities involved. The extent of this group is shown by the number of weekly and daily papers that have a political correspondent and devote a large part of their coverage not so much to news as to stories about how and by whom public issues are settled.

Nor is this interest confined to the politics of one's own country or situations likely to have a direct personal impact on the observer. When the Labour Party lost the 1959 election (and I failed to get elected), I was so disillusioned with British public life that I took a post in Africa in order to study the working of 'the Westminster Model' in a strange environment. Once I got to know the pattern underlying Nigerian politics, once I could place the personalities involved, make fairly accurate guesses about motives and future eventualities, the same fascination gripped me and indeed all the other commentators, and investigators. Back in this country, I find that if one old 'Nigeria-hand' detects another in a party, they immediately get into a huddle in a corner in a way which engineers, traders or doctors who have served in Africa do not. 'When were you out?', 'Did you meet this or that soldier or politician?' and then they try to piece together an account of the last two coups.

Irrespective of the validity of my suspicion that a passionate interest in politics is more wide-spread and more deeply felt than the absorption with which other men regard their occupations, the point remains of why this degree of interest exists at all. The answer cannot be a simple assertion about the wish to wield power over others. As has been shown, many who fall victim to this obsession are not practising politicians at all and may have no professional connection as students or commentators. Also for a large number of those who are actually elected to the House of Commons, there can be few illusions about the amount of power they are likely to enjoy. In my own case having written a book one of whose major themes was the miniscule influence of backbenchers on government in no way diminished my desire to be elected. Nor is there a great deal of power available for junior ministers. Men who enter politics, not because they enjoy it but in order to grasp some authority, are likely to be very miserable. Aneurin Bevan said he came to Westminster to seek power and that having risen as far as the Cabinet, it had still eluded him.

So while the Churchills, the Bevins, the Wilsons and the George Browns of politics clearly revel in the exercise of their offices, many of the obsessed know they will never grasp power and some positively shrink from the idea. Lord Butler might well have had the Premiership in 1963 had he been prepared to accept the offers of several senior ministers to unite in a refusal to serve under Sir Alec Douglas-Home but, in the last resort, he preferred to act under or with another leader. He was not willing to make a positive bid and really fight for power for himself.

The fascination of politics is that besides its intrinsic importance, it has so many different aspects. In its essential form it becomes an argument over values, over man's relations with his fellow men, arguments which can never be settled but which never lose their appeal or their urgency. I was first interested in this way by the 1945 election campaign. Up till then the war had been on and I had had no experience of political issues. Then suddenly arguments arose for the first time: – could someone buy land and claim to own all the coal, stone or oil embedded underneath it? Should the government collect money from the healthy people so that the sick were assured of proper treatment or should it be left to the sick to pay when they fell ill? Should there be a United Nations? Were the Indians entitled to govern themselves? These were so absorbing, especially for one whose mind was just starting to operate, and this excitement grips each succeeding generation. I am worried about racial discrimination, child poverty and Vietnam but I am not surprised that the students of today find these topics quite overwhelming.

Perhaps a slightly later development is an interest in the machinery of politics. One finds some systems (like econometric or logical models) give positive pleasure; it is good to be able to move around in a series of assumptions, to use the language. But in politics the system is infinitely complex and always changing. One has to learn about the electoral system, to grasp the working of Parliament, the methods of the civil service and the intricacies of local government. While knowledge can be complete, there is a clear gap between the initiates, those who have grasped the main relationships, and those who have not.

In addition to the intensity of ideological arguments and to the pleasures of understanding the system can be added the fascinating study of personalities. Some of the most intriguing men in Britain are drawn into politics. Mr Harold Macmillan may have been branded at one time or another as a fop, out-of-date, inscrutable or as 'supermac', just as Mr Wilson has been called brilliant, deceitful, irresolute and determined but the commentators are again and again drawn back into their orbit, lured and held by their style of government.

The detective instinct can also be satisfied as so much, particularly in British politics, is secret. Who devised the Selective Employment Tax: – a Hungarian economist, the Secretary to the Cabinet, or Mr Callaghan in his bath? It is not surprising that some political columns are called 'Insight', 'Close-up' and 'Inside Story'. How many of the Cabinet are opposed to entry to the Common Market? Did Sir Anthony Eden (as he then was) have a secret pact with France and Israel? Was Sir Alec Douglas-Home forced out of the leadership of the Conservative Party or did he decide it was time for a change?

For those who start to take an interest, there is a continuous stream of new material. The position never remains the same. A Party may be doing fairly well, the polls improving and the foreign situation calm. Then a Minister is found to have had relations with a girl who has a friend at the Russian embassy, a rebellion in a state on the borderline between the Russian and American spheres of influence produces a 'missile confrontation' between East and West or the Prime Minister dies and the governing party is torn in pieces choosing a successor. Politics requires patience but the situation is continually changing and no-one need ever lose all hope.

Finally, the issues are so important. What could be more important than preventing a nuclear war, abolishing poverty, getting the races to live together in amity, and the fact that these problems are not solved once and for all but require continual attention does not reduce either the significance or the fascination of the task.

These qualities can attract all interested in politics; there is rather a special situation for the much smaller group who actually take up politics as their profession. For MPs the life has particular difficulties. It is not financially rewarding, it means living away from one's family for most of the week, the work is hard and the hours long and peculiar. Few backbench MPs would seriously argue that they contribute more than a successful teacher or lawyer, while the artist or writer whose works live on has left behind him something of much more lasting value.

Yet there are compensations for MPs. In his constituency and in Westminster, the member is given some status. He sits on the platform at local events, his speeches are mentioned in the local paper. At the House, the public come to watch him work and the press hang around him asking if he has any gossip to impart. He has a ringside seat for the major events in the country's history and there is always the chance that he may graduate to play an influential part, he may become one of the few ministers who do really have an effect on policy.

If all the present backbenchers could see their future in a crystal ball, some of those to whom it was revealed that they would never become ministers might leave the House, many would stay, but whether they left Westminster or not, they would all retain their passion for politics. It is perhaps as well that the future cannot be foreseen, for the more people who are both obsessed by politics and are prepared to devote themselves to the profession, the more likely that the government will be vigorously conducted and the public properly served. The day that no-one wants to stand for Parliament and that the press and the citizens lose interest in our national affairs, not only the democratic system but the whole will of the country to survive and make its way in the world will be in danger.

1.2 'Forty years on?' (From *The Political Quarterly*, Jan.–Mar. 1968, pp. 42–55)

Being forty is a happier event for a Journal than for its contributors. Before this age, I found no special difficulty in putting ideas across to students or young voters – it was just a matter of clear and convincing exposition. The audience might agree or object but there was no problem of communication. One could assume the same approach and the same general objectives. Moreover, before the age of forty, there seemed to be less need to explain or to work out one's own ideas. If they were wrong, if it was a blind alley, there was always time to try again. After forty this also changes and soon it will be necessary to decide what type of contribution one can most usefully make and settle for it.

For some people, this problem occurs only in terms of their own beliefs and purpose, but for anyone who has taught and practised politics, who is a Labour MP and wonders whether this is a worthwhile occupation, who is continually trying to persuade others to take an active interest in politics, the issue is somewhat wider. Not only has the personal aspect to be straightened out, but it must be fitted into a reasonably convincing account of what left-of-centre politics are about in Britain. But to attempt this now is to venture into a most unfashionable field. The Labour Party's chief ideologists, Crossman and Crosland, are busy Ministers and in any case seem to have lost interest in this kind of thinking. No one has taken their place and there are no very coherent theories in the various sections of 'the left' or among 'the radical right' of the Labour Party. The problem spreads far beyond Britain. The Scandinavian, German, Australian and New Zealand Labour or Social Democratic Parties have all drifted far from their original beliefs without discovering any satisfactory substitutes. Very few people now consider that there is a single form of society that can be labelled as 'capitalism' or that there is an alternative package called 'socialism' which can be put in its place. Perhaps it is that we have become more mature and realise that Western industrial society is too complex a development, that there are more sources of change than just political or governmental pressure, that the direction of development is hard to calculate or guide and that the process could never be halted with the announcement that at last the desired condition had been achieved.

And yet one still wants motives and directions in which to go. Pragmatism is not an alternative because it assumes, first, that as new difficulties arise there is the will to tackle them, a will to act that is impossible without some convictions and, secondly, it assumes the existence of principles to apply in each case. Given the current lack of doctrine, perhaps the best way of gathering one's ideas together is to work out how one reached the present position both in personal and in broader party and national terms.

In my own case my views were formed at school in Edinburgh during the war and at Edinburgh University after 1946. The underlying tone of Scottish lower middle-class life (my father was an insurance agent) was deeply impregnated with presbyterian morality. I encountered few practising Christians, the Church meant mainly gloomy Sundays with nothing to do but walk along wet, empty, grey streets, but this in no way weakened the prevailing doctrine that everything a person did was good or bad, it either contributed to or detracted from the total well-being of the community. And the war strengthened this atmosphere. It was wrong to leave food on your plate; sailors had died bringing it to Britain. It was wrong to idle, as your parents had sacrificed to pay the fees at the school and it was better to have one's Leaving Certificate before going into the forces at seventeen and a half.

At the same time, Edinburgh was (and is) one of the most class-conscious of cities. Each station of society had its own accent, its own residential areas, and for each section there was an appropriate group of schools. There were the free corporation schools for the working class and two well-known corporation schools which charged small fees and were filled on a highly selective basis by the abler and more ambitious sections of the working class. Then came several grant-aided schools, which had ranges of fees and location enabling them to cover the spread from lower-middle through middle-middle to the verges of the upper-middle class while the wealthier lawyers, medical consultants and professors sent their children to private and expensive day schools or even to one of the three English-style boarding schools in the City. As children, we knew exactly where anyone was placed in the social scale; once their accent, address and school were known, they were categorised. Being at a middle-middle-class fee-paying school, I never encountered a working-class child, the school rugby teams having no fixtures either with the ordinary corporation schools (they played soccer, anyway) or with the purely fee-paying private schools.

The last major influence was the rigid discipline enforced by a bullying headmaster who took great pleasure in corporal punishment and encouraged the senior boys to administer it to the juniors. The headmaster was quite clear that he was training the officer class, he refused to have history taught beyond 1815 because it then became 'controversial' and he made the whole school sing 'Land of Hope and Glory' every morning at prayers. I can recall arguing that if all boys in all countries sang 'wider still and wider shall thy bounds be set', there would be nothing but wars and in any case why should our boundaries be wider than our own country? This was treated as a sign of total mental aberration, not worth discussing; but it was punishable simply because to argue at all on such an issue was an act of insubordination.

The only time I encountered people outside my segment of the middle class was on youth hostelling holidays. In the summer of 1945 I met a London schoolmaster who liked teaching in a tough area and was fresh from an active part in the recent General Election campaign. Up till then I had heard nothing of politics. While walking across Skye, he put over a simple case. Why should people be divided into classes, why should they be set against each other when everyone was entitled to the same treatment, the same respect? It was all the result of conflicts built into a system based on private property and competition when co-operation would produce better results, and the kindly relations one already had with people one knew and trusted could then spread throughout society. In addition, the people were entitled to a fair share of the wealth they produced and why should men who owned land also own the coal underneath it? Why should shareholders who did no work have easy lives at the expense of those employed in the industry concerned?

All these ideas fitted my dislike of authority and my assumptions that work was meritorious, that people were essentially good and would want to co-operate and to eliminate social tensions if one could only get through to them, and that all problems could be settled by discussion and rational argument. I became a convert, indeed a fanatic, eager to dispute the issue on any occasion with all comers and rapidly reached the conclusion, which I have never entirely abandoned, that anyone who was a Conservative was either not capable of argument or not willing to see reason.

This development came just when I entered Edinburgh University and began to live instead of merely existing and when the post-war Labour Government was in its most constructive period. There was the tremendous excitement of discovering that in history (my subject) one could have different opinions, different assessments and explanations and not be wrong, as opposed to the school system I had endured with its lists of memorised facts which were either correct or not. The man who influenced me most was Professor Richard Pares who, with steadily failing health, worked away in front of us; his mind could amost be seen grinding down towards the truth, rejecting any explanation that did not stand up, revising his own theories and evading no objections.

The university Socialist Society in 1946-47 contained all kinds of left-wingers, including some convinced and able Communists. Those, like myself, whose position was vague and unformed, did not feel very closely linked to the Labour Party. It seemed self-evident that industries that had failed in the 1930s should be nationalised and run as large efficient units with good labour relations and a proper concern for the needs of the community. A Health Service seemed a splendid idea and independence for India was obviously the only acceptable solution. Conservatives stressing the value of personal rewards and the importance of remnants of Empire were simply ridiculous, though the Labour Party, as an organisation, seemed a bit dull and pedestrian.

At that stage I was, like most students, unimpressed by material problems and much more interested in abstract questions. Above all, I was puzzled by historical change. Why had the West moved from feudalism towards mercantile and then industrial capitalism? Why did society change its form and could the whole process go into reverse? Why was it assumed that change went forwards into new historical situations? Why had Germany, moving into a kind of parliamentary system before 1914, suddenly plunged into the horrors of the Nazi régime? Was the Soviet system the way the West would go, or was it on its own course and would it become more democratic or not?

At the time I was taking a course in economic history and the lecturer explained the 'materialist conception' of history. It seemed to give the clue. At any one time the way the community made its living determined the classes into which people were divided and conditioned the system of government and the pattern of beliefs. Then when easier methods of production became possible, the society began to change and if the new system spread through the community, the rest of the structure would likewise be changed. I read Tawney's *Religion and the Rise of Capitalism* and felt that it explained such phenomena as the Reformation. I thought I understood why the early industrial nations had turned to doctrines of self-help, individual initiative and the sort of Protestantism I had known since my childhood. (In middle-class Edinburgh it was assumed that those with money must also have virtue because they had worked and accumulated and in any case God would not have permitted a system where the unrighteous prospered.)

Probably my acceptance of the materialist conception of history went too far as the theory reduced the role of reason in social development to a level which was inconsistent with my belief in people's capacity to change their own circumstances. I also had an uneasy feeling that certain values, such as respect for human life and the rejection of categories of cruelty, had a deeper basis than just being the top dressing on a given economic system, though I could never prove this to my own satisfaction. Looking for a justification for these values, I became a Christian for a short period, but the idea of mass punishment of the ungodly and the improbability of this kind of divine intervention in history drew me back out of religion. But I still wish I could establish the values on which I operate and I still feel a great longing for the confidence and the qualities exhibited by some of the more progressive Christians.

The other aspect of the economic interpretation of history which I could not accept was the dialectical element which some of its Marxist exponents included. To argue that since the middle classes had taken over from the aristocracy and created a new type of society, the next stage had to be workers' take-over from the middle classes was most unconvincing, as was the further point that all further development would, at that stage, suddenly cease. The book that answered all these problems for me was *The Managerial Revolution* by James Burnham. He threw out the dialectic arguing that new systems of production produced new class systems. Classic capitalism was a mid- and late nineteenth-century product and had been giving way to a managerial economic system so that the old owner-capitalists were disappearing as a force, the managers of the big combinations were taking over and this same process was occurring in Russia as well as in the United States.

This seemed eminently sensible to me. It explained all that had happened in the Soviet Union and was happening in Britain and America. It also meant that the ownership of property or the form in which production was organised was much less important than the values governing distribution, the degree of freedom allowed and so on. A successful managerial super-state could be fascist, communist or the American mixture of monopoly and enterprise, so that it was how individuals were treated in the society that mattered. This put economic change back in its place as an important technique for increasing wealth but it was not an end in itself. Personal liberty, the right to some control over factors affecting one's own life, security and many other qualities of life were much more significant for socialists of my general outlook. Later I noticed Boris Pasternak made the same point when Dr Zhivago criticised the Communists as always living for the end of the next five-year plan, the building of some new industrial complex or the achievement of some production target, when what really mattered was the kind of life they lived in the meantime.

Just at this stage, student politics had to come down to earth. The Communists on the left decided that NATO was anti-Russian and that the Labour Government had 'sold out' and must be denounced. As a result there was a split between them and the Democratic Socialists, the latter either taking over or leaving the old Socialist Societies to form Labour Clubs. This was not done without a bitter battle and I had my first experience of in-fighting and the personal denunciations that have been such a feature of left-wing politics. Relations were severed and things were said then in 1948 that still make it difficult for those involved to be reasonable about each other twenty-two years later. It is not clear who introduced into the Left this idea that honest disagreements are unlikely and that differences of opinion are to be explained by the sudden discovery of moral corruption dating back into the person's earliest history, that many desperate careerists disguised themselves as socialists only to be discovered and denounced every time there is a crisis. I recall some otherwise intelligent people who explained Hugh Gaitskell's policies by alleging that he owned shares in South African companies; and only a few months ago a left-wing MP pointed at some of his colleagues who had not abstained in a division and shouted 'office-seekers'. This type of condemnation has done great harm because one cannot create a more confident society with an instrument riven by suspicions and jealousies.

The 1948 split put the Social Democrats into Labour Clubs. I joined the Labour Party and some of my friends began to look for candidatures for Parliament. This was still too remote and institutionalised for me, or I was still too immature, but the value of democracy was becoming a most important part of my socialism. As part of my work, I wrote a study of the Chartist Movement in Scotland and came to admire the Chartists with their desire to use democracy, not as a method of bolstering an existing system but of pushing through revolutionary changes. The politician I admired most was Aneurin Bevan. His book *In Place of Fear* took the line that poverty, property and democracy could not co-exist. People were bound to use their democratic powers to ameliorate their conditions by insisting on a reasonable distribution of property and a society which could, in this way, eliminate fear, class suspicions and envy, would thus be moving in a socialist direction.

When Bevan resigned from the Labour Government in 1951, I was at Oxford and at once sent him a telegram congratulating him on his stand. I was a Bevanite in that I was sure he was right that the levels of Western rearmament the Americans wanted at the time of the Korean War were both unattainable and would sink the Labour Government. Bevan also seemed to have the moral fervour, the belief in egalitarianism and the vision to carry the Labour Party – always a slow, lumbering, unexciting body – a stage further. Also Bevan seemed to be

standing out against the kind of ideological imperialism that characterised the United States during the Korean War, that was evident in
General MacArthur's speeches and later in the policies of John Foster
Dulles. As an historian, the idea of countervailing alliances and sensible defence precautions seemed proper to me. The great indictment of
the Conservatives in the 1930s was that they had not built up an effective power block to stop Hitler. But the idea that there was an inherent superiority in the American way of life and that people all over
the Western world should adopt its outlook and atmosphere seemed
not only silly but offensive.

For these reasons I was a Bevanite, but at this stage in the early
1950s this did not mean the belief in nationalisation as an end in itself,
in Clause 4 fundamentalism, which was later imported into the Gaits-
kellite-Bevanite controversy, nor did it imply the element of wishful
thinking about defence which was also incorporated when the Campaign for Nuclear Disarmament became active in the later 1950s.
When these things happened, I found myself agreeing with the Cros-
land-Gaitskell point of view, though I always thought that Gaitskell
need not have forced certain confrontations, particularly over Clause 4
of the Labour Party Constitution.

Also, although the Labour Party wishes to remove class barriers, it
is itself a prey to class feelings and there was something of this in the
Bevanite-Gaitskellite dispute. As I had wanted to extend my education
and read some economics and philosophy, I had obtained a scho-
larship to Oxford and reacted very strongly against the class atmosphere which is so much a part of Oxford. I had left a university with
abler scholars than I encountered at Balliol, yet the young dons who
taught me, besides being relatively lightweight, were so full of themselves, so clear that it was an act of condescension that they undertood
any teaching at all, so lacking in any interest in their pupils, particularly those without connections or titles, that I came to dislike the
institution intensely. My dislike tended to rub off on those Labour
Party members who managed to remain left-wing and yet at ease in
such a blatantly élitist part of the establishment. Though not always
true, I tended to identify some of the Gaitskellites with this kind of
person and, while I accepted their arguments, I suspected a lack of
concern of ordinary individuals and a touch of upper-class paternalism.

A curious side-product which affirmed my democratic or populist
leanings was that I found I had more in common with the American
Rhodes Scholars than with many of the English at Oxford, and this
despite my Bevanite battles with them over the Korean War. As a

result, I went for a year to Princeton and was delighted with the egalitarian and idealistic atmosphere in the United States. Although this was at the height of the McCarthy era, it was a pleasure to live in a street where the neighbours were plumbers and joiners, where playing the superior-class trick did not pay off and where there was such determination to eradicate abuses. While the Americans might not accept some of the criticisms outsiders made of their society, once they did recognise an injustice, they were determined to root it out. There was a sense in which the dumbest freshman on the campus mattered as much as the most distinguished professor – all of which was tremendously refreshing: the United States seemed so dynamic, so open to reform compared with slow-moving and traditional Britain.

I returned to teach history first at Glasgow and then at Edinburgh universities, starting in a pall of gloom about the willingness in Britain to accept discomfort, ugliness and injustice and the lack of any sense of urgency even among reformers and socialists. Still, the only way forward was to buckle down to work in the Labour Party and in my university. In the first case I became candidate for the Pentlands Division of Edinburgh in 1956 and in the second penetrated to a non-professorial seat on the Senate of Edinburgh University and on its Steering Committee.

Both seemed hopeful after a year or two. In a Scottish constituency, the candidate's energies were spent not so much on internal controversies about socialism – this was more a London-based activity – as on combatting the Conservatives, reacting to the Suez invasion, to the Hola camp episode in Kenya, to the imprisonment of Dr Hastings Banda and on pressing the need for better housing and more humanity in the administration of the social services. Just as the Conservative establishment at Westminster clung to the vestiges of Empire, in the university the older professors clung to their largely despotic powers. I was told, after a speech on the Senate, that the non-professorial staff were present to listen and learn, not to speak; and at one meeting of the Faculty, the first item on the agenda was a resolution 'to instruct Mr Mackintosh's professor to find sufficient teaching and research to keep his mind off the affairs of the university'. Struggles of these kinds can be exhilarating provided there is some degree of progress.

Politically I was in practice a total Croslandite, his book *The Future of Socialism* appearing in the year I was adopted as a candidate. I shared his view that the form of economic organisation was less important than traditional socialists supposed, that the Labour Party had to run a managerial economy on its own terms but that this was compatible with much greater social equality, fairer opportunities in education, better industrial relations and a much more comfortable, attractive pattern of life for the majority. By this time I was becoming impatient with the machinery of democratic control, so in articles in the Press and in my 1959 election address, I advocated a regional elected assembly for Scotland in order to bring the local civil service and the many *ad hoc* administrative bodies under the control of a popularly elected body.

Then came the 1959 election result – a shattering blow. After what seemed to me to be one of the most immoral, cynical governments of all time, nine months of prosperity had blotted out the record of Suez, of Conservative colonial policy, and of years of domestic inactivity. What was worse, Labour had been deserted, above all, by the prosperous working-class voters. For the first time, I had to face the fact that the working classes might not be radical. I began to realise, as recent voting studies have shown, that many are conservative, anti-foreign, anti-reform and want to end class barriers only in the sense that this would improve their own earnings. In the middle of writing my first major book, *The British Cabinet*, I felt impelled to include a paragraph in which I pointed out that if a short electoral boom was enough to carry a majority of voters, a reasonably competent and self-confident Conservative government need never lose power.

To add to this set-back, I found that while I was allowed to carry the administrative burden of my university department, the Professor would not yield the real power and above all he would not appoint men to vacancies whom I would have regarded as kindred, radical spirits. This was a lesson which I should have appreciated, that however competent one's administrative capacity, to run an organisation in part in sympathy with the consumers, the rank-and-file, the students in this case, can only be done from a secure power base. Otherwise one is labelled as 'difficult', 'prickly', 'obstinate' and the establishment will always prefer competent orthodoxy or even inactivity and incompetence to such distressing attributes.

In a mood of deep depression I cast around and decided to go to Africa. New universities were being started, I had had some most able and enthusiastic Nigerian pupils and I felt that in newly independent countries there would be a desire to forge ahead, to avoid the mistakes of the past, there would be energy, vision and the excitement of creating a new state. So I threw up Edinburgh (and a trade union nomination for a safe Labour seat that had just become vacant at a by-election) and sailed for Nigeria, to teach in the Politics Department at the University of Ibadan.

This was, perhaps, my greatest disappointment. Gradually as I collected material for a book on *Nigerian Politics and Government* (published in 1966), I found that, in my terms, there was no vision. The old Nigerian tribal concepts of administration were that the state existed as a method whereby those lucky enough to be in control milked the rest of the people, and these concepts were reasserting themselves. While I was studying the Action Group, the most Westernised and 'socialist' party in Nigeria, its leaders were found guilty of the most elaborate series of frauds by which they had managed to pocket £6 million of the impoverished peasantry's money. My students wanted degrees, not to build a new Nigeria, but to get a job, a free house, a car allowance and a chance to collect enough money to pay back the relatives who had put them through university. My book became a compendium of corrupt practices and a chronicle of the collapse of democracy, the slow death of any hope of non-tribal national government in Nigeria.

By 1963 I could see no further purpose in staying and came home, to find the atmosphere totally changed. The Conservatives had suddenly discredited themselves. The country or at least the opinion leaders were turning to the critique that some of us had made before 1959 – that British society was slow, old-fashioned, uncomfortable and often unjust. By being abroad, I had missed the peak of bitterness between Gaitskell and his opponents. The party was now united under Mr Wilson (for whom I would certainly have voted as leader in 1963) and was looking effective and confident. The public seemed to accept the message of books such as Michael Shanks's *The Stagnant Society*, and the Penguin, *What's Wrong With ...?* series. Harold Wilson seized on this mood with his Scarborough speech combining science, modernisation and socialism and it looked at last as if the Labour Party, on a programme of Croslandite policies with a Wilsonian left-wing top dressing and much more emphasis on domestic reform, was actually going to win power.

As a total addict, a compulsive participant in the public affairs of any body or country with which I am associated and encouraged by the revival of all the policies I had pushed between 1956 and 1959, I rushed back into the arena and found a candidature in one of the three seats left in Scotland. This was just lost (by 625 votes) in 1964 but, after Mr Wilson's brilliant tight-rope act on a majority of six, was won in March 1966 by 1689 votes. Now what has come of all these hopes sustained from 1963 to 1966? Has it all gone wrong?

First, what has gone right has been the emphasis on public expenditure. Despite a lower rate of growth than had been expected, the programmes for welfare, health, education and roads were maintained

43

until 1968, thus producing a definite shift in the direction of public or social investment. The mistakes of the Government have been primarily in economic management. As the Gaitskellites had argued, a Labour Government has to run the modern economy even better than the Conservatives in order both to pay for its social expenditure programmes and to increase personal living standards. The reasons for the failure to do so had nothing to do with the old left-right battles on socialist theory. The errors were simply of technical judgement centering around the refusal to devalue and the reliance on politically crippling doses of deflation till the sterling crisis of November 1967 finally convinced the Prime Minister and the Chancellor of the Exchequer that sterling was overvalued.

The other errors were that, like its Conservative predecessors, the Government clung too long to the trappings of Britain's former world role and to the heavy cost of keeping forces in the Persian Gulf and the Far East. Finally, the democratic reforms of the Government were half-hearted. A few hesitant changes in House of Commons procedure ran into ministerial and civil service opposition and were halted before they had any real effect. An outburst of frustration about the lack of democratic control outside London produced nationalist by-election victories in Wales and Scotland and signs of discontent in England but, instead of this hastening the progress of devolution and local government reform, all these problems were shelved till after the next election. Now, in early 1970, the Government is left with its chances of winning an election depending on its capacity to do what Mr Macmillan did in 1959, to run a short pre-election boom which blots out the memory of earlier disappointments.

Is it all then dust and ashes? Not in the sense that the political philosophy worked out in the 1950s has proved wrong. On the contrary, it seems clear that the managerial groups in control in Britain in industry, finance and the senior civil service will go on trying to block any effective sharing of power with the people. They will face odd outbursts such as local nationalism and protest movements but if there are to be any concessions, these will have to be extracted through the normal machinery of politics. The trouble is that a party of protest has to perform the dual role of being part manager and part critic of the system, it has to govern the people and also to represent their resentments and their desire for some share in the processes of government. The reason for the setbacks of the last three years is that the leaders of the Labour Party have been so anxious to show that they can perform the governing role (and for some of them a centralising, dogmatic tone is not alien) that they have tilted the balance too far against the representative anti-government traditions of the Left.

In terms of policy there are similar problems. Now it is no longer possible to blur the distinction between altruism and working-class demands. If poverty is to be alleviated, if there are to be proper pensions and hospitals, if there is to be adequate aid for the underdeveloped countries, it must be paid for in part by the better off workers. That they are not all socialists, that they are as open as any other section of the community to the 'I'm all right Jack' type of appeal, should always have been apparent. Indeed, it is becoming clear that considerably prosperity for the majority in Britain could be combined with a most unpleasant social atmosphere including racial prejudice, intolerance of the weaker sections of the community, increasing xenophobia and anti-youth, anti-student outbursts.

Nor has increased wealth removed class barriers. Subjectively in terms of defensive attitudes and mutual misunderstandings, they still mar community relations. The rebuilding of city centres as one-class consolidated housing estates, the remaining divisions in education, the division between the South-East and the provinces and the variation of accents and of manners have all militated against genuine equality of treatment and of respect for the individual.

These points may be regarded as ammunition by socialists who feel that democracy and checks on an over-powerful government can be overdone. Real local government reform, they argue, would mean that Conservative local authorities will be able to maintain conservative educational systems, effective parliamentary reform and the Government could not slap through its measures. In short, the people are not to be trusted. But while it is true that the mass electorate has many unpleasant reactions, surely it is better to proceed by carrying the electorate, even if the process is slow. It is the oldest of fallacies that people can be forced to be free and they never are: in the long run the electorate will want something the establishment objects to and then these powers will be used to enforce obedience. Laws, such as the Race Relations Act, are highly desirable and point the way to better behaviour, but there is no escape from the need to persuade the electorate to want to end discrimination and to face the consequences of prejudice and persecution. While democracy does not maintain that the people are always right – far from it – they are as likely to be right as a Government that pushes through the Kenyan Asians Bill and defeats its own constituency reorganisation orders. And any long-term improvement in the quality of society depends on an interaction between leadership based on the right principles and a community that responds to these pointers.

Looking ahead, the more practical problems facing Britain are serious in terms of the style of life that democratic socialists have always wanted; but the major requirement remains an intelligent and compassionate combination of public opinion and private energy. If our cities are to be renewed, if the countryside is to be preserved, if motor-cars are to be kept as devices that increase rather than ruin the average citizen's comfort, if labour relations are to be improved and the pollution of the environment prevented, then effective left-wing government is required which can combat sectional and selfish interests, make the large concerns, private and public, listen to what the consumers want, and do so in a manner which emphasises the general welfare.

A political party capable of winning a majority of votes must be a complex and representative body. The task for socialists is not just to defeat their Conservative opponents but to keep up discussion inside the Labour Party which goes beyond the question of who wins the next election. It is at times like this that I am grateful for the echoes of Carlyle and the Scottish worthies of the past with their constant emphasis that nothing worth doing is ever easy, and that the value of any endeavour lies as much in the effort made as in the end result.

1.3 'How much time left for parliamentary democracy?'
(from *Encounter*, Aug. 1974, pp. 48–52)

We are in a first-class muddle about our politicians, about the kind of people we want and the way they ought to behave. The old 19th-century view was clear. Politics was about the running of the country. Every responsible person ought to have his opinion, and those with strong views, a gift for leadership, and reasonable ability ought to be ready to enter public life; to do so was both an honour and a duty. No one thought that politicians should give up their estates, directorships, or other interests; MPs had to have outside means and their political activites were an addition to these normal pursuits. Also, this meant that they brought a variety of experience to Parliament and had an independent existence on which they could fall back when they left the House.

The alternative view, perhaps more appropriate today, would be that politics is a full-time occupation in which people must spend a considerable period to acquire the appropriate expertise. If this is the case, then they cannot hold outside jobs and must be paid accordingly. There is the subordinate question as to whether it would be best for men and women to embark deliberately on such a career at an early stage and remain in it most of their lives, as one would in medicine or in academic life, or whether they should come in later in some cases, having achieved a reasonable degree of seniority in another occupation, and then put in a more limited period in the House.

It is important to be clear which is the most desirable pattern as, if politics is to be a career stretching from early adult life to retirement, then this affects the pay structure, places greater importance on the possibility of transferring from local to national politics and means that there must be some security for those who are defeated or who retire. If, on the other hand, a measure of inflow and outflow is required, then MPs must be as well paid as those in the occupations from which they are to come (assuming that politics, being full-time, these outside jobs must be abandoned) and their opportunities to return to their previous occupations must be safeguarded.

Part of the answer to these questions depends on the kind of work politicians are supposed to do. If their task is to give the reactions to national problems of those engaged mainly in other pursuits, then the part-time nature of the job can be accepted. This is the old tradition, and it still influences the organisation of the House. It is why there is no entitlement to an office, no provistion for a full-time secretary or a separate telephone; and why men such as Enoch Powell still regard these appurtenances as unnecessary and indeed wrong. The art of politics, on this theory, is the expression of opinion on the great issues of the day, and the man who succeeds is the man who strikes a sympathetic chord in the country and thus wins mass support. According to this view, the MP should not contemplate acting as a local welfare officer or ombudsman. Clement Attlee, for example, used to be adamant that there were local councillors to do this work (he had been in local government himself); and for other matters redress is through the courts. Again, this older approach still dominates our institutional arrangements. The MP has no special position or authority in dealing with the affairs of his constituency. Any letters he may write to the local councils have no greater legal force than those sent by any other citizen, and if the MP receives a reply when he writes about other people's affairs, this is simply an act of courtesy. He could well be told to mind his own business.

On the other hand, constituencies are becoming less and less interested in what their MP says on national questions. Electors seem to think this is the task of the handful of leaders who appear regularly on television. Perhaps the electors despair of our politicians solving national problems and feel that talking about international affairs is largely pointless when Britain's role in world affairs is greatly diminished. But they do increasingly expect the MP to look into and take action about local issues.

The Liberals have built this into a theory called 'the Politics of Involvement' or 'Community Politics'; but it is practised by an increasing number of MPs of all parties. According to this, the MP does not only hold 'surgeries' every Saturday but he joins and takes part in neighbourhood councils and tenants' associations. He sets out to involve people in working with him and with the local councillors in applying pressure on central and local government over all kinds of issues, particularly those concerned with planning and local amenities.

All this takes an inordinate amount of time and energy. It is much more easily practised by prospective candidates than by those actually elected (which is why the Liberals have done most to develop the idea). But if this approach spreads, then the MP must have a properly staffed office both in his constituency and in the House. At present the Palace of Westminster – for such it is – virtually shuts during the recesses and the MP may find himself locked out of his office, if he is lucky enough to have one in the first place. Mrs Marcia Williams, secretary to Harold Wilson and now Lady Falkender, was once denied access to his office – he was then Leader of the Opposition – on the grounds that during the recess MPs and their staff had no right of entry.

In a curious way, the refusal to provide for a staff (each MP can claim £1000 a year towards the cost of a secretary) puts a premium on retaining an outside source of income so that the MP can pay for proper services out of his own pocket. In the 1960s the two MPs who were reputed to do most for their constituencies were Harold Lever and Gerald Nabarro, both of whom were very wealthy men who could afford an adequate staff.

In addition to this refusal to consider and be clear about the nature of a politician's work, there is a total muddle as to whether the practice of politics is in itself reasonable and desirable. In the 19th century the word 'politician' denoted an activity but had no derogatory overtones. Some men went into the House and, whatever their motives, it was accepted that to want to do so was a laudable ambition. Those outside the House who were well-known and successful were often prepared to be identified with one of the political parties. Indeed, W. S. Gilbert could satirise the position by saying:

> *I often think it's comical,*
> *How Nature always does contrive,*
> *That every boy and every gal*
> *That's born into the world alive*
> *Is either a little Liberal*
> *Or else a little Conservative.*

But in recent years, the idea has crept in that to be committed politically means surrendering part of one's independence and judgment; that it necessarily involves the support of some untenable propositions and thus builds an element of dishonesty into all those who are associated with a party. The curious aspect of this is that being opinionated, even in extreme forms, is no handicap or evidence of any failing, but to be an avowed member of a political party, however mild and middle-of-the-road one's opinions may be, is held to be a disability.

In part, obviously, politicians have contributed to this. Those who regularly lambaste their opponents for pursuing policies they had themselves been following only a few months before; those who never admit any mistakes; those who constantly claim more credit than they can possibly deserve – all, no doubt, help earn this reputation for them and their profession. Also, politicians often suspect their fellow -practitioners just as much as the outside public do. They may prefer to confer with civil servants and trust the advice they get from this source more than the opinions of party colleagues simply because they think that civil servants are in some sense objective or independent. When I was a Professor of Politics in Scotland, I tried to start a centre of local government studies. Some time later, in the House of Commons, I met the minister charged with local government reform heading for my old university to consult 'a professor who has shown some interest in the subject.' On discovering that the professor was me, he abandoned both the trip and the consultation.

But if politicians are partly to blame for this state of affairs, the attitude of the public makes the situation worse. To be identified with a party is held to imply not only a suspect judgment but an inherent tendency to put across tendentious propaganda and to seize illegitimate advantages. It is also assumed that no one identified with one

49

party could work loyally and wholeheartedly with someone identified with another party. Thus, the civil service must 'stay out of politics' rather as one advises a child on a wet day to keep out of the puddles. There is no objection to a civil servant having strong views or expressing them; he just has to avoid the label of a party.

A radio or television newscaster or interviewer can be opinionated – but, again, he must avoid identification. The ground rules of the Independent Broadcasting Authority require the resignation of any such person if he announces party membership or candidature. This rule was questioned on the then ITA Advisory Council in the late 1960s. It was pointed out that what mattered was evident and offensive bias and it could exist without the person concerned ever having any party connections. On the other hand a man whose approach was respected on all sides, who then became an avowed party member, or an adopted party candidate, and was still as fair and reasonable as before, had committed no crime and should be allowed to retain his job. This view was actually accepted by the Council; but it was rejected by the ITA on the grounds as they put it, that TV commentators must be 'like Caesar's wife, above reproach.'

Anyone who has been in the House of Commons and then leaves finds out that he must go through a cleansing ritual, like a Mohammedan who has had sexual relations with an infidel, or at least a period in quarantine before he is readmitted to normal life. Interviewing boards, trying to be helpful, say that 'no doubt you had to get this desire to take part in politics out of your system but we assume that this episode is now behind you. . . .' As the period of active political life recedes, one slowly qualifies once again as an independent critic and commentator 'safe' enough to be used on the media. Indeed, one may get so far as to be consulted again as 'an expert' by one's former colleagues. After a few years – who knows? – one may even be appointed to a Royal Commission set up to consider some topic that is too important to be left to those biased partisan fellows, the regular politicians.

In the institutionalisation of all this, there are first the exclusions by law or professional rule. Civil servants and local government officials above certain levels must play no overt part in politics. School teachers may not stand for local authorities which control education; and, indeed, no one can be elected to a council if he holds a paid office under that council. Similarly, no civil servant or member of the armed forces (in peacetime) can be elected to the House and, in practice, they have to resign if they become candidates. Many other occupations apply the same rules which not only exclude people from playing a part in politics but, if they persist with this folly, drive them into subterfuges. It leads the would-be politician to conceal his candidature as its announcement would mean resignation and unemployment from that moment till an election which could be two or three years off and which he might not win.

Contrast this approach with that adopted in Germany since the War where civil servants can be active in politics and may stand for parliament. If they do so, their posts, with the appropriate levels of promotion and superannuation, are held open for them as long as they serve in the *Bundestag*. And the same rules are enforced outside the civil service, so that teaching posts are also kept open for those elected. The general approach is to encourage an interest in politics by making it easy and safe for people to stand for elective office, those doing so being assured that this will in no way be regarded as a disqualification from returning to their previous careers. The result has not led to any disintegration of the German administrative machine or to difficulties between Civil Servants and Ministers, but it has meant an increase in the level of expertise in the *Bundestag* and has facilitated the movement of men as brilliant as Ralf Dahrendorf into politics, out into the European Commission, and then back into academic life.

The most extreme example of the current confusion about the role of politicians has come up over the current demand for a register of MPs' interests. In the first place, the demand grossly overestimates the influence of members. The House of Commons has no executive functions; it cannot award contracts or decide in favour of one group of interests as opposed to another. In over 90% of votes, the 'party line' covers all MPs. Parties are thinking about the public's responses and the next election, not about making money for one or two out of the 635 members. If one considers the cases in which private MPs can have some influence, they fall into a tiny handful of categories.

First, there is the occasional private MP's Bill on issues like Abortion, Capital Punishment, etc., where the parties find it too difficult to impose a party line on all their members. Then there is the question of a controversy within a party as to its line on a particular controversial question. Should the Conservatives come down in favour of commercial radio or not? Should the Labour Party decide in favour of reform of the liquor licensing laws or not? Finally, there are the rare great issues which cut so deep that MPs are prepared to break ranks, the best recent example being the vote (on 28 October 1971) about

British membership of the Common Market. Of these, the first and third are so much matters of conscience and are so much issues on which the MP will be called in question by his consitutents that there is not the smallest chance of financial inducements having any effect.

In the interim category, deciding the line to be taken by a party on smallish issues over which there is some sympathy but no clear-cut position, it is worth those outside interests retaining the services of one or more MPs, to put their 'point of view.' This is particularly true of taxation arrangements where governments introduce Finance Bills without prior consultation (to prevent forestalling) and are then prepared to make adjustments, given effective presentation of their case, during the committee stage of the Finance Bill. For these purposes, a number of outside interests pay one or two MPs retainers and brief them – but, compared with legislatures such as the US Congress where the members have real power, this is of tiny significance. Also, there is a strong case that these views should be represented, and they will only gain the day if they have some merit; for if the party spokesmen apply the whip against them, they are doomed.

There are one or two other motives for giving some small retainer to an MP. One is simply a little prestige gained from having one's annual dinner at the House of Commons or having someone to take distinguished foreign guests around the House. The ironic thing about these various motives for retaining MPs is that they are worth so little that the sums paid are trivial – *viz.*, the £250 recently mentioned in the T. Dan Smith case. The easiest way of stopping the whole thing is not to ask for a register of interests but to pay MPs properly and to prohibit retainers. The simple fact is that on £4500 a year now, the MP who has two homes to keep and, if he is involved in constituency work, a secretary to 'top up' out of his own pocket, is so hard-up that he is keen to snatch at every £250 a year that passes under his nose. I repeat: proper pay (say the same as a GP, an Assistant Under-Secretary, or a Professor) plus the government providing a proper office in Westminster and in his constituency, and all MPs would be delighted to agree to a total prohibition on any payments from outside interests.

The most flagrant example of the present muddle arises not even in the case of private MPs but over the official Opposition. They receive no financial help apart from special payments to the Leader of the Opposition and the Chief Whip. The original theory of the British system was that, in opposition, a party had time to reconsider its position, to work out new policies, and thus come back to the struggle for power revived and re-equipped.

In practice, the very opposite happens. In Government, ministers are relatively well-paid and very well served for advice and assistance. Out of office, they fall back to the position of private members with the added handicap that so-called Shadow Ministers have no help and no extra resources but a much greater burden. As a result, they become more divorced from the facts, they learn less, and parties in opposition tend to fall back on the more primitive aspects of their original ideologies and to produce unrealistic schemes which are only discarded after some period in office.

A good example was the contrast between June and July 1970. In June, the Minister of Agriculture, Fisheries, and Food (on a salary of £13,000 a year) had a large and expert staff to brief him on the vast range of complex problems falling under his charge. A month later, he was the Shadow Minister down to £4500 a year with no staff and a marginal constituency on his hands. Yet he was supposed to rise in the House and put constructive questions and counter-proposals to the Minister. Such a person might be 'tempted', though not by money. But, suppose a fertiliser company offered to pay for the services of one researcher for him, or suppose the National Farmers' Union offered him simply some expert opinion on difficult points? As it was, the person concerned had to go back to work privately as a barrister to pay for his constituency secretary and to get himself a little help in his Shadow duties. Is this work as a barrister to be registered as a corrupting influence, a derogation from his purity as an MP?

The whole Labour Opposition between 1970 and 1974 was serviced by a tiny handful of research assistants paid for, if you please, by the Rowntree Trust. It is to be hoped that no one suggested this foundation money from the confectioners influenced the Opposition's attitude to VAT on cocoa and chocolate. This is yet another example of our clarity of thought a hundred years ago – and our confusion now. Then we were clear that what mattered in politics was opinions, not money. As a result, the amount that could be spent on an election in each constituency was limited to a small sum per elector. This remains the law today long after elections have ceased to be determined constituency by constituency and what matters, in terms of money, is the *national* campaign. But no limits are set on expenditure at *this* level – so that money now does have an influence. Industry subscribes heavily to the Conservative Party (though many industrialists dislike the process) while the Labour Party is saddled with a massive obligation to the trade unions.

Here again, the Germans thought the position through after the War and set up a publicly-financed fund to pay for the central machines and campaigns of the political parties, allowing them to draw out of the total in proportion to the votes they obtained at the last general election. As no one has been prepared to think through the position in Britain, we continue with 19th-century rules which are supposed to reduce the influence of moneyed interests but actually produce the opposite effect.

All in all, the present situation induces one to despair. The only hope is if the nation realises that so much of its thinking is indeed muddled and so many of its institutions and rules are in fact hopelessly antiquated. Will it ever be ready to take a grip on itself, in terms of our industrial, social or political organisation and recast the system in the light of first principles? Alas, the problem is that these principles also need to be thought through. This could be a lengthy process. Is there so much time left for parliamentary democracy?

1.4 'Smaller politicians' (From *The Listener*, 1 June 1978, pp. 5–6. Review of *The Performers: Politics as Theatre*, by Norman Shrapnel, Constable, 1978)

The idea that politicians should be judged by their personalities as they come over in the House, and by the way they handle their colleagues, is not a new one. In this book, Norman Shrapnel, as befits his record of 20 years in the gallery, writes a slight, perceptive, anecdotal and affectionate series of pen-portraits, dating from Churchill to Callaghan.

The result is good light reading which does recapture the atmosphere of time now gone. It is hard, thinking of the pessimism and victory by boredom of Harold Wilson's last years, to remember the young, new, dashing figure of 1963, just become leader of the Opposition, tearing into the demoralised remnants of an aged and tiring Tory administration. The reader is reminded of Wilson's curious affinity with Macmillan, and of some of George Brown's glorious efforts, where the warmth and dynamism of his personality came over with such force.

The book makes only a few serious points, but they are worthy of thought. Why was there such a collapse in the quality, in the sheer size of the front-bench performers in the 1960s? I sit in my study looking at the mass of volumes on 'The Life and Letters of' one 19th-century cabinet minister after another – all in their way informative, and some really good reading. It would be invidious to list individuals, but no one would dream of writing or reading the life and letters of two-thirds of this or recent cabinets.

Has there been such a decline in quality and, if so, why? One reason is that Britain is no longer a world power, the House of Commons spends very little time on crucial world events, and more and more debates are about boring and detailed problems of economic policy. No country as insular and introverted as Britain can produce great statesmen. Then there is the curious preference for the mediocre among politicians, particularly on the left. It is amazing how far the House of Commons has gone in rejecting oratory, historical knowledge and literary allusion. On the left, a man of real powers of speech who can lace his speech with recollections of similar issues arising in the late 19th century is suspect. He is élitist. He is a Whig, longing for the past. When the devolution bills for Scotland and Wales were debated, anyone who pointed out that the UK had framed independence bills and constitutions for over 30 countries, many of them on a federal basis, was treated with contempt. What possible relevance could this have to the current problems of Wales, Scotland or Ireland? To quote Gladstone's solutions for what became known as 'the West Lothian problem' (of having Scots MPs legislating for local English affairs when English MPs post-devolution could not legislate for similar Scottish affairs) was to invite derision or boredom.

On the right, similarly, the Conservatives prefer the young, hard men of the advertising agencies and stockbroking firms who are equally new to Parliament and government. The Tory MP from an ancient family who says 'My grandfather, who was then First Lord of the Admiralty, used to say . . .' is inviting comparison with Peter Sellers, and does not score points with first-generation politicians of the Heath -Thatcher type.

So, as Britain has been reduced in stature and world significance, British politicians have been diminished. They long for preferment, and are not as colourful or individualistic. They speak on more trivial matters. The ambassadors' gallery is not crammed with representatives of foreign powers awaiting the word from Britain's leaders. Even the sense of humour has gone. Churchill's witticisms about Lady Astor ('I may be drunk but the Hon. Lady is ugly and tomorrow I will be sober') or about Sir Clive Bossom ('What a name; it is neither one thing nor the other') would not go down well now. Indeed, even unconscious humour is not appreciated, as I recall when I was the only person to laugh when Mrs Thatcher pointed a finger at Jim Cal-laghan, then Chancellor of the Exchequer, and said: 'No wonder the Hon. Gentleman's policies are all wrong: he needs a woman under him at the Treasury.'

The one point I doubt in the few general remarks made by Mr Shrapnel is his assertion that, to all the people he portrays, the House of Commons was the central and only vital institution. I doubt this, because all those who, in earlier years, brought a little quality, a little depth and a little gaiety to the House had other lives. They read books, they lived outside as well as inside the House, they had non-political friends, and they could bring some perspective to debates. Part of the decline he notices is due to the fact that so many of the faceless men and women on the front benches have no other lives. Outside the House they would be nothing; they do not paint, write, fight, build, or all the host of other activities which gave Churchill and his contemporaries and predecessors their larger-than-life qualities. Like so many current developments, it is all a bit disappointing.

Part 2

Parliamentary government and its discontents

2.1 'The Westminster model' (Extracts from *The Government and Politics of Britain* (4th edn), Hutchinson, 1977, p. 244)

The pattern of government which evolved in Britain between 1870 and 1914 was regarded then (and by many since then) with particular satisfaction. Not only were a large number of books written about it, but most of the commentators assumed that there could scarcely be any improvement. There were several reasons for the belief that the system prevailing at that time was close to perfection. In those years Britain was particularly powerful and successful, the dominating mood being one of confidence that progress would continue and that Britain's peculiar and powerful position in the world would always remain. Looking back, it seemed clear to the Victorians that Britain had been through the social and political phases or overcome the difficulties then besetting most other nations. Personal liberty and equality before the law had been established. A respected monarchy gave continuity and an aura of authority to the government, yet all personal or arbitrary rule had been eliminated. The aristocracy had never been marched to the guillotine, yet their powers had been tempered and shared with the other classes in the community. As late as the 1860s, there had been serious worries that any move towards democracy would introduce class warfare and political instability but, by the 1880s, these fears had faded. It was accepted that Britain had managed, apparently with unique success, to combine a proper degree of governmental authority with responsiveness to popular opinion, that patriotism, property and stability had been fortified rather than endangered by bringing all sections of the population into a continuing debate about public policy.

Exemplifying this self-confidence, late nineteenth-century historians tended to regard all aspects of British history as stages in an inevitable march towards this happy conclusion. They thought they had discovered that the Anglo-Saxon tribes, even before coming to Britain, had always proceeded by open decisions at 'folk moots' and that these albeit rudimentary democratic practices had tempered the Norman autocracy introduced into England after 1066. Any further attempts at despotic rule were countered by baronial revolts which forced respect for basic liberties upon recalcitrant sovereigns. These concessions and rights were embodied in Magna Carta. Then the practices of presenting grievances, of agreeing to grants of taxation and of making proclamations clarifying ancient custom, were all brought together in periodic Parliaments dating from the time of Simon de Montfort and Edward I. The Lancastrian kings, it was alleged, were involved in a 'constitutional experiment' of rule with Parliament while even the Tudor despotism only served to confirm these trends since Parliament was used to carry through the Reformation and to show patriotic support for Queen Elizabeth. From this point of view, Charles I may have had a tragic history but he was guilty of attempting to halt the country's steady progress towards constitutional monarchy and the emergence of the House of Commons as an essential partner in government. Charles II and James II had the same failings and the English genius for non-violent progress was revealed when the latter monarch was allowed to escape. A new monarch was installed and what these historians dubbed as 'the Glorious Revolution of 1688' established simply that Parliament could not be set aside or over-ruled. Next, it was argued that the late seventeenth century saw the invention of the two -party system, the descendants of the Roundheads and Cavaliers becoming the Whigs and Tories who were content to fight it out at the hustings and in the House of Commons. According to this version of British history, George III's great error was to try and restore a measure of personal rule but luckily this was abandoned by his successors. The Reform Bill of 1832 created a uniform right to vote for men of property who were thus brought into the political system without any sharp break with tradition. Then the Reform Acts of 1867 and 1884 carried the process further and gave all established male householders a voice and a vote.

This, known as 'the Whig theory of history', viewed the system of government in practice in Britain between 1880 and 1914 as virtually the last word. The pattern then established was regarded as not only the culmination of fifteen hundred years of progress but was itself so simple, so logical, so effective and satisfactory, that the accounts of it had great force. These accounts filled the books and the minds of students of British government long after much had changed and were still regarded as largely correct until the 1940s. Thus the conventions and practices of the late Victorian period were not considered as merely true for that time, they were regarded as proper or normal. When further changes occurred, they were noticed with reluctance and tended to be regarded as departures from the norm, the main features of this system, which may be called 'the Westminster Model', still dominating the textbooks in use after the Second World War. It then became the basis of the constitutions which were carefully written up for emergent nations of the Commonwealth on the grounds that if this system was the most advanced yet produced, why not hand it on in its complete form to the new states of Africa and Asia? Also nationalist leaders who learnt their politics in Britain or from British books and teachers were so convinced by the merits of the system that they would settle for nothing less. Any adaptations to meet special historical or social conditions in their countries would have been regarded as insulting, as suggestions that they were not capable of the most advanced form of democracy. . . .

Since the 1880–1914 period, the organization of life in Britain and the factors in society affecting the political superstructure have been altering very rapidly. . . .

While the Westminster Model was never reconstructed or revised, the continuation of trends such as the extension of the right to vote, the consequent growth of parties, the new demands of the electorate and the complex administration required to fulfil these demands all affected it, introducing new elements and finally altering the balance between the institutions. As regards new elements, the tremendous increase in government intervention in the economy meant that many sectors of private industry formed pressure groups to put their case to the government. At the same time, the growth of a mass electorate and of a fairly rigid party system so reduced the power of the House of Commons, that these pressure groups preferred to deal directly with Whitehall. Under the Westminster Model, all direction on matters of policy was supposed to come from politicians so that civil servants in the 1860s and 1870s thought it improper for them to see pressure group representatives – everything had to go through the House of Commons and the appropriate minister. The executive committee of the Trades Union Congress was originally called the Parliamentary Committee because the point of unions coming together was to press for favourable legislation and this, in turn, meant lobbying Parliament. Likewise the various groups of industrialists dealt primarily with favourable MPs. By the end of the century, this attitude was changing and pressure groups have found it increasingly worth while to deal directly with Whitehall. On the Civil Service side, inhibitions about such contacts have declined and since the 1940s, it has been accepted that departments should always consult with recognized pressure groups, most items of legislation being worked out in this way before they are ever placed before the legislature. (A fascinating example of the hangover of the old proprieties is that it is thought to be 'unconstitutional' to show the draft of a clause in a Bill to the spokesman for a pressure group. They can be told the content of the clause and can bargain as to whether it is acceptable or not, but they are not allowed to see the final wording because of the old conventions of the Westminster Model which require that Parliament must be the first to see the actual words of the government's legislative proposals.)

But the cardinal virtue of British government in its classic period had been the delicate balance between authority and popular control, between the Cabinet and the House of Commons. And it was here that the responses to new political demands and to new administrative tasks produced the most important and perhaps least appreciated changes; least appreciated because the words used and the outward forms remained the same. Yet the trends and their effects can be clearly discerned. While governments in the 1850s and 1860s could rely on something approaching a consensus of backbench support and only faced defeat if they seriously antagonized distinct bodies of MPs, by the 1890s the opposition was indulging in systematic attacks and governments had to rely much more exclusively on their own back-benchers. The number of party divisions in the House (defined as cases where nine-tenths of each major party voted together) rose from around 30 per cent in the early 1860s to 60 per cent in the early 1870s to over 90 per cent in the 1890s. Because of this 'state of bloodless civil war', as Lord Salisbury put it, governments were able to command the support of their backbenchers and so assumed control of the House of Commons. This was achieved by stages between 1882 and 1902 when Mr Balfour carried his procedural reforms or 'parliamentary railway timetable', so called because it was possible under his revised Standing Orders to know just what station along the road to enactment any item of legislation would have reached by a given date.

These changes all increased the power of the executive so that by the turn of the century, the government could rely on voting down any undesirable motions in the House. This enabled the government to cut down the flow of information to MPs, stopping, for instance, the nineteenth-century practice of regularly publishing sets of documents (Blue Books) explaining or revealing the recent conduct of foreign policy. Detailed scrutiny of the financial estimates ceased. Question Time developed as a less satisfactory substitute for the right to raise debates, whenever a member so desired, on motions to go into committee and on other procedural opportunities. Forty years later, after the Second World War, the limited value of questions began to decline as so many members wanted to intervene in the same period of time that the Speaker decided to limit each member to one supplementary question and the whole process was speeded up so that any reasonably competent minister has little difficulty in withholding information. Also, Question Time became less of an occasion for backbenchers to press ministers on specific, often constituency, matters. Instead, the frontbench opposition spokesmen took a larger part and questions became increasingly an aspect of the party political battle between the two sides of the House.

The complexity of legislation and the practice of prior consultation with pressure groups, already referred to, had the same effect as did the very large extension in the Prime Minister's patronage in the form of ministerial appointments. Governments in the 1880s had some 35 ministers in the House of Commons. By 1918 the figure had risen to 60; in 1945 it reached 71, while Mr Callaghan in 1977 had 97 jobs to distribute among his backbench supporters. At the same time, the outlook of members had altered in that many came into politics in order to have some influence on public life and could see no way of achieving their objective unless they held office. Being an MP does not in itself confer sufficient opportunities or satisfaction on the more ambitious and capable members. Also few MPs have the wealth or social prestige of their nineteenth-century predecessors so that they have fewer satisfying alternatives to the quest for political advancement and ministerial office.

Thus though so many outward features of the Cabinet and of the House of Commons remain the same, the balance between them, which was such a central and admired feature of the Westminster Model, has been steadily altered in favour of the executive as a result of the trends that have been described. Whatever is thought of the virtues and failings of British government today, it cannot be denied that relations between the executive and the legislature are quite different from the relations existing a hundred years ago. The capacity of the Commons to remove one government and install another, to amend legislation, to pick off ministers, to extract information and to push the government into changes of policy, has largely disappeared. While this may or may not be a desirable development, the mistake is to go on talking as if these powers existed or, and this is a more sophisticated modern twist, to admit the present situation but then to assert that the use of these powers in the last third of the nineteenth-century has been greatly exaggerated or misunderstood; in short, that there has been little change.

The reader may wonder why it is necessary to spend so much time explaining that the Westminster Model, the idealized version of British government in the 1880–1914 period, has changed in the last sixty years. This is partly because, as has been explained, its language is still used and misleads current observers and its maxims are still quoted either to cover up or to try to accommodate current practice. But there is a further point. The pace of development of the two sides of government, one being the executive or the administration, and the other the system of supervision or control, seems to alternate. Up till the late eighteenth century, there had been almost no administrative reform, no innovation or renovation in government. The process began in the 1780s under the Younger Pitt at a time when all reform of Parliament or local government was anathema. It was resumed in the 1820s and 1830s, under the influence of Bentham, the radical reformers and the free traders, many of the old cobwebs being swept aside. Administration was grouped in a few departments all under ministerial control, urban local government was reformed, the legal system was tidied up and financial organization was focussed on annual accounting of all the money that flowed into and out of one Consolidated Fund.

Political reform was begun in 1832 and accelerated after 1867, the distinctive feature of the late nineteenth century being that, apart from the reorganization of the Civil Service and its recruitment by open competition (1870), there were no further extensive changes in the practical operation of government. The new departures were not administrative or organizational but political. What was carefully elaborated was the system of popular control based on the moral doctrines of equality of respect for the individual and of the individual's right to make his own judgement of political issues. As Gladstone put it in 1864 when he 'set the Thames on fire', 'I venture to say that every man who is not presumably incapacitated by some consideration of personal unfitness or of political danger, is morally entitled to come within the pale of the Constitution.' This doctrine underlay the extension of the right to vote in 1867 and 1884, the introduction of the secret ballot in 1872, the Corrupt Practices Act of 1883, much of the intense battle over Irish Home Rule and the final adjustment of relations between the House of Commons and the House of Lords in the Parliament Act of 1911.

Since the turn of the century, however, the pendulum has swung the other way and the vast administrative developments noted at the opening of this chapter have altered the whole shape of British government, but there has been no new political theory and almost no new machinery of scrutiny or control to match the increased scope and power of the executive. Ostensibly Britain still adheres to the democratic doctrines enunciated by the late-nineteenth-century liberals, but with flagging conviction. There are strong undercurrents which, though not often brought to the surface in public discussion, run strongly in favour of keeping decisions in the hands of limited groups of experts, men chosen for their knowledge, training or existing authority.

The curious result was that by the 1960s, when it began to be recognized that the system of political control was outdated and when some of the forms of government built into the Westminster Model began to prove administratively inadequate, there was no strong ideology to provide guide lines for the necessary reforms. For instance, local government of the old county and borough pattern had become barely capable of carrying on the tasks assigned to it by the central government and demanded by the voters, so the structure had, by common consent, to be changed. But there was no agreement as to whether a reformed system should involve more devolution or more central control, whether it should be based on the doctrine of genuine local democracy or whether the role of elected members should be largely advisory. Similarly the Treasury found the House of Commons' system of annual provision of part of the money needed for government (which the Treasury had abandoned in 1962 in favour of a five-year rolling programme covering the whole of public expenditure) a nuisance and sometimes so misleading to foreign financial circles as to be positively damaging. But this dissatisfaction did not mean that there was any agreement about the nature of a reformed system; that is whether it should lead to a restoration of the House of Commons' former actual capacity to scrutinize public expenditure or whether this should remain a formality. Again the public sensed that the role of backbench MPs had altered to such an extent that reforms of parliamentary procedure were necessary and ministers found some of the older aspects of procedure tedious; but there was no doctrine which gave a ready answer to the fundamental question of what backbench MPs were supposed to do, how much influence they should have or whether the object was to make it easier or harder for the executive to manage the House of Commons.

In all these cases, the governments of the 1960s and 1970s either tended to hand the task over to a Royal Commission or began piecemeal pragmatic changes in the hope that such difficult and unanswered questions would resolve themselves. Needless to say this did not happen and while most of the value judgements still repeated the old slogans of democratic control, the actual effect of the reforms proposed usually left these issues open. . . .

The doctrine that is usually referred to in the opening pages of these Royal Commission or Ministerial Committee Reports is a watered-down version of the late-nineteenth-century belief in democracy which inspired the system described above as the Westminster Model. Genuflections are still made towards these old gods. Thus every time a nominated board is established to perform some administrative function, it is felt that some sort of democratic check is necessary and as elections cannot be run for each *ad hoc* board, another nominated body is created called an 'advisory council', the idea being that this acts in lieu of democratic control. In fact, these advisory councils neither have the strength conferred by expert knowledge, nor the experience of full-time work in the field, nor the responsibility conferred by direct election, but they cover up for the assumed need for some outside, popular supervision of these administrative agencies. At the same time, this adherence to the remnants of old political beliefs can add to the complication of government. For example, in the interests of efficiency, there should be amalgamations of the many regional and local authorities responsible for planning, development and the major environmental services. One solution, to do all this from Whitehall, which is allegedly under the scrutiny of the House of Commons, is impossible because of the extent and variety of the work. To hand the work over to elected local authorities covering an extensive area would be to set up bodies with a genuine degree of independence and power and this is suspect. The result is the present multiplicity of bodies producing confusion both at the administrative level and on the part of the electorate who are left wondering where and by whom decisions are actually taken. The same problems inhibit reform of the Commons. If it were possible to be clear about what power or general role the House should have, the relations between MPs and the executive could be adjusted accordingly. At present the fiction that each MP acts on his own judgement and takes a discriminating part in legislation is preserved by insisting that members must be present and pass through the lobbies night after night, though in fact such activity makes no material difference, but seriously impedes MPs in their task of keeping up to date with their special interests and with their constituency work.

It would be perfectly possible to recast the system of democratic supervision so as to restore a considerable part of the power of the Commons and to provide a devolved system of regional and local elected councils which would mean that every important administrative body was subject to checks and examination at one or other of the three levels – national, regional or local. At the same time, the doctrine of ministerial responsibility could be limited, the degree of independent influence already existing in the Civil Service openly recognized, the Fulton reforms on management implemented and the Commons given powers of direct scrutiny of these sub-sections of the public service. The reason all this has not happened has not been because of technical problems but because there is no clear view of how government should be organized or controlled. The public are not very interested in such issues. They are used to politicians listening with some care to their demands and the evidence of this attention and the obvious impact of general elections is usually sufficient to make them feel that the old maxims of the Westminster Model still have some meaning.

If the present drift in ideas and in practice was recognized and accepted, the British political system could openly be established on a popular plebiscitary basis, with a quinquennial election to put one party or the other in power checked only by 'advisory committees' at certain levels – the Commons in the centre and similar nominated or elected bodies at suitable subordinate points in the administration. But though the machinery of government is developing in this direction, there is insufficient willingness to face the facts, to give up some of the pretences left over from the old period of vigorous, participatory democracy in order to remove the anomalies and rationalize the system.

If some clarity of purpose and coherence of action is to take the place of this drift, the ideas and energy ought to come from the political parties because, in theory, they are supposed to provide the driving force in political development. Yet the parties are rooted in the community. The old view of the party organizations dating from Ostrogorski's great work, *Democracy and the Organisation of Political Parties* (translated by F. Clarke in 1902), was that these bodies had a life of their own. They were organizations which could operate on the one hand on the electorate and on the other on the MPs, thus directly influencing policy. In fact, this is to elevate a small group of officials or 'caucus', as Ostrogorski called them, into a prominence they do not deserve. In Britain, the party machines are relatively weak and only hold meetings, choose candidates, run election campaigns and hold conferences. But the parties are also deeply influenced by the two ends of their operations, the one end being in the constituencies and the other in the Cabinet or Shadow Cabinet. The parties' greatest area of freedom and influence lies in the local constituency activists' power to choose the candidate for a parliamentary election. This is normally a once-and-for-all choice as it is unusual for the sitting MP to be refused renomination. But in making the choice, the selection conference in the case of the Labour party, and the constituency executive in the case of the Conservative party, are not easily moved by pressure from outside and even the leaders of the parties have found it hard to get close friends and political associates nominated. Senior party figures (such as Creech Jones on the Labour side after 1951 or Christopher Soames on the Conservative side after 1966) have found it almost impossible to be selected. Thus this is one important way in which the parties must reflect the opinion of the more active local members, a necessity which keeps the parties tied fairly closely to their local connections.

At the other end, the parties are tied to promulgating the views of the parliamentary leadership. In the Conservative party, the organization is directly under the control of the leader while in the Labour party, the organization serves the National Executive which is elected by the annual conference. In practice, being elected to the National Executive does give its members a degree of power and position. Some are elected because of their independent standing in the party and because of specific positions they have adopted on certain issues. A combination of the loyalty of trade union members, of the distribution of ministerial posts among MPs on the Executive and of personal persuasion by the Prime Minister and senior colleagues helps to keep the Executive and the Party leadership together though there can be tension and even open conflict as occurred in 1976–7.

These two ends of the parties, in the constituencies and in the Cabinet, are brought together at regional and national conferences where the activists meet and exchange views with their leaders in the company of their MPs. On such occasions, there is a process of mutual education and stimulation which can at times descend to mere manipulation of the delegates by the leadership and can also rise to a high level of discourse about the basic problems confronting the nation. The activists are usually to the left, in the case of the Labour party, and to the right, in the case of the Conservatives, of their parliamentary leaders. But there is a recognition by both activists and leaders that the party's task is to win an election and this means carrying the less opinionated sectors of the electorate with them. On the other hand, the leadership appreciates that it cannot indefinitely trample upon the deeper convictions of the solid party supporters. . . .

The question that remains is whether any of these parties is likely to impose some pattern on the development of British institutions in the foreseeable future. Will there be an attempt to restore more complete democratic control? Is there a preference for efficiency as a criterion? And what, if any, are the parties' attitudes to the specific problems of government that have not been resolved? The answers are confused.

Looking first at the Labour party, its doctrine or beliefs are, in 1977, by no means as clear cut as when the party constitution was adopted in

1918. Clause Four declared that the objective of the party was 'to secure for the producers by hand or by brain the full fruits of their industry, and the most equitable distribution thereof that may be possible, upon the basis of the common ownership of the means of production and the best obtainable system of popular administration and control of each industry and service.'

Underlying this was a mixture of beliefs and of desires to remedy particular situations. British society was condemned by the early Labour leaders as being selfish and cruel. There was too much poverty, and hardship fell on those with the fewest reserves and resources. The accepted explanation was that the capitalist system of production was based on selfishness since only some in the community could prosper as their prosperity had to be at the expense of others. This was because these capitalists lived in part or in whole out of the profits which should have been shared with all those who had helped in the process of production. The solution was to end the capitalist system by turning to public ownership, where community interests could be considered first, where profit would be eliminated and where work and reasonable prosperity could be guaranteed to all. But there was also a strong democratic element in the doctrine. The early Labour leaders supported votes for women, home rule not merely for Ireland but for Scotland and Wales, and were deeply concerned about the respect that should be paid to individuals, about the sense of freedom that was lacking in the nineteenth-century employer – employee relationship.

In the 1930s, the emphasis changed. The misery of the inter-war years in the areas of declining heavy industry left their mark, while the intractable nature of the problem was revealed by the failure of the first two Labour Governments. As a result, Labour thinking began to lay more stress on State control, on the need to take over at the centre and then to redistribute wealth and plan for the whole country. This drift of thought was emphasized in the 1940s by the Beveridge Report recommending a comprehensive pattern of welfare organized on a national basis, by the new emphasis on Keynesian planning and by Herbert Morrison's concept of the large national corporation as the best method of organizing nationalized industries. The populist element in the party's thinking remained but focussed more on the party conference than on the degree of scope to be given to the House of Commons or to local government. On the whole, the Labour party took the old radical view that the task of Parliament was to enact the legislation foreshadowed or promised in the party's election manifesto. A Labour majority in the House of Commons should rally round the executive and protect it against the array of hostile capitalist forces, the Conservative Opposition being merely the front-line troops for the captains of industry, the financiers and the press barons.

These ideas came together and were put into operation by the 1945–51 Labour Government. Some of its politicians were backward-looking in that their major objectives were to remedy inter-war problems. The older declining industries were nationalized, the Beveridge plans enacted, a National Health Service started and full employment maintained, the emphasis all being on the results of these policies, on their effects on people's lives. Little attention was paid to the machinery of government and Aneurin Bevan abandoned any attempt to re-form local government. There was a considerable growth in the size of the central government, many *ad hoc* organizations were created and there were complaints about bureaucracy and controls. The tendency was to dismiss these as Conservative propaganda, since for many Labour activists, controls and rationing were what had brought fair shares during and after the war. At the same time, the Government had to grapple with newer or less anticipated problems of regional development, of a weakness in the overall balance of payments and of a rapid change in Britain's international position, all of which combined to prevent any basic rethinking of socialist doctrine. . . .

The Labour party entered office in 1964 committed to a more rapid rate of growth, improved welfare benefits, more expenditure on schools, houses, roads and health and one major measure of public ownership – the renationalization of the steel industry. Mr Wilson had also said a good deal about modernizing the machinery of government. He had proposed a more extensive No. 10 staff, a smaller Cabinet and many of the modern techniques of business management in the Civil Service which were later elaborated in the Fulton Report. In 1966, he went further and proposed two new Select or investigatory Committees in the House of Commons. But after four years of difficulty and unpopularity, the attitudes of the Labour party were more mixed. In economic affairs, fiscal controls were being practised by the Treasury to try and maximize the advantages gained by the 1967 devaluation of the pound. The new Ministry of Technology, on the other hand, was using more positive methods of intervention, injecting public money into industry, encouraging mergers and pushing technological innovation. At the same time, welfare benefits were increased but this did produce complaints about 'idlers' and 'scroungers', across-the-board welfare payments were becoming increasingly expensive and some Labour party members began to press for more selective methods of eliminating poverty.

By the early 1970s, it remained true that the Labour party was identified with the interests of the working classes, with the need for a reduction in class barriers and for the maintenance of the welfare system. But there was less confidence that rapid growth could be ensured and less assurance that the gaps between the really poor and the better-off workers could be narrowed by the traditional remedies. There was some evidence that Labour's emphasis on regional development had reduced the contrast between the prosperous midlands and southeast and the older industrial areas. But it would be hard to identify a coherent or clear-cut Labour or socialist philosophy in the sense in which such philosophies had existed before 1914. The democratic element in the party's thinking was mainly a conviction that 'the people must be right' but popular views were indicated by the act of choosing every four or five years between the two major parties. The Labour Government had tried small items of parliamentary reform, experimenting with morning sittings and with a limited number of Select or 'specialist' Committees. But these experiments had come at a time of internal tensions in the party and were associated with more relaxed attitudes to party discipline in the House, tendencies which angered the older, loyalist backbenchers. In the Labour strongholds of Scotland and Wales, there had been challenges from the Nationalist parties which made major gains in the February and October 1974 elections. As a result, these sections of the party turned reluctantly towards devolution but without any great conviction or enthusiasm.

The interest in institutional reform in the Labour party has tended to be concentrated on the right or social democratic wing of the party. That section was severely mauled in the battle over British membership of the EEC and lost ground in the Parliamentary Party at the two general elections of 1974. Despite the popular victory of the Europeans or moderates in the 1975 referendum, the left was stronger in the National Executive and in the party. The moderates were worried by the pro-union stance of the party when Heath was struggling to maintain his anti-inflation policy.

But the party fell into the hands of those who saw it as the spokesman of the organized workers in politics, a view which combined the left and centre. This was embodied in what was called 'the social contract' with the unions. When Harold Wilson retired in March 1976, the candidate of the radical right, Mr Roy Jenkins, got only 56 votes and soon left British politics for the chairmanship of the European Commission. Interest in the machinery of government waned and as prices started to rise more rapidly and unemployment rose to over a million and a half in the winter of 1976–7, the party adopted an increasingly defensive posture. Apart from turning again to referenda as a way of passing the devolution decision on to the electorate, there was little interest in radical reform of any kind. The left had its philosophy and fought to change party policies in that direction while the actual direction of the party under Mr Callaghan, aided by Mr Foot, was in the hands of those who believed its main task was to represent the unions in politics, to look after their interests. But even this got strained as prices rose faster than earnings and the need to stem inflation clashed with the unions' desire to return to free collective bargaining. All that is left for the Labour party is to appeal to its traditional loyalties. Although the class divisions in British society are weakening or blurring at the edges, the parties and the public have tended to fall back on these divisions as the only touchstone they have in politics.

The Conservatives, in contrast, have always been a party more accustomed to government and less interested in theories but they have been equally class identified. Although the party had a strong aristocratic and agricultural interest, by the 1930s it was becoming closely connected with industry. Conservatives strongly held the Victorian belief that there were large areas of social organization in which it was simply improper for government to meddle. The government did not have to concern itself with the balance of payments (which was always expected to be favourable or self-adjusting), free trade meant that there was no need for elaborate connections with industry, the level of employment had to be left to the supply and demand for labour and all that the government should do was elementary regulation in the interests of those sections of the community unable to defend themselves. With this view, the Conservatives in the inter-war period were for small-scale government and low taxes – the less done by government, the better and cheaper. At the same time, those public health, welfare and property protection services which the central or local government did provide, should be efficiently administered. Thus, though Neville Chamberlain personified the Conservatives' connection with industry and with these *laissez-faire* ideas, he was a most effective and efficient Minister of Health from 1924 to 1929. In addition, the Conservative party was closely identified with Britain's overseas empire, with the armed forces and with a foreign policy resting on a balance of power in Europe and elsewhere on the use of appropriate force to defend British interests.

In the 1930s, this Conservative outlook (rather than philosophy) did not face any very serious challenge from the Labour party's ideas but events did inflict certain serious blows. The first was the pressure for independence or at least for a measure of internal self-government in India. But more serious was the alarm and despondency caused by the 1929–33 slump in which the confidence of British industrialists, already sapped by the doldrums of the 1920s, was seriously shaken. Some of the beliefs in the limited nature of government activity were abandoned. The Conservatives turned to protection disguised as imperial preference in 1933 and adopted a series of State measures to aid the reduction and consolidation of the declining heavy industries. This whole experience was so shaking that though the Labour party had failed in both its minority governments and had shown no sign of making radical changes when it was in office, the Conservatives were seriously worried by the possibility and consequences of losing office. This sense of self-doubt also had some part in convincing Conservative leaders that neither Britain nor Western society could survive another trauma of the seriousness of the First World War and thus, for the only time in its history, the party abandoned its usual reliance on strong defences and the balance of power in Europe, adopting a policy toward Nazi Germany known as appeasement.

Although Conservative morale rallied under the pressures of the Second World War and first accepted and later was thrilled by the leadership of Winston Churchill, some of the other aspects of the War constituted a serious challenge to Conservative ideas. Wartime experience seemed to show that the government could control industry, produce full employment and higher output and then share the available produce more fairly. Also the movement of people involved in wartime adjustments, the identification of the Conservatives with appeasement and the 'fair shares' aspect of rationing all helped to undermine laissez-faire doctrines. As a result, the Conservatives found themselves badly defeated in 1945.

In response to the early activities and enthusiasm of the Attlee Government, the Conservatives mounted little challenge. Their older emotional attachments suffered with the decision to grant independence to India, Burma and Ceylon but the new post-war MPs who came into the party (particularly at the 1950 election) were more exclusively concerned with domestic policy. In part, they developed the traditional Conservative view that government was inherently inefficient and undesirable, particularly fastening on the record of the nationalized industries. Also, because they were continually looking to see whether a service or a subsidy could be removed, the Conservatives were less interested in any machinery which might have been set up to permit some element of popular control or consumer representation in these industries and services.

However, the thoughts that did occur went in two directions. At first Conservatives suggested that the regional hospital boards should be directly elected. They were also protagonists of greater parliamentary supervision of the nationalized industries and supported the creation of the Select Committee on these industries against Labour resistance in the mid 1950s. But the Conservatives are also by tradition believers in a strong executive. They have felt this was necessary to conduct proper policy and, while in power, they trusted their own leaders. For most Conservatives, there was no need for elaborate control systems built into Parliament. Normally, having chosen a leader they were prepred to leave everything to him. If there was trouble and they became unhappy, a direct visit to the leader or the Chief Whip would usually suffice. So there was no need for specialist committees, or reformed local government. As for the Civil Service, it has to be cut down to the lowest level necessary. But if a service was necessary, for example at the Ministry of Defence, then it should be supported against interference, particularly by a parliamentary committee which might well contain several busybodies, ultra left-wingers or just cranks. Thus the Conservatives wanted a smaller, efficient and cheap executive but were then ready for a strong executive. And each time there was a surge forward in governmental activity, for instance during the war or under the post-war Labour Government, they were prepared to extend their view of what was necessary to cover some if not all the machinery which had been established. . . .

After Labour won the general elections of 1964 and 1966, the Conservatives were on the defensive until the consequences following on the deflation of July 1966 began to make the Labour Government unpopular. But, unlike the last years of the Attlee Government, the Conservatives developed no critique of the form or extent of government. Rather, they called for tax reductions, firmer enforcement of law and order and legislation to reduce the number of unofficial strikes. At the same time, the Conservatives looked on the possibility of decentralization a little more favourably than the Labour party. The Conservative ex-Prime Minister, Sir Alec Douglas-Home, chaired a committee which proposed an elected assembly to debate the early stages of purely Scottish legislation, the estimates and general Scottish questions. The difficulty for the Conservatives was that while they were prepared to look with some favour on proposals which reduced the size of the central government machine, the particular solutions of elected assemblies in Scotland and Wales would produce Labour-dominated authorities with considerable power even when Britain was under a Conservative Government in Westminster. By the time the Devolution Bill was actually introduced in 1976, their opposition was overwhelming.

Thus Conservative views had changed very little since the 1950s. There was a willingness to accept most of the new social and economic measures but to administer them as tightly as possible and to cut the cost of government. Within this framework, the Conservatives wanted to retain a strong executive and to strengthen similarly the hands of private authorities, particularly the employers, in dealing with the unions. Some Conservative leaders when in opposition said that they would like to improve the Commons' capacity to scrutinize public expenditure and to appoint some more select or specialist committees but this ceased to be their policy once in office again in 1970. The Expenditure Committee was made permanent but the atmosphere was no longer favourable to reform as it had been in the mid 1960s...

All this goes to show that both major parties are chiefly concerned with the product of government, the level of taxes, welfare benefits and wages, the degree of unemployment and the standards of the public services and are less interested in the machinery of government, the ideas behind it or the quality of public life and debate. Nor is this surprising. All this means is that the parties reflect the attitudes of the public. The voters are only interested in the machinery of government if the existing institutions fail to do what they want, if there is serious inefficiency or injustice, in short if their lives are disrupted. And most politicians are normally only interested in these subjects if the voters are reacting strongly.

The Liberals are much less interested in the major class-based attitudes that distinguish the Conservative and Labour parties. They have no distinctive economic policies and are not identified with the interests of any specific social groups. But the Liberals are deeply concerned about the institutional structure of British government, about parliamentary reform and the rights of individuals. They advocate a type of federalism for Scotland and Wales, England being divided into a number of large provinces with a second tier for immediate local government. In practice, the Liberal party draws most of its support from the rural areas of the Celtic fringe in Scotland, Wales and the West country where the normal British class divisions are weaker. In these areas, there is a remnant of the old anti-landlord, anti-aristocratic feeling which has been the basis of historic Liberalism. Also, in these areas, there is no industrial base for the Labour party, the Liberals thus reaping the benefit of these older social cleavages.

The whole experience of the Liberal party shows that the distinctive institutional reforms and causes which that party has espoused are of interest only to a small, largely middle-class minority and probably the Liberals do not in this sense represent majority opinion even in the seats which they hold. However, the party has struggled to become a factor in what its leader, David Steel, hopes will be a realignment of political forces. It made the first major step in this direction when Mr Callaghan's Government lost its overall majority (due to one death and one departure) in March 1977 and had to reach a formal accommodation with the Liberals or face defeat in a motion of no confidence. It was significant that the two major measures the Liberals asked for in return for their support were not social or economic. They were both concerned with the machinery of government, one being a renewed effort to enact devolution for Scotland and Wales and the other being a Bill for direct elections to the European Parliament with a free vote on proportional representation. At the time of writing it was not clear whether the Labour Government could deliver on either of these points and therefore whether the accommodation with the Liberals would last beyond the autumn of 1977.

Unlike the Liberals, the Scottish National Party did make major inroads in the industrial and urban areas which were normally the preserve of the Labour party as well as in agricultural areas which had been controlled by the Conservatives. The Welsh National Party had its main successes in rural and Welsh-speaking north Wales. The main plank of these parties is basically a solution to the problem of local government, albeit an extreme one in that they advocate total independence. But in practice, the appeal of these parties was a combination of impatience at remote or impersonal bureaucracy and disappointment at the economic performance first of the Labour Government of 1964–70 and then at that of the Conservatives between 1970 and 1974. Only some 50 per cent of those voting Scottish Nationalist wanted total independence though over 60 per cent of the entire electorate declared a desire 'for more say over our own affairs'. Thus the rise of these parties is a symptom of the element of alienation from 'the system' which does exist, of the weakening of class loyalties, of the decreasing confidence and pride in being British and of the desire for a way of escape from the dilemmas that have confronted British politics in the 1960s and 1970s.

This survey of party attitudes to the problems of government in Britain both helps to explain and confirm why the situation is as it is. The major parties reflect the public's concern with their own conditions and in this, the chief determinant is still the social structure. The fact that the cleavages are not deep also reflects the large measure of agreement over the major problems affecting the society at any one time. Those who regard the division between the parties as bogus are merely asserting that they feel that other issues which cut across both parties, rather than between the parties, are more important to them. This may be true for them but it is clearly not true for the majority whom the parties represent. Nor is there much evidence that the present basis of social and political divisions is disappearing. Butler and Stokes have argued, almost certainly correctly, that it is weakening but it still remains as the principal guide to and determination of political loyalties.

The result of this investigation does not, however, help answer the question of how British government is likely to develop in the next decade. It shows that the community has not gone through dramatic experiences (of rapid industrialization, defeat in war, or class or race conflict) which would produce a powerful political philosophy, a philosophy which would then provide the answers to the major problems of political organization. There are remnants of old beliefs, a new hedonism, an interest largely in the outcome of government, an impatience with authority, a dislike of élite assumptions, all mixed together. As a result it is likely that the solutions adopted will be mixed but will on the whole confirm the present drift towards centralized executive power, towards a weakening of the system of representative government in favour of plebiscitary government while the major decisions are taken by the centralized executive relying on the Civil Service and in conclave with the powerful external pressure groups which represent the public as producers. The public as citizen, taxpayer and consumer will probably continue to feel bemused, neglected and somewhat alienated.

2.2 'What is wrong with British parliamentary democracy?' (From *Westminster Bank Review*, May 1968, pp. 20–35)

Recently there has been an outburst of criticism of politicians and of the political system in Britain. According to a National Opinion Poll when voters were asked to name the most useful members of the community 53% chose doctors and only 4% named MPs; 78% of respondents thought that most politicians would promise anything to get votes, 71% considered that Britain would be better off if there were some businessmen in the government and 66% said the politicians cared more about their party than about their country.

To examine these criticisms, BBC Television put on a series of three programmes in December 1967 and January 1968. They were called 'Change or Decay' and in introducing the first Mr Ian Trethowan said that 'more and more people are worried, indeed fed up about the way the country is being run'. Appearing on the first programme, Lord Robens thought that the explanation for the public's disillusionment with Parliament and politicians was that everyone was 'sick and tired of double-talk' and then, as on several other occasions, he argued that the country should be run in an entirely different fashion 'as a vast corporation'. On the 29th of February 1968 Lord Robens returned to the subject and said that the Prime Minister was 'pedalling a penny-farthing bicycle in a jet age in terms of government' and that what was wanted was not 'a businessman's government but a businesslike government'. During the second of the BBC programmes, Lord Butler put most emphasis on the spirit in which government is run but agreed that 'there is a good deal wrong with the system as well'; while in the last programme, Sir Paul Chambers argued 'that democracy . . . is becoming less effective' and that 'the machinery of government is becoming increasingly inefficient'. Three months earlier, Sir Paul had founded an Industrial Policy Group because of 'a deepening disquiet at the way in which our mixed economy is being governed' and a feeling that businessmen should make their views and values explicit. Mr James Callaghan, then the Chancellor of the Exchequer, thought that this body was 'potentially sinister'; but Sir Joseph Lockwood, one of the members of the Group, explained that its purpose was to study current problems and to pose solutions. He did, however, say that he had 'some doubts about democracy' and thought it would be better, once a Government had been elected, to 'close Parliament down for six months and let them get on with it'.

All this may not amount to much; but it is the first set of explicit objections to the Parliamentary system to break surface in Britain since the 1930s and there may be evidence of a groundswell of disenchantment that is still growing. The Nationalist Movements in Scotland and Wales are ostensibly democractic in that they want separate parliaments but there is also a strain of contempt for parliament, a tendency to refer to Westminster as a farce, a mere 'talking-shop', a strain which could easily become predominant. That half of those questioned in the poll referred to said they could detect no real difference between the parties, indicates a detachment which could turn to a rejection of this form of politics. In part the talk of a need for a coalition amounts to the same thing, a distrust of or a disbelief in party politics and a suggestion that neither party has sufficient capable men to form a full government and that neither can be relied on to put the national interest above party considerations.

Both a cause and an effect of these views is that service in public life, that is in politics, is no longer accepted as a natural and honourable objective for men who have proved their worth in other occupations. On the contrary, there is a positive reluctance on the part of those who have made their mark in industry, in the trade unions, at the bar or in the professions to accept nominations; and there is also a steady drain of men of ability out of the House of Commons into other occupations.

What then, are the critics of British democracy saying and how serious is this challenge? The first problem is that there is no single theme and indeed many of the objections are confused and contradictory. One obvious element is that the politicians have repeatedly failed to solve certain central problems such as maintaining steady growth without periodic balance-of-payments crises. They have been unable to devise a new international rôle for Britain after the dissolution of the Empire or to achieve their most recent objective in foreign policy, entry into the European Common Market.

On a slightly different level, the democratic machinery of government has seemed to be weak in the face of some of the other powerful institutions in the country. Neither Parliament nor the Cabinet could stop some recent damaging strikes or assert control over the prices charged by some industrial combines. The increasing use of the motor car crams and spoils our cities whatever transport bills are passed; and Lord Thompson buys up more newspapers whatever the preferences of the public for one kind of newspaper or another. Above all, the politicians seem to find it hard to control the civil service, the vast bureaucratic 'they' who do things to 'us', much the same things whatever party is in power.

While these general criticisms may be widely shared, any agreement breaks down once a more detailed analysis is attempted. Some argue that there are no great men left in politics and those who remain are of low quality or have few evident principles. The National Opinion Poll found 53% claiming that there were no outstanding men in any of the parties; but Lord Butler felt that a problem in managing Parliament was that 'we . . . are getting people of higher distinction in the Commons'.

Most of those with any knowledge of government have agreed that, while more men of ability in the Commons (and in local government) would be most desirable, there are enough of marked capacity to fill a Cabinet and that any weakness lies not in the men but in the machinery.

Here again there are divergencies. Lord Robens wants a two-tier Cabinet with the direction in the hands of ministers who are non-departmental, who can think and plan ahead. Both Lloyd George and Churchill went some distance with this idea in the two world wars; but in peacetime it has always broken down simply because the thinkers must have departmental knowledge to work on; and, conversely, the heads of the key departments can take decisions which will condition all future thinking. Many senior politicians would agree that they have too little time for reflection, that the information at their disposal is not always adequate and that there tends to be a dogfight at top levels over money and priorities when many of those taking part have not been able to study all the issues. Yet the solutions are not easy and lead in very different directions. Thus, while some advocate more parliamentary control, particularly of the civil service, others would like to give the government an even freer hand.

It is implicit in the views of many critics that the House of Commons is a nuisance, that its powers have prevented ministers doing their job properly. The talk about a businessman's government or a businesslike government often includes the analogy of a board of management and the annual meeting of shareholders. The latter can throw out a bad management but the executives get a year in which to prove themselves, with no need to explain each move and debate each decision. The only criterion is results in an annual balance sheet.

Sometimes this view, that the Commons interferes too much, that it has too much power and takes too much of ministers' time, confuses or combines the House with outside pressure groups. For instance, the present Labour Government appeared to be divided over the degree of control it wished to impose on wages in 1967. Part of the trouble was the difficulty of carrying such legislation; but the difficulty was a compound one of persuading trade union MPs to vote for a measure and also of carrying the TUC and of preventing a split which might have made things difficult at the party's annual conference where trade union votes were needed. Similarly when Mr (later Lord) Derek Heathcoat Amory had to abandon a section of his 1960 budget, this was not just due to pressure from MPs but to a combination of their efforts with City influence on ministers and the fact that the

Conservative Party organization was closely linked with and in part maintained by these interests. Nevertheless it is this type of combined capacity to resist unpalatable measures that has led some critics to look enviously at the powers exercised by General de Gaulle. He, it is said, was able to make devaluation work after 1958 just because he could rule by decree. Once the French had taken a cut in living standards and solved their balance-of-payments problem, steady expansion was possible and then the General won his vote of confidence.

On the other hand the opposite criticism is often made that the Commons is not strong enough to control the machinery of government. Britain had a number of failures in her Middle Eastern policy, from the Palestine Question just after the second World War through the Abadan crisis to the Suez War but, while one government succeeded another, no one knew who was giving the advice which led to these failures, what the advice was or whether these influential posts were still filled by the same men. The contrast with the time when the House of Commons had some real power in the nineteenth century is marked. Then members could force the Government to lay all relevant despatches on the table of the Commons and could insist on searching inquiries if there was inefficiency or failure.

In recent years there have been complaints about the power of the Treasury and its capacity to dominate the politicians, arguments put most strongly in Samuel Brittan's *The Treasury under the Tories, 1951– 1964*. The arguments had an influence on Labour thinking and it was to avoid a single source of advice on economic policy that the new Labour Government set up the Department of Economic Affairs in 1964. Since then, however, there has not been any marked improvement in the method or success of British economic policy though the Treasury has gradually reasserted its control. It was the Treasury, apparently, that urged a measure of deflation in early 1966 and that compiled the package of cuts in expenditure announced in July of that year. With the departure of Mr George Brown, the DEA declined in influence, the process being carried one stage further when Mr Shore took charge of the Department (which then lost a number of its powers) and again further when Mr Roy Jenkins became Chancellor of the Exchequer. It might not be inappropriate if Mr Brittan were to call a second volume of his study *Labour under the Treasury*.

Faced with all these confused and contradictory criticisms, is it necessary to conclude simply that when the country is not doing well each critic turns on the aspect of the system that he dislikes most, that all depends on value judgments? The development of political studies in recent years establishes certain points. For instance, despite totally different conclusions, commentators such as Professor Bernard Crick, Mr P. G. Richards and Mr Ronald Butt all reach much the same conclusion on the actual power of the House of Commons. It will help if the general lines of the discussion are set out.

To ascertain the power or influence of an institution, it is necessary to separate its effects from those of other allied or connected pressures; and this means asking again and again, 'what would have been different but for the activity of the Commons?' This is hard because, as has been mentioned above, the House or a section of members may be working with an outside pressure group whose influence has to be estimated and discounted. Or backbench agitation may coincide with by-election defeats, or a slump in the opinion polls, so that what appears to be a concession to certain members may be due more to evidence that the members are speaking for a body of voters who may change their allegiance on this issue.

The fact is that once the hardening of the party system stopped cross-voting in the Commons and every division became virtually a matter of confidence, the direct power of the Commons ceased and it was reduced to exercising influence. The extent of this influence can be established only by endless case studies; and the difficulty of these examples is that, after extensive research and interviewing, some of those most closely involved (such as ministers and officials) can still disagree about which pressure really led to a particular change of policy. Perhaps the Prime Minister changed his mind or there was a shift on a Cabinet Committee, a row on the government back-benches, outside representations or a report from constituency agents. In some cases all factors may be present and then it is very hard to allocate the shares of influence.

Nevertheless the influence of the Commons can be established within certain limits. Some commentators can and have argued that the Opposition have no influence at all. There is certainly very little evidence of any government listening to the official Opposition in the last twenty years. Those who claim some influence say that they can detect a similarity between clauses in one year's Finance Bill and amendments which they moved and had rejected in previous years. It can also be argued that if the Opposition hit on a line of policy with definite appeal, such as the Labour Party's superannuation plan of 1958, the Government may in time take over some of the ideas. This is all that can be said for Opposition influence during the lifetime of a government.

The main function of an Opposition is to put their own anti-government case to the electorate and they have about a third of the time available to the House in which to do this. Yet it would be wrong to list among the values of an Opposition that they can drive an unpopular government from office. It was often said that Lord Woolton's reorganized Conservative Party so harried Mr Attlee's weak and dispirited Government in 1950 and 1951 that it collapsed. There are naturally two sides to any battle; but most historians now agree that Attlee's Government fell to pieces, it more or less surrendered power, and that, while Conservative attacks hastened the process, the decision to dissolve at a bad time without any pre-election build-up was entirely the Prime Minister's. Similarly in 1963–64 Mr Wilson led the Opposition with great tactical skill but the key factor was whether Sir Alec Douglas-Home had suffficient time to restore confidence in the Conservative Party. Had he been able to delay the last legal date for the election by a further few weeks, he might well have won rather than lost by four seats. At present, when the Opposition are leading by 22½% on one opinion poll, this is due again to the failures of the Government rather than to credit being won by Mr Heath and his colleagues. Nor is this surprising for it is the Government which is making the news, they set the pace, produce or fail to produce results, explain their policies and choose the time at which to go to the country.

So the Opposition are there as the alternative should the Government fail; they try to spend their ideas and to create a climate of opinion; but they are in a relatively weak position and exercise only the most marginal influence over the activities of a Government.

The main influence possessed by the Commons is exercised by government backbenchers. They have a number of methods of approaching or pressing ministers. This can be in open debate (including questions, adjournment debates and the general 'sense of the House'), by deputations to the Prime Minister or the Chief Whip or by speeches in the meetings of the full parliamentary party held 'upstairs' in the House. When the Conservatives are in office their backbench 'subject groups' on agriculture, defence, foreign affairs and so on have some influence; but, though such groups also exist on the Labour Party side, they are less active and influential.

In assessing the degree to which the use of these channels has affected government policy, the problem is the variety of different estimates given by the ministers concerned. Some senior politicians, even including Prime Ministers, can be found who sincerely assert that they never gave way or altered course because of the views of their backbenchers. To do so, they declare, would be to abandon their task of governing. It is true that, whenever a ministry has decided that a policy is essential, it has pressed on whatever the reactions of its followers. The Conservatives forced through the abolition of Resale Price Maintenance in 1964 although their majority at one stage dropped to one. Both parties pushed ahead with applications to join the Common Market despite considerable doubts among sections of their followers; and now Mr Wilson is bent on imposing prescription charges and a statutory control on wages though these are anathema to a considerable number of Labour MPs.

On the other hand, it is possible to collect a series of cases where it appears that government policy has been adjusted to meet backbench objections or anticipated objections. Looking solely at the period since the 1966 election, it seems likely that the Government's dissociation of Britain from the bombing of Hanoi and Haiphong occurred to fore-stall left-wing hostility. It is probable that a factor which helped the 'soft-line' members of the Cabinet to carry a very mild form of wages legislation in 1967 was the opposition of the trade union group of MPs. It is quite certain that the closure of certain coal mines was delayed by the activity of the miners' MPs, though again a factor was the desire to retain the support of the NUM outside the House. Individual members can sometimes mount a campaign which exposes a weak case about which the Government themselves have doubts or where there are inconsistencies. Thus members showed that the Selective Employment Tax would not operate as intended on agriculture and would deal unfairly with charities; and in both these cases alterations were made. The weight of indignation inside and outside the House led Mr Callaghan to make a concession on Clause One of the Immigrants Bill, a concession which could have a considerable effect on the working of the Bill. Earlier, feelings on the backbenches were invoked in the Cabinet dispute on whether arms should be sold to South Africa or not. The withdrawal from East of Suez and the cut back in arms expenditure would almost certainly have led to the abandonment of the Aldabra base and the cancellation of the Anglo-French variable-geometry aeroplane, yet both steps were hastened by the campaign waged by Tam Dalyell MP against these projects. Dr Dun-woody followed up the ban on advertising cigarettes on television by obtaining a promise that the Government would legislate against the provision of gift coupons with cigarettes.

This is the total of instances in two years when backbench pressure from the Government side appears to have made some difference to government policy. There may be other cases which have escaped observation but they can have little effect on the general estimate of the influence of the Commons which is derived from comparing these cases with the total of decisions taken by the Government during this period.

The Commons has other effects besides its rôle in the formation of policy. It is the reservoir of manpower from which three quarters of the places in the Government are filled, including all the most important posts. Its collective reaction to a minister can make some difference to his career, as total failures in debate or at Question Time may (but need not) lead the Prime Minister to remove the minister; while notable successes may hasten promotion. The one important electoral function performed by MPs occurs on the rare occasions when the leadership of either the Government or the Opposition falls vacant and the respective parties meet to elect a successor. Finally, at moments of extreme crisis such as in late 1916 or May 1940 when Government failures reached the pitch of making an enemy victory over Britain an immediate possibility, the Commons were able to revert to their pre-1885 conduct and indicate dissatisfaction so strongly as to precipitate a change of Government.

This then is the total effectiveness or value of the House of Commons at the moment, a value which it renders at an annual cost of just over £3 million (out of an annual government expenditure of £9503 million). In these circumstances, is it worth maintaining Parliament? Should it be told to go home for a while (as Sir Joseph Lockwood suggested) or be reduced to receiving and approving an annual report on the state of the country like a shareholders meeting; or should its powers be increased and the Commons have restored to them the much stronger influence they had a hundred years ago?

The arguments for reducing the powers of the House even further are based on the belief that it slows down, hampers or diverts ministers from carrying out the policies that would be in the national interest. They assume either that a combination of ministers and civil servants knows best what is good for the country or that the only check that is necessary can be provided by pressure groups such as the CBI, the TUC, the BMA and so on. This argument rejects the view that an important aspect of government, even if considered only in terms of efficiency, is whether the public at large understand and accept policies. It is assumed that national affairs would proceed more smoothly

85

if governments did not have to carry even the present very docile House of Commons with them and that the idea that a policy has been approved by freely elected representatives is unimportant in getting it accepted and worked.

Is there any evidence for these views? The one occasion in recent history when senior politicians have suggested that they deviated from what they knew to be the correct path was in the late 1930s. Stanley Baldwin and some of his apologists have argued that rearmament was delayed only because the House and the electorate were unlikely to accept it. In fact this is a thin case because the famous 'confession' on rearmament applied to the period of the East Fulham by-election in 1933; and Baldwin made no great efforts to educate the electorate on this issue afterwards. Rearmament was not stressed in the 1935 election which the Conservatives won comfortably; and once Neville Chamberlain became leader in 1937 he did all he could to play down any danger from Germany. The main reason that rearmament was so slow in these years was not the House of Commons or the electorate but the considered priorities of the leading ministers.

It might also be argued that trade union reform since the Second World War has been held up by Conservatives' fears of antagonizing bodies which contain considerable numbers of Conservative voters and by Labour's close connection with the unions. On the other hand, it is not easy for any government to alter the structure of complex private bodies if their functions are not to be taken over by the state. It is one thing to say that certain types of strikes are to be made illegal or to be open to actions for civil damages but it is another to demonstrate that such changes can be enforced.

Apart from these two very dubious examples, there is little evidence of ministers being held back or thwarted in their policies by MPs. Indeed one of the most marked features of the British political system is the power it confers on governments to act as they like subject only to the sanction of the next general election. If, then, it seems to be true that British policies have failed too often in recent years, this cannot be blamed on the House of Commons. And if the arguments of the critics are carefully examined, this case is never seriously made. The irritation against MPs, and against democratic practices, is more a rub-off of criticisms of 'the system' as a whole. Most of those who have worked the system either ignore the House of Commons or argue that it should be stronger. Mr Maudling was neutral on this point; but Mr Crossman, Lord Butler and Lady Sharp all agreed that Parliament could act as a more useful stimulant, critic and countervailing power if certain reforms were made.

The arguments for this second proposition, that the House of Commons should be stronger, fall into several categories. One is that legislation must be understood by, and be acceptable to, the public if it is to work smoothly. Too many of those framing laws or taxes have lived all their lives in Whitehall and do not appreciate how some provisions may affect the public. They may not always have worked out all the implications. To be forced to explain why a measure is needed, what background work was done, which alternatives were considered, what the outside groups had to say and how each clause is to operate, is an essential part of the process of efficient legislation. There is considerable evidence that some recent taxes and laws have been too hastily prepared (SET, the Immigration Bill, the Transport Bill) and that further explanation, discussion and amendment would have produced more workable Acts.

Secondly, the present legislative process takes into consideration most organized interests but neglects the taxpayer and the consumer simply because their only representatives are the members of parliament. Perhaps the best example is the determination of agricultural policy. Every year, the Minister of Agriculture and his officials meet the National Farmers Union about the beginning of the year. First the costs and trends in agriculture are established. Then there are negotiations about the money to be provided by the taxpayer to achieve certain levels of farm income and output; and the result, the Annual Price Review, is announced in March. During the two months when the critical decisions are being taken the Minister, as one holder of the office has put it, 'goes into purdah'. He virtually refuses to see any MPs, even from agricultural constituencies, in case it should bias his view or spoil his negotiations with the NFU. MPs are told 'come back and see me by all means, once the decisions are taken'. This is perhaps the most complete example of a general tendency to try to exclude the House of Commons from major decisions.

When a Bill is prepared, every interested group is consulted, except the public because they are not organized. The body that is supposed to undertake this task, the House of Commons, is not called in at the critical formative stage but is presented with a *fait accompli* when any changes would cause the government to lose face.

A further argument in favour of increased powers for the Commons is simply that the size and activity of the Civil Service has increased so greatly that it can no longer be effectively supervised by sixty or seventy ministers. Officials may know best on many issues; but where policy is being made down to the level of Assistant Secretary, it may also be advisable to know who is making which decision and to ensure that all the research necessary for decision-making has been done. In recent years there has been a great deal of evidence of legislation based on no thorough study of the background, of Rent Acts based on no adequate survey of the state of rented property, of estimates of the effect of sanctions on Rhodesia that have been wildly out, of preparations to enter the Common Market without a detailed understanding of how its rules actually operate and so on. If 'the system' makes mistakes, and these are mistakes of unknown officials, there is no use cursing ministers or MPs who have equally little idea of who is at fault. Far better to turn to the one agency with the right to investigate in the public interest, the House of Commons, and give it this task to be conducted by specialist committees armed with powers of interrogation.

A particular example of this general point is that the Commons has lost almost all control over finance. When the Finance Bills were simple, small measures and members could vote as they liked, a system of annual control was established which matched the annual budgeting of the Treasury. This worked very well till the 1890s when public finance became more complex. Now the government operates a five year system of forecasting of public expenditure and the House of Commons is left deliberately with the old annual calendar which bears virtually no relation to what actually happens. Thus control is impossible except through the two committees on Estimates and Public Accounts. The worth of even this limited degree of control has been demonstrated again and again, as when excessive profits on sales to the government were detected (the amount being more than sufficient to pay the cost of the whole of Parliament for the year).

Lastly, no one has suggested that Britain should give up being led, at least mainly, by men trained in politics, which means men who have come up through the House of Commons. Yet there is a serious danger that the supply of adequate talent for political leadership will cease if politics is continually denigrated, if the House of Commons is belittled and if the influence of MPs is further reduced so that the life of a backbencher offers little to men of ability and ambition. At the moment, the leading trade unionists will not stand for election; and senior businessmen are not ready to let their brightest junior executives serve. When either party looks like being out of office for some time, some of the best men leave for posts that offer a chance for creative activity. Labour lost a number of men of Cabinet timber in this way before 1964; and if the Conservatives were to lose the next election, many of their leading spokesmen (some already part-timers in the City) might be tempted to depart. The result could only be to weaken the standards in British politics and to lead to more failures and more public criticism.

It would seem that, without entering into any value judgments about democracy, arguing purely on grounds of efficiency and results, there is a far stronger case for increasing the power of the House of Commons than for reducing it. Also one would have thought that this case would appeal to all sections of the community, from businessmen with their suspicions of officials to rank and file voters who are exposed to the decisions of a far-flung bureaucracy. Yet this is not the case. As has been shown at the start of this article, many of the objections are aimed at MPs, at the House of Commons, at the one portion of the machine which gives the public some right to intervene and be heard.

The reasons for this can only be guessed from personal impressions. A careful attitude survey would be needed to produce an accurate account of them. Part of the explanation is simply that when the nation has suffered disappointments and set-backs, there is a desire to blame someone and while the MP is seen and known, the officials responsible are covered by the anonymity of Whitehall. Part is that the public have been fed on old accounts of the sovereignty of Parliament. They were told MPs were elected to represent them, but are now beginning to realize just how powerless the Commons and its members are, a realization which makes them say, rightly enough, that they have been deceived. Politicians want to persuade people to support the parties, to canvass and collect dues, and to come out and vote; and so they stress that the result of the next election will make a real difference, which leads to an inevitable wave of disappointment if it does not.

Another factor, which is more serious and more difficult to pin down, is that the gaps in communication in our society appear to be widening despite increased standards of living and of education. At the time when British democracy was establishing itself, Gladstone had no hesitation about speaking for two hours to assembled villagers on the complexities of the Eastern Question. Now there is a sense, particularly among senior professional men, business executives and officials that it is hard to explain the actual facts of a situation to the public, that government by secrecy and slogans is the best way of proceeding. The opposite side of this coin is the popular belief that there is an inner élite who govern but who do not reveal all the facts, a belief which irritates voters. The House of Commons loses every way. It is excluded from the essential information because ministers, officials and pressure groups fear that their precious secrets will be leaked and that the public will hear the real arguments underlying decisions. Yet the public fasten their resentment on MPs because they feel politicians ought to know and to have told them the facts rather than come back later on apologizing because election promises could not be kept.

British Parliamentary democracy is in real danger because it is being ground away by these two pressures. Too weak, too much under the control of the respective front benches to act on its own or to help itself, the House of Commons is having its influence steadily reduced by the increasing power and secrecy of Whitehall and the outside pressure groups with which Whitehall deals. At the same time the public still expect the House of Commons to exercise a measure of control and if it seems less and less capable of doing so, their confidence will continue to decline. There is not much time left in which to arrest this process.

2.3 'The Member of Parliament as representative or delegate' (From *The Parliamentarian*, Jan. 1971, pp. 14–21)

This question has aroused controversy since the Greek city-state, since the first recorded discussion of political problems. The dilemma was put in its starkest form by Rousseau when he said that 'Sovereignty, being no more than the exercise of the general will, can never be alienated and . . . the sovereign . . . can be represented by no one but himself . . . Sovereignty cannot be represented, for the same reason that it cannot be alienated . . . The Deputies of the People are not, nor can they be its representatives.' Yet in a modern mass democracy men cannot represent themselves, so there must be a process of representation and the problem arises: how should the system work and how far should the representative be bound by external elements in his constituency or in his party?

As evidence that this is no academic question, it happens that the author's own constituency party of Berwick and East Lothian met on 13 September 1970 to discuss a paper submitted by one of the party activists. Headed 'Democracy within the Labour Party: Some Observations', it included the following section:

Constituency Political Action:

Our MP is our representative at Westminster. He serves all his constituents and yet is already under severe constraints when making political decisions.

 i Patronage (especially when Party is in power).
 ii Chief Whip and discipline of Parliamentary Labour Party.
 iii As a Labour MP he accepts party manifesto and by his party ticket he
     declares to his constituents his allegiance to the Labour Movement.

Like local councillors the MP is clearly in Parliament as a result of the work of activists and yet at the same time we are a good deal less informed about the national situation than we are about local affairs and therefore cannot as yet expect to control the actions and decisions our MP takes. However, we do have a right and duty to participate in their formation.

Proposals:

1 The MP should attend all meetings of the General Management Committee
  and Executive.
2 The MP should inform us in detail of the business of Parliament and his
  voting record in the House. He should also keep us fully informed of the
  business and meetings of the Parliamentary Labour Party.
3 All major items of forthcoming business should be discussed and the
  attitude of the Constituency Labour Party to these issues established.
  The MP should inform us in advance if he is to vote against these
  decisions.

The proposals would result in a greater flow of information which would enable us to formulate our ideas on national politics; they would also enable us to participate more fully in the making and implementation of these decisions by our MP.

In order to analyse the problem, it is best to begin from the two most extreme cases and narrow the situation until a reasonable accommodation is reached. The most extreme case of the representative theory is still the famous address delivered by Edmund Burke to the electors of Bristol in 1774:

Parliament is not a congress of Ambassadors from different and hostile interest, . . . Parliament is a deliberative assembly of one nation, with one interest, that of the whole . . . You choose a Member indeed, but when you have chosen him, he is not Member of Bristol, but he is Member of Parliament . . .

Certainly, gentlemen, it ought to be the happiness and glory of a representative to live in the strictest union, the closest correspondence, the most unreserved communication with his constituents. . . . It is his duty to sacrifice his repose, his pleasures, his satisfactions to theirs. But his unbiased opinion, his enlightened conscience, he ought not to sacrifice to you, to any man, or to any set of men living. These he does not derive from your pleasure; no, nor from the law and the constitution. They are a trust from Providence, for the abuse of which he is deeply answerable. Your representative owes you, not his industry only, but his judgement, and he betrays, instead of serving you, if he sacrifices it to your opinion.

There is no equally eloquent statement of the attitude common among party activists that the MP's task is to transmit his constituency's view, to explain his own position to his supporters, and to be prepared to modify it if his constituency declares to the contrary that he is there to communicate opinions rather than to contribute his own but the document submitted to Berwick and East Lothian Labour Party and quoted above is a good example of this kind of thinking.

Of these two positions, Burke's is by far the most tenable as he allows that there must be overall harmony. If this did not exist, then the electors of Bristol could choose someone else at the next election. Burke had grounds, in the days of a small electorate, for saying that the electors knew him (or any other candidate); they had formed opinions as to his views and the quality of his judgement before he was elected and he had therefore been elected in large part because of these qualities. Once elected, he was therefore entitled, indeed instructed, to use his own judgement.

On the other hand, the extreme theory of delegation breaks down more or less at once when it is asked 'who delegates?' So many answers are possible and the machinery of delegation, the machinery for ascertaining views of the delegators, is so hard to devise that the concept runs into immediate difficulties. Indeed, as the constituency resolution printed above recognizes, pressures on the MP to act according to fixed rules or instructions come from quite different and sometimes contradictory sources. Some can be said to come from below, that is in the constituency, and some from above or from the party organization in Parliament. Often the two are linked but sometimes they are opposed.

It is worth starting by looking at the pressures from below and examining the various bodies and sectors of opinion which might feel entitled to mandate or instruct an MP. The widest sector of opinion is the entire constituency and such pressures can arise in Britain with its relatively small single-member constituencies. For instance, where a seat includes either a single economic interest or has geographical problems affecting every voter, this may happen. There are, and have been, constituencies based so completely upon mining villages in Nottinghamshire, Durham, and South Wales that it is reasonable to argue that the welfare of that industry affects virtually every voter. Similarly, to represent Orkney and Shetland is to accept a concern for transport to the mainland which is shared by every islander. But the vast majority of constituencies in most countries contain a mass of interests and geographical considerations, some of which may be contradictory, and this leaves the MP to weigh and consider which he will support, which aspect of his constituency he will represent, or what position he feels it correct to adopt.

A second group who may claim the sole right to instruct the MP are his party voters. They elected him and may claim that he owes a primary allegiance to them. Mixed town and country constituencies sometimes reveal these feelings. The author was asked recently by a burgh in his constituency to press for the rating burden to be raised on agriculture in order to make things easier for townspeople. One argument made was that the townspeople elected him and since, it was alleged, the farmers largely voted Conservative, he should give his backing to those in the towns who were predominantly Labour voters.

Apart from the actual merits of the argument, one difficulty of this kind of pressure is that the group claiming credit for the return of the MP can be further refined, the extreme position being reached in the resolution quoted above when it says 'the MP is clearly in Parliament as a result of the work of activists', a group which, in most constituencies, would number under 200 people. As this particular seat was won by 641 votes, the same argument could be made by any cohesive group of 641 who could have been persuaded to abstain or by any 321 who could have unitedly switched their votes to the Conservative candidate. Thus the fishing community in one village, or the tightly knit Catholic community in another part of the constituency could both claim to have been the marginal group who sent the MP to Westminster, thus being entitled to his undeviating support.

Finally, in the Labour Party there is the question of nomination and sponsorship. A candidate may be selected for a seat because he was the nominee of a certain union or a certain group within the party and they may feel that, as a result, they have a special claim upon his time and his influence. Some MPs continue to be sponsored by bodies after their election and these bodies may pay the Member an addition to his salary or they may contribute to his election expenses or to the running costs of the constituency party. There have been cases where such organizations have threatened to withdraw this help unless the MP votes a certain way. Such threats are usually held to be breaches of privilege, but it is legitimate for an organization to refuse to renew its sponsorship or support in consequence of the way an MP has voted or the views he has expressed in the past.

These, then, are the groups which might claim to instruct a Labour MP (it is only slightly different for Conservatives) and the effectiveness of the pressure is greatest at both ends. Clearly an MP will not wish to fly in the face of the cherished interests of his entire constituency and he may feel the direct pressure of his own constituency party and his sponsoring body, each of which has a machinery for bringing its views to bear.

Turning to the other end, the pressures from agencies inside the parliamentary party, they can be related to those exercised by the constituency. The leading example is the possession of the party label. This can be forfeited if the MP has the party Whip withdrawn and the result, in every case except one since 1945, has been defeat at the subsequent election. Because the MP has the party label and relies so completely on it, he is obliged to vote with his party on most issues of confidence in the House of Commons. Certain exemptions on 'conscience grounds' are allowed, but it has always been hard to define such cases. It has boiled down to mean any issue on which the MP feels so strongly that he must dissociate himself from his party. But the MP knows that if he does this on purely political questions, if he votes with the Conservatives and if he can be singled out (either for acting alone or for being incorrigible), he risks the withdrawal of the Whip. The Conservatives have not taken such action since 1942 but they usually find it is as effective to allow the constituency party to act and to threaten the MP with replacement at the next election.

The second form of pressure comes from the Whips' control of patronage but this is of a somewhat different kind because, if it is accepted, it is self imposed. While there is nothing dishonourable in an MP wishing to become a Minister (or to qualify for trips abroad, knighthoods, or chairmanships of certain Committees), there is no reason why any Member should alter his conduct in order to achieve such objectives. But it must be admitted that this pressure can sometimes run counter to constituency and local party desires that the MP should press a certain case, especially if the case irritates the MP's own leaders and embarrasses them politically.

This leads to the difficulties of what the MP can and should do when a group or section in the constituency wishes to delegate him to behave in a certain way and his party in Parliament has the opposite point of view. For instance, in a few months, the Conservatives may be placing a three-line Whip on their Members to vote for entry to the Common Market with some constituency associations wishing to instruct their Member to vote against entry. And the constituency parties may go further and say that besides being the group that chose the MP, besides being the activists whose work secured his return, they are also reflecting, in this instance, the views of most Conservative voters and, according to opinion polls, the views of most voters of all parties in the constituencies. The MP, if he is merely responding to pressure, may turn to his Chief Whip and make these points, to be told that without the official backing of the Conservative Party, without his party ticket, he would never hold the seat, as the electors' interest in this one issue is not as persistent as the Labour-Conservative cleavage, and it is on this overall question of allegiance that his subsequent re-election will turn.

To this conflicting group of claims on the loyalty and actions of the MP, two further issues or factors must be added. One is that the Member has to do more than just speak and vote. There are further claims on his time and energy and he can do other things for his constituents, such as provide information about his own activities and about what is happening inside his party and inside Parliament. His party may not wish to direct him how to act, but is it entitled to be told how he acts, for instance, when he votes for a leader for the party? The second, and most difficult item is the allowance to be made for the MP's own views, judgement, and opinion. Basically no one can have respect for men who repeatedly advocate causes of action with which they disagree. Yet this has, to some extent, to be done by Cabinet Ministers and by party politicians. But both observers and participants expect that at some point the Member's own judgement of what is correct can and should come into operation. The question is when and under what circumstances?

The problem is made more difficult if the MP is given a special degree of security. The answer was not so hard for someone in Burke's position. It was realistic for him to say: 'Leave me to judge what is right but I accept that, if my constituents often dislike the outcome, they are entitled to turn to another candidate at the next election'. In the eighteenth century this could and did happen. Now, however, the party ticket means almost automatic victories in safe seats and it has become the practice in Britain that once an MP is selected, he will in almost every case be readopted unanimously and automatically until he dies or retires. In two recent cases, the constituencies have rebelled, in one refusing to renominate Mrs Margaret

Mackay because of her ardent advocacy of the Arab cause, and in the other refusing to renominate Mr S. O. Davies because he was 83. But given that normally MPs have security of tenure (unless actually defeated), the case that they must accommodate themselves to certain levels of feeling in their constituency parties becomes stronger.

Even then it is hard to fix any limits. The constituency party rejected Mr S. O. Davies, but he was re-elected when he stood as an Independent. The local activists may be highly unrepresentative both of the loyal party voters and of the electorate as a whole. And the smaller the party membership the more this is likely to be the case. There was a time recently when, in the fifteen Glasgow seats (thirteen of them held by Labour) the total number of reasonably active Labour Party members was estimated at under 500. . .

The first duty of a Member under these circumstances is to explain his position to his local party. Burke was correct in arguing that the MP should make every effort to carry the local party with him and he should be given every facility to do so. Attempts to devise actual machinery to allow appeals from the local party activists to all party members or to the mass of party voters have always run into serious difficulties. When populists, who believed in direct democracy in the United States, tried to remove the power of the local party executives, they turned to the primary. But this has not proved very satisfactory because it only pushed the battle back one stage to the question of who is capable of organizing the primary and bringing out the voters? In practice all that can be said is that the MP must try and the local association should help him to explain his views as often and as fully as possible.

Where an MP is a deeply committed party supporter but disagrees with specific policies, the national leadership should lean over backwards to protect him. If any such move is made, it is usually for the rather different reason that the publicity which quarrels of this kind evoke can be politically damaging. The more satisfactory reason is that all parties should (but rarely do) welcome men of independence of mind and deep conviction and there is always the possibility that these dissidents may be right. The minority of despised anti-appeasement Conservatives in the late 1930s happened to be right. So were the Bevanites in the early 1950s when they said that the level of rearmament proposed by Mr Gaitskell was unattainable and, insofar as an attempt was made to attain it, would destroy the Labour Party's social programme.

The counter may be made that the individual MP is not likely to be right – after all he is overworked, gets no special information not available to the public, and has little chance to form a detached opinion. But the Government, once it embarks on a policy, has great methods of preventing discussion. Ministers are bound by collective responsibility, by the feeling that it is 'not their pigeon', and by the desire for promotion. The local activists, although their sources of information are as good as those of the average MP, are not on the job full-time, have far less to lose, and do not know the personalities involved in any direct way. So the pressures against MPs caught in such a pincer movement are great, the dangers so obvious and threatening that anyone who stands out under such circumstances deserves the greatest consideration.

Burke is basically right. A man who finds himself out of sympathy over a considerable range of issues and period of time with the vast majority of his constituents, or with the body of his (national) party, should give up the job. But while he holds the job it would be disgraceful to take up positions he at heart believed to be false or contrary to the public interest simply because of the demands of his local party or the Whips in the House of Commons. Such are the pressures against men who take these stands, that they should be aided and respected wherever possible. This is in sharp contrast to the disagreement with the leadership in Parliament that is applauded in the constituency parties. Such disagreements are, no doubt, genuine but they can bring great political rewards of notoriety in the Labour Party, election to the National Executive and even office (after which the disagreements naturally tend to disappear). But the MP who disagrees with both his party in his constituency and his party in Parliament is taking his life in his hands. He must be respected and supported by all in a position to do so, whether they agree with his particular views or not. Nevertheless, there is a point when such opinions, genuinely held, should lead the Member to realize that it is no longer appropriate for him to represent his constituency in the House or to carry his party label. The precise point at which this realization should occur to the MP cannot be fixed. It would be better for such a decision to come from the MP rather than be forced on him from outside and it is to be hoped that those involved in such disputes realize that what matters is the long-run direction of their representative's political views and actions. In the short-run it is very hard to tell in such disputes who is being true or false to his party, and reasonable judgements of this kind can be made only when the period in question can be seen in perspective.

2.4 'Anybody still for democracy?' (from *Encounter*, Nov. 1972, pp. 19–27)

With President Nixon's recent visit to Moscow – and with the growth of worries about the internal political health of some Western countries, the old Cold War slogans about the inherent superiority of 'the democratic way of life' seem to be less appropriate. And this will be no loss, as they were usually a substitute both for thought and real feeling. But such sloganising was about the only time the West ever emphasised its political system and its beliefs. It is true that throughout the 1950s Western institutions were exported to the former European colonies, but probably only a minority of Left-wing liberals believed that democracy had world-wide value. The departing colonial officials set up elections, courts, and parliaments, partly because they were told to, and partly because they found it hard to think of any coherent alternative. Only when Western observers were confronted by Khrushchev's 1956 revelations to the Twentieth Congress of the Soviet Communist Party (so vividly confirmed later on in the novels of Solzhenitsyn), by the Berlin Wall of 1961 or by the forcible suppression of Czech socialist freedom in 1968, was there any return to or reflections about the real value of the democratic system.

A symptom of this situation is that today most academics, writers, and politicians would be hard put to it to make a coherent defence of democracy, to explain the theory and distinguish between essentials and mere machinery. It is a curious but well-known fact that the writing of political philosophy has virtually ceased since the Second World War and though student Left-wingers have returned to Marxism or neo-Marxist adaptations, this only emphasises the vacuum in current political thinking and the lack of ideological support for the way in which most of the advanced industrial nations seek to organise their societies.

Indeed the same drift into uncertainty, not on party-political dogmas so much as on the basic principles of social action, has overtaken many contemporary British politicians, most of whom formed their opinions during or not long after the last war. At that time politics, in the sense of how the country should be run and peace preserved, seemed vitally important; and it was taken for granted that these goals could be achieved by Parliamentary means. The heroes of the non-Communist Left were men such as Stafford Cripps or Aneurin Bevan; even rank-and-file MPs were regarded with respect; and the common objective was to retain or win a majority in Parliament. It was in these years that the House of Commons established the National Health Service and nationalised several major industries, so that there was no real fear of a conspiracy of money interests which could upset the result of a general election.

Now many of these attitudes have gone. Even those youthful students who will join a Labour Club shrug their shoulders over the leading members of the British Labour Party; the average MP is used to the public's mild contempt for politicians; and winning a majority in the Commons is not seen as a major step in any direction. The idea that the Parliamentary system can be used to make positive changes in our society has dwindled, not because it is thought that the City or Big Business or Whitehall would deliberately challenge a Left government, but because the House of Commons and both political parties tend to be written off as part of the same rather flabby, immovable, complacent establishment.

One subject on which democrats did feel a spurt of excitement and renewed commitment after the War was in the late 1950s and early '60s with the rush to independence and self-government in Africa. This was a real vindication of their underlying belief in the rights and dignity of man. It was evidence that without formal education and without the penumbra of a developed industrial society, people still aspired to run their own affairs. Perhaps this sentiment reached its peak in 1958 when Harold Macmillan's Conservative Government put the newly-returned Dr Hastings Banda in prison and accused the African Nationalists in Nyasaland of having prepared an elaborate 'massacre plot'. That venerable and ancient gathering, the General Assembly of the Church of Scotland, came alive that summr as the missionaries back from Nyasaland, aided by a Left-wing group among the clergy called the 'Iona Community', battled with their more conservative or quiescent brethren on the basic issue of whether Africans could be 'trusted' and whether they were 'fit' to govern themselves. There was much rejoicing when the progressives won, and soon after they were vindicated by the Devlin Report. Since then, as is well known, Dr Banda has exiled his opposition and has become the symbol of collaboration with South Africa.

Those excited by African democracy shifted their admiration first to Kwame Nkrumah and then to Jomo Kenyatta, followed by Kenneth Kaunda and Julius Nyerere. Though *apartheid* remains a major enemy and African self-government still gets the support of liberals and radicals, the Congo fiasco and the Nigerian Civil War, the military coups and the mass deportations throughout Africa have transformed their original enthusiasm into a rather weary realism.

In Britain itself, the last time there was a mood of reform and renewal was the early 1960s leading up to the 1964 general election. But, in retrospect, though there was a feeling that Britain was 'out-of-date' and needed 'renovation', the principles on which reconstruction was to be based were not at all clear. It was an eclectic movement, sometimes calling for more Managerial Efficiency, sometimes anticipating unnamed improvements as the result of the application of Technology, while in other cases accepting the need for greater popular control or 'Participation'. This confusion came out in the somewhat muted call for parliamentary reform, it never being clear whether the objective was more efficiency (*i.e.* rapid action by the executive), or the abolition of medieval parliamentary forms, or increased power for back-benchers in the Commons to watch over the executive.

The kind of doubts held by politicians themselves, by civil servants, and by the interested public about the meaning and value of democracy were, however, fairly evident. A small but revealing example is the belated reform of the Health Service which eventually emerged in 1972. When the Service was being set up in 1947–8, many hospitals were owned and managed by the local-elected borough and county councils. It was then argued that these units were 'too small' to run a proper Health Service and so the hospitals were taken away from the local authorities and placed under the control of a number of nominated regional hospital boards. The Conservative Party, in opposition at the time, said it was quite wrong to give this kind of responsibility (including the power to allocate and spend so much public money) to non-elected bodies, and it proposed that the member should be elected. Aneurin Bevan resisted this on the ground that he was establishing a national (if somewhat de-centralised) service for which the Minister was responsible and could be questioned and controlled by the House of Commons. In fact, while this has been true of the overall policies of the Health Service, in their own regions the boards have been largely laws unto themselves.

So, when in the late 1960s the reform of local government was proposed – the new units being larger authorities of almost exactly the same size as the regional hospital boards – it seemed as though a return to an element of democratic control in the Health Service would be possible, a united Health Service in each region could be made the responsibility of the new, elected councils.

But first the Labour Government, and then its Conservative successors, decided on exactly the opposite course of action. Newly nominated area Health boards were to be created, but instead of being under the control of the elected councils, they were to be on their own; and what remained of the local authority Health Services – the Medical Officers of Health, District Nurses, School Health Service, etc. – was to be taken away from the elected councils and given to these *ad hoc* boards which would be, for practical purposes, under the control of the medical profession.

Why did this happen? Part of the reason was the deep distrust of both the senior civil service and MPs for local elected councils. A major influence was the pressure of the medical profession who detested the idea of explaining their proposals and adjusting their priorities to meet the demands of elected representatives. They argued that, while it was entirely proper to have the educational service controlled by councillors, it would be quite improper to have the same arrangement for the Health Service, a view which suggests that the allocation of priorities in health is purely a matter of professional expertise. In fact the same value-judgements and essentially political decisions are involved as in any other allocation of resources among different sectors of the community.

If democratic procedures are regarded with this degree of doubt or suspicion in Britain today where did the original belief come from and what precisely did it amount to?

In political terms, the basic step towards democracy was the Reform Act of 1867 which enfranchised all urban male householders. The serious debate which led to this result was begun in 1864 by Gladstone. When contemplating the refusal of the Lancashire mill workers to turn against the anti-slavery cause despite the unemployment produced by the North's blockade of the South during the American Civil War, he asked:

What are the questions that fit a man for the exercise of a privilege such as the franchise? Self-command, self-control, respect for order, patience under suffering, confidence in the law, regard for superiors; and when, I should like to ask, were all these great qualities exhibited in a manner more signal, even more illustrious, than in the conduct of the general body of the operatives of Lancashire?

Soon afterwards Gladstone began to put the proposition in the negative and to ask: on what grounds could it ever be right to exclude a man from the franchise? He concluded that a share, however small, in political power meant that each individual was able to take sides in the great issues of the day, and that these were essentially moral questions. Gladstone's deep religious views left him in no doubt that each individual was responsible for his own moral judgements, and therefore no one could claim that their superior education, or property, made them fit to take these decisions for other people. It was this line of reasoning which found such a response among industrious working men, steeped in non-conformist religion. The remark that was said to have 'set the Thames on fire' was Gladstone's comment:

that every man who is not presumably incapacitated by some consideration of personal unfitness or of political danger is morally entitled to come within the pale of the constitution.

His strongest opponent was Robert Lowe, later Lord Sherbrooke. Lowe referred to John Stuart Mill who (in 1865, he said) spoke 'of every citizen of a State having a perfect right to share in its government' and pointed out that such an argument:

appeals to some *a priori* considerations. . . . But where are those *a priori* rights to be found? . . . If they do in reality exist, they are as much the property of the Australian savage and the Hottentot of the Cape as of the educated and refined Englishman.

But not all Englishmen were educated and refined. He asked his fellow MPs:

Let any gentleman consider the constituencies he has had the honour to be concerned with. If you want venality, if you want ignorance, if you want drunkenness and facility for being intimidated . . . if . . . you want impulsive, unreflecting and violent people, where do you look for them in the constituencies? Do you go to the top or to the bottom?

There followed the clear conclusion:

Once give the men votes, and the machinery is ready to launch these votes in one compact mass upon the institutions and property of this country.

These extracts come from different speeches but in the dispute between Gladstone, Bright, and Mill on the one hand, and Robert Lowe
on the other, the underlying issue was clearly revealed. If government
is a matter of *technique and expertise*, then some people are bound to
know more and be better able to comment than others. If, on the
other hand, the main political decisions are *value-judgments*, then no
man can take this kind of decision for his neighbour. Gladstone would
not for a moment have said that one person is no more likely to be
right than the next, for he believed profoundly that there was one
truth, one proper course of action in each situation, but that every
individual is responsible for seeking his truth; the obligation to
do so cannot be confined merely to those with titles, property, or
education.

These views would seem radical even today; and, in the sense that
they reveal an equal respect for each individual, they are. But this
doctrine has to be added on to the rest of the views and practices that
Gladstone and his Liberal followers took for granted. Thus there was
no suggestion that every working man was equally competent to govern, or equally competent to pronounce upon complicated matters. It
was the task of leaders to explain and to administer, to bring out the
salient value-judgements at stake, and then it was the electors' duty to
give their verdict.

Such political doctrines implied clear rules both for leaders and for
the public at large. It was quite immoral, Gladstone thought, for a
politician to go looking for issues, to go constructing programmes. His
task was to explain how the government should be conducted and if
injustices became apparent, he should explain how they should be
remedied. If the electorate agreed, they would support him. If not,
there could be no question of altering his views to win votes. Time
and the follies (or successes) of his opponents would reveal who was
right. And, of course, the electorate could make a wrong decision –
after all, had they not once given Disraeli a majority? – but, in the
end, truth must triumph. History showed zig-zags but also a discerni-
ble progress towards truth so that the politicians who said 'what was
right' were bound to win in 'the long run'. In politics, as in private
life, virtue brought the appropriate rewards.

It was on these very simple moral ideas and optimistic assumptions
that British democracy was based. The result was being a steady extension of the franchise; the democratisation of local government; the
foundation of the Labour Party; and the first suggestions that, in addi-

tion to the Irish, even Hindus and Hottentots would eventually be entitled to self-government.

Then came a series of blows to the optimistic assumptions, of which the worst were the 1914–18 War, the rise of Fascism and the drift of communism into totalitarian tyranny. In addition, democratic methods were abused: referenda led to a pseudo-populism, and the mass media could be manipulated to bolster evil régimes. While none of this actually invalidated democracy and no alternative political system suitable for Britain has been suggested, the total effect has been to weaken any positive belief. In the last twenty years, and there can be no denying it, confusion and apathy and disillusion have crept in. The old democratic maxims remain; but, because there is little real vigour behind them, they do not appear as a coherent body of thought.

One confusion or corruption of democratic theory that has become common is the assertion that Majorities are Always Right. A Fleet Street advertising slogan insists: '*A paper with five million readers cannot be wrong*'. There is a fond illusion that a general meeting of students, or the annual conference of a political party, must always produce the correct policy proposals.

In any attempt to sort out the essence of the theory, it is first necessary to ask: Which majority is entitled to speak on what issue? As a candidate for the rectorship of a Scottish University – a post representing the students on the University court – I was asked repeatedly if I would always accept the majority opinion. This turned out to be the views of a majority of that minority of students which came to a general meeting. There are 11,000 at this university, and general meetings rarely reached 1000. In any case, on issues of university policy, the academic staff are also part of the community affected; the money comes largely from the general taxpayer; and should these groups not be reckoned as part of the constituency from which a majority should be drawn?

Another example has arisen recently where Mr Dick Taverne has been asked to stand down as Labour MP for Lincoln. He was rejected by a majority of the constituency management committee. But he claims (as did Nigel Nicolson, the Conservative MP who was similarly dismissed by his Bournemouth Constituency Party) that a majority of Labour Party members, a majority of Labour voters, and a majority of all voters in Lincoln would prefer to retain him.

Thus the same issue can often be decided in different ways, not on the merits of the case but by asserting that a 'majority' is entitled to have its way, and then by arranging the constituency so that the appropriate majority is created. For instance, should the Royal Ulster Constabulary and the British Army be denied entry to the Bogside and Creggan areas of Londonderry? A majority in the Catholic enclave says 'Yes' – a majority in Northern Ireland says 'No' – a majority in a United Ireland would say 'Yes' – a majority in the United Kingdom of Great Britain and Northern Ireland would say 'No'. . . .

The point of my illustrations is that an issue cannot alter from being right or wrong simply because the group consulted is changed. Clearly, in certain cases, some groups are *more* entitled to consideration for their views, and on some matters the support of those 'closely concerned' is necessary. But none of this is a substitute for a decision on the merits of the issue, and the founding fathers of British democracy would have concentrated far more on the issue itself than on manipulating the constituency in order to get the answer that they wanted. Basically, they would have believed that when 'the facts' were established and the 'moral issues' at stake clarified by extensive debate, then there should be only one correct answer and it would be the duty of political leaders to win support for this conclusion whatever the composition or extent of the audience being consulted.

A further difficulty connected with the assumption that the majority is always right is: What kind of issue should be presented for popular decision and what is the appropriate machinery? It has often been contended that it is proper to settle the allocation of a disputed territorial area by conducting a plebiscite. The reasons for advocating this method are that the outcome touches the life of every individual and that, in most border areas, the issue at stake is something the people involved have 'lived with all their lives' and on which they are therefore 'well informed'. So the inhabitants of the Saarland – or Fermanagh & Tyrone – could properly be asked whether they wanted to be a part of France or of Germany – or whether they wished to belong to Northern Ireland or to Eire.

But it is worth remembering that, in both these cases, there was no elected legislative body which fitted the exact area and which could be consulted. The same would be true of the consultation of the African population of Rhodesia (recently carried out by the Pearce Commission). The older variety of democrats always preferred to consult elected representatives, if at all possible. They recoiled from the kind of 'government by referendum' now advocated by some exponents of popular participation.

The reason was *not* fear of public opinion. It was because

governmental decisions can rarely, if ever, be reduced to simple *Yes/No* answers. It is not just the problem of framing the question and of avoiding what is called 'the band-wagon effect', though this is, nevertheless, a grievous difficulty. For example, on the issue of whether a referendum was desirable on Britain's entry into the EEC, the question likely to get the biggest percentage of '*Yes*' answers is:

Before taking their final decision about joining the Common Market, Norway, Denmark and Ireland will each have a referendum in which all the people will be able to say whether they want to join or not. Do you think that Britain should do the same?

While this question would almost certainly produce the desired result, the way of putting it which would be as likely to produce the *opposite result* from the same respondents would be:

When France, Germany, Italy, Belgium, Luxembourg and Holland decided to form the Common Market, they each left the decision entirely to their Parliaments. Do you think Britain should do the same?

In addition to the difficulty of framing a neutral question, there is the much deeper problem of explaining or asking for a decision on all the consequences. For example, not to join the EEC would leave the government of Britain to pursue its economic and political objectives as part of a changing Commonwealth (and with the EEC developing on its own Continental lines). On the other hand, to join would mean such alterations in the context and methods of British politics and administration that a single question (or even a 'depth interview') could not encompass the situation, even assuming the respondent was fully informed on all the details. In contrast to this, if the decision is left to the political leaders of the country, they have to live with their judge-ments, to work them out in all their ramifications and then they have to ask the public something on which voters can give a judgement – has the total result been beneficial? This is why the pioneering democratic thinkers in Britain always preferred to emphasise that decisions came from the Government supervised by the legislature, and that both of these were ultimately responsible to the electorate. They never seriously contemplated the proposition that individual governmental decisions were to be taken directly by the voters.

Lastly, on the issue of majority rule, there is the question of what is meant by saying that a majority is 'always' right. Although the 19th–century democrats fought to extend the numbers entitled to vote, they were clear in their reservations on this point. They also believed in the 'rights of individuals' and of 'minorities', and realised that majorities could be dictatorial and oppressive. Since then there have been many tragic cases to prove this. The way the Americans treated US citizens of Japanese descent during the Second World War is a depressing example. And legislatures representing majority opinion can also be oppressive and remove individual rights – as the British Parliament did when it passed the 1968 Commonwealth Immigration Bill and denied British passport holders of Asian origin the right to enter this country.

Nor is this all. On matters of policy, as well as on questions of minority rights, majorities can be wrong. It is not merely that there has been support for aggressive military actions – a majority of Germans probably supported Hitler from 1934 till the tide of the War began to turn in 1942 – a majority of the British electorate probably supported the invasion of Suez in 1956. Majorities can also be wrong about the ways of achieving acceptable objectives. The desire to avoid another World War in the 1930s was entirely laudable; but it is almost certain that a majority of the electorate supported the Appeasement policy and, in particular, the Munich settlement, though in retrospect they were probably wrong in thinking this 'the best way of maintaining peace'. What is much more common, and more difficult to resolve in terms of domestic policies, is when the same majority wants incompatible objectives. Thus, it is probably the case that a majority of trade-unionists are opposed both to a government-enforced Incomes policy *and* to run-away Inflation.

All these limitations on the maxim that a Majority Must Be Right can be made tolerable if the majority operates through an elected assembly. This process encourages a certain level of debate and recognition of minorities and their rights. It affords time for the electorate to assess the total impact of policies and the motives and capacities of the competing politicians. If, after all this (as may happen), the electorate takes the wrong decision, provided there is a vigorous political dialogue, the voters must in time get closer to the truth by rejecting leaders who have failed to provide adequate solutions, either through incompetence, errors of judgement, or through unacceptable values.

There is another confusion – or corruption – of democratic ideas, and

107

it has to do with the propriety of defying laws or using force 'in certain circumstances'. There is, at first, an apparent contradiction between saying that majorities are always right and then arguing that force or law-breaking could be permissible, since presumably a majority in a democratic system can get the laws it wants.

Consider the advocates of Sit-ins or Strikes in breach of established procedures, of refusals by local authorities to comply with laws they do not like (e.g. on school milk, or rent increases) or of the resort to force in Northern Ireland. One argument is that there *is* an appropriate majority for change but that those in control are so 'deeply entrenched' that only physical force will extract any concession. A variant is the allegation that democratic procedures are 'so slow' that the majority can only lose heart unless a quick demonstration of their feelings produces instant victory.

Then too we hear that the 'wrong' majority has been consulted. If there was one issue that the Conservatives stressed at the 1970 election, it was the need for a reform of Industrial Relations. But the trade-unionists who advocate resistance to the subsequent Act of Parliament have argued that it was unacceptable to a majority of their members, thus appealing from the whole electorate to one minority group involved.

A third version is the suggestion that a majority is in fact in potential agreement – but this is not explicit because the public are not 'aware of the facts' or have not 'concentrated' on the issue – so that some sort of intervention with their lives (e.g. blocking the roads leading to an airport, or a lightning strike on commuter trains) is necessary in order to bring the matter home to the majority who will then, it is alleged, demonstrate their true support.

Only a few of those advocating force are prepared to say that they do not really care what the majority think, that they will persist in disrupting the community in order to get their demands accepted – not on their merits, but simply out of fear of the consequent disorders. The shining example of this approach is the IRA. But even in this case, many of the IRA Provisionals would claim that they were appealing to or serving the cause of a 'future majority' in a United Ireland. Now it is clear that in accepting a cease-fire, they have bowed to the will of the present majority in the Catholic areas.

If it could be established that a deep-seated wish of the electorate in Britain could not be achieved after a period when both parties had been in Parliamentary office, then one of the assumptions of the supporters of a democratic system would be seriously challenged. It must be stressed, however, that the desire or objective in question must be attainable. There is no point in the British electorate returning governments to power which promise to put this country back into (say) the 'super-Power class', if our size and resources as a nation make this impossible. It is no use voting for parties which promise to 'double the standard of living' if the economy cannot conceivably produce this quantity of wealth. The check – for democrats – is that prior discernment (or subsequent disillusionment) among the electors should lead to the rejection of those who make such utopian promises. But if *attainable* objectives are withheld from the electorate by some 'conspiracy' of those with special access to power, then the democratic system can indeed be judged a failure. In such a situation the use of force could be justified.

There is, however, no evidence at all that this has happened. The examples cited where 'nothing has been done' are usually cases where a real and effective majority has been objecting to the proposed course of action. In situations where the policy is reasonable and there is adequate popular support but the existing machinery is very slow (or, as with the early claims for student representation, there often was no machinery), the use of force nevertheless is hostile to the whole philosophy on which democracy is based.

For two reasons. The first is that force is a substitute for rational argument and assumes that a good case cannot win on its merits. It also disarms those with a good case when they encounter superior force. I have heard students say that there is 'no point' in establishing their case on rational grounds, and they have proceeded to organise a sit-in. But what answer have they had when a strong-arm squad ejected them?

The second reason is that one of the grounds for adopting democratic procedures is the atmosphere – the methods – the humane attitude to other people – which it induces. To proceed by discussion, through an elected assembly which accepts the possibility of rejection by the electorate, means a respect for the views of one's opponents. How can one create a society which has a regard for individual rights and for the day-to-day well-being of its members when one goes in for terror or riot or even a little rough 'manipulation'?

A university was designed to cultivate free inquiry and the pursuit of truth – how can it thrive if, at any moment, a disagreement between a professor and a faction of students is settled by the shouting of slogans? In industry, factory relationships which offer an element of security and respect for the workers cannot be created if negotiations are likely at any time to give way to disruption and confrontations based on force. It is true that members of the minority (Catholic) community in Northern Ireland had to wait rather longer for housing, and often got less well-paid jobs, than members of the majority (Protestant) community. But the kind of social situation in which both groups can receive equal treatment and live free and satisfactory lives is made less likely so long as recourse to violence is considered legitimate, 'progressive', useful. On all this, Gladstone, Bright, Mill and their followers were both clear and correct. Since the argument for democracy was based on the right of each person to make their own moral judgements, the machinery of democracy had to be operated in a manner which confirmed and supported these rights; and any short-cuts to policy objectives desired by the electorate, which involved the undermining of these rights, damaged rather than enhanced both the cause of democracy and the well-being of the community.

One last confusion and corruption of the older theories of democracy occurs over the question of leadership. Nowadays the word itself seems to have an odious connotation. It is the habit of many advocates of 'popular participation' to turn on anyone who suggests that political leadership requires training, or skill, or experience, and to denigrate them as 'élitists'. The merest hint that any MP knows a little more about government than the man-in-the-street is scoffed at as an arrogant assumption of middle class intellectuals.

It is, as has been said, correct that when the franchise was being extended, those favouring democracy argued that each citizen was entitled to 'pass judgement' on the conduct of the politicians. But it was never held that each voter knew as much about the technicalities of government as Messrs Gladstone and Disraeli. And the electorate today are still prepared to respect expertise in certain fields, viz. in medicine, the law, science or technology. So much is this the case that (as over the structure of the new Area Health Boards), they are prepared to overlook the essentially political questions of how much is spent on health and whether services for the elderly get priority over heart transplant experiments, and so on.

I would be prepared to argue that much local and national administration requires skill and experience as hard to acquire as the expertise of the surgeon or the scientist. The public are right to press politicians and officials to explain their policies. The answer that it is 'too complicated' for the voter to understand is properly resented but, on the other hand, it should be appreciated that to press for *accountability* and *open goverment* is not to suggest that ministers do not face problems as or more difficult than those encountered by, say, the managing directors of multi-national companies.

It is, rather, to stress that being in public life adds to the need for expertise in management and in diplomacy, the further expertise of communication. Nor does this mean the ability to see superficial explanations, or to curry favour with the voters, or simply to say what people want to hear. Gladstone explained his budgets and his objections to Conservative Near-Eastern policy with long speeches of infinite complexity, making no concessions to those of inferior stamina or intellect (this was a great mark of respect for his fellow men). If the public did not like what he had to say, his answer was not to 'trim' in order to hold his party together (Gladstone split his on Home Rule for Ireland), or in order to win an election. The politician ought to persist in saying what he believed to be correct until either he disappeared from public life or the voters realised that he was right and finally rallied to his support.

The idea current in certain political circles today that an MP who has strong views and retains them when they are unpopular is guilty of 'arrogance ... élitism ... and undemocratic behaviour' would have been quite incomprehensible to the originators of the democratic doctrine in England. Democracy was based on the quest for truth by the leaders and the allocation of support by the electorate. After all, the opposite position – attributed to an American local politician who said: 'These are my views, ladies and gentlemen, and if you do not like them, I will change them' – would make parties and elections and debate unnecessary. A country's leaders could simply adapt their views to the results of the latest opinion polls. Yet the *Tribune* group on the Left of the Labour Party considered that Labour MPs should give a prior undertaking to follow the decisions of the annual conference of the Labour Party whatever these may be and whatever the MP himself believes. Alas, this is an attitude which is widespread. I have mentioned the contested election for Rector of a Scottish University, because, though a Labour MP, I had voted for British entry to the Common Market, and I was asked by students whether I would promise never to exercise my own judgment in this way again but always simply to reflect the opinion of (I think it was) the last general meeting of students.

There is talk on the Left just now as to whether the Labour Party should be a 'socialist' or a 'social democratic' Party. If the latter term means that in addition to propounding a policy of social change, the

Party ought to rethink and reaffirm its democratic philosophy and give its attention to preaching the meaning and virtue of democratic politics, the time is clearly overdue. But surely the necessity for such thought and action spreads far beyond the confines of one party.

It is, I fear, basically unhealthy for a country to depend on a political system which is not backed by positive conviction and understanding, and whose original principles have become corrupted and confused. At present I fear they lack coherence and the power to win and retain the support of new generations.

2.5 'Taming the barons' (from Chapter 5, 'Political Institutions' in *Reshaping Britain*, PEP Broadsheet no. 548 Dec. 1974)

It has often been said that while the executive arm of government has grown out of all recognition, compared with what it was a century ago, the mechanism of democratic control has failed to show a similar extension of its powers. But the contrast is more glaring and more complex than is indicated by this analogy of rapid growth as compared with stagnation or even a degree of atrophy. A hundred years ago Parliament included representatives of the most powerful interests in the country. It is true that the landowners had been defeated by the Anti-Corn Law League in 1846 but they were still present in the House of Commons in large numbers. So were the railway company directors who needed an Act of Parliament in lieu of the modern planning permission and compulsory purchase orders to build their lines. The old West India interest had given up trying to buy seats after the 1830s as this became too difficult and they had lost their sugar monopoly, in part owing to the strength of the East India Company in politics, which lasted till it was discredited by the Indian Mutiny. But all these forces wishing to influence the government focussed their attention on the two Houses of Parliament. The corollary was a convention which held that it was quite improper for civil servants to see pressure group spokesmen; any communications between officials and such people should be by correspondence only. When the unions combined to form the TUC to put their case for certain legal changes, the executive was named 'the Parliamentary Committee' because its chief job was to lobby Parliament, and if a deputation wanted to see the government, they always called on the appropriate minister and not on the officials of the Board of Trade.

The changes that have occurred have not merely been the vast extension of the numbers in Whitehall and of its responsibilities and activities. In addition, as Parliament's capacity to amend and reject laws and to influence policy has declined, the powerful groups in society have shown less interest or have even opposed the election of their leading members to the House of Commons. They prefer to send them to deal directly with the civil servants, which increases the latters' power and further diminishes that of Parliament.

It is well known that this process started between the wars, grew rapidly under the pressure of the wartime emergency and became established after 1945. The official guide to civil servants' duties came to include a section on their obligation to consult all recognised interest groups. The criteria by which a group became accepted and put on the list of bodies to be consulted were fairly simple. The group had to represent the bulk of the persons or companies or organisations in the area of activity and had to accept that all negotiations were to be kept confidential, even from its own members. In return, the leaders of these interest groups were consulted before any government plans were published and they could thus make their representations at a formative stage when plans were still open to argument and when no loss of face was involved in making changes. Those groups which wanted new laws (which had been the usual objective in the nineteenth century) would go to Whitehall if what was wanted arose out of existing policies: that is if the matter was not highly controversial. On the other hand, if the proposal was in this category, then the pressure group could not deal directly with government departments. It had to turn to open advocacy of its case through the media, trying to reach the public and MPs. Those groups whose sole or main objective was a 'cause' requiring legislation clearly still had to try and influence Parliament, particularly if it was an issue on which the parties were not committed, such as penal reform or the abortion laws. But these groups constitute a small minority. The majority are interested in the development and execution of accepted policies and they are on the consultation list and deal directly with government.

In one case, the form and propriety of these dealings was laid down in an actual law. The 1947 Agriculture Act prescribes an annual meeting between the government and the National Farmers' Union at which the prices for the coming year are to be determined. Other bodies, such as the British Medical Association and the National Union of Teachers, do not have quite such a legal right to consultation, though it is unthinkable that anything should be done about the Health Service or about education without the views of the BMA or the NUT being obtained. The same is true of the representatives of industry and the TUC.

There are two consequences of these developments. One is the diminution of the influence of Parliament which has already been noted. It would now be hard to find in the House of Commons men sufficiently prominent in industry, either on the management or on the union side, to be accepted as the spokesmen or as the mouthpieces of these interests. In any case because MPs' votes can usually be taken for granted, an MP who had such a connection would not be seen as the kind of representative who could speak for an outside group. As a result, ministers wanting some evidence of the views of an organised section of the community consider that they are obliged to look outside the House. Pressure group leaders, for their part, will not seek membership of the Commons, partly because of the diminished influence of backbenchers, but largely because they do not wish to face conflicts of loyalty when party discipline pulls one way and the demands of their organisation another.

The second consequence follows naturally from the practice of regular consultations between pressure groups and government departments. If there has been an interruption of the process, it is regarded as something highly abnormal and means that the legislation concerned has not been through the usual procedure taken to be necessary when policy decisions are being made. If this happens, it may be an indication that the government expects serious opposition from the group and has decided either that there is no point in meeting just to register disagreement or that there is no time for a prolonged conflict. The other situation, which will cause less anxiety and friction, but which is nevertheless undesirable, is when consultation does take place but the government ultimately decides to turn down all or most of the advice of the pressure group. In these cases, what can a pressure group do to indicate to its members that on this occasion it either was not consulted or had its advice rejected? Pressure groups are not allowed, by the convention of consultation, to reveal the precise points put to the government or its responses. Yet, somehow, pressure group leaders will want to indicate either that they were not consulted or that part or all of their advice was rejected and that they object strongly to what the government has done.

The National Farmers' Union solved the problem after each annual determination of agricultural prices by announcing that the outcome was 'agreed' with the government or that it was 'not agreed' and, in one case, they would not say either that they agreed or did not agree; they simply reserved their position. It seems that governments going through these negotiations with the farmers hold a certain sum (reputedly about £2 million) in reserve and offer it as an additional bonus if the NFU is prepared to say the final outcome is 'agreed'. Similarly, the TUC has objected in the strongest terms on the very rare occasions when it was not consulted (as over the 1972 Industrial Relations Act) while the CBI has indicated reservations on Fair Trading Bills and on legislation on monopolies. ...

If there is a major breach between the pressure group and the government and if there has been either an avoidance of the normal processes of consultation or a breakdown, the leaders of the pressure group may claim that they are under no obligation to recommend their members to co-operate with the government. They may go further and say that members need not obey the law as, in some sense, it is not legitimate. The denial of legitimacy is a clear consequence of two concepts, first that passage by the House of Commons is not, of itself, an adequate indication of the consent of the community and second that prior consultation with recognised groups has become an essential part of the legitimising process.

Several other developments have added force to these concepts. The old assumption that passage by the House of Commons was adequate evidence of public consent has been seriously damaged during the controversy over British membership of the Common Market. When Mr Heath said that he would not consider it proper to take this country into the EEC without 'the full-hearted consent of the British people', he was apparently suggesting that passage by the House of Commons was not enough. The Labour Party then carried this downgrading of Parliament much further by proclaiming the necessity for a referendum. Yet if ever there was a free and deliberate expression of opinion by MPs it was on this occasion. Party lines were broken, 60 Labour MPs voting with the Conservatives and 20 more abstaining, so that entry was endorsed by a majority of 112, yet this was not taken as 'full-hearted consent'. The evidence of opinion polls showed that a majority of the British people was opposed to entry and that, in consequence, the verdict of Parliament was inadequate. Usually, those who argue that Parliament's consent is not enough point to the strength of the party hold on MPs so that the verdict of Parliament can be taken for granted. If this is a weakness, it has been intensified in recent years with the increasing tendency for party conferences (which are, in practice, much less representative than the House of Commons) to set out detailed programmes which are held to be binding on MPs, whose task is simply to push these policies through. It seems as though the unfortunate MPs lose both ways. When they assert themselves, break party ranks and vote according to deeply held convictions, as they did over the Common Market, they are asked 'Whom do you represent? You are simply asserting your own personal opinion'. When they enact the points in their party programme endorsed by the party conferences they are told 'Your vote meant nothing; you were committed to this by the party manifesto'.

This devaluation of the process of parliamentary democracy has been carried further by many well-meaning people who have advocated greater public participation in decision-making, since one of the implications of their case is that the traditional and normal channels of representation are inadequate. If there are strong objections to a third London airport, the arguments ought to be pressed on MPs as they have to reconcile the conflict of interests between airline passengers and local residents, between London's development as a world commercial centre and the demand for peace and quiet in nearby villages. Yet the current tendency for those who feel strongly on such matters is not just to lobby MPs, the assumption being that if the party whips are put on, there is little the MPs can do. In such cases, an 'action committee' is formed and while it will seek the support of local MPs, it will also appeal to the public, press the government directly and possibly even contemplate some kind of 'direct action'.

In addition to these doubts about Parliament, there is a disenchantment with the political driving force which operates through the House of Commons: the political parties. In recent years, the membership of the two main parties has declined and the same accusations of being rigid and unrepresentative are levelled against these bodies. Thus active citizens who wish to further certain public causes may feel it is more effective and appropriate to join pressure groups such as Shelter to get something done about housing and the homeless; they may join the Child Poverty Action Group or Amnesty rather than belong to a political party. While these bodies, like local amenity societies and consumers' protection groups, will seek the support of particular local or well-disposed MPs, they will also use many of the methods of the economic and professional pressure groups in attracting attention, spreading information and pressing for action in specific situations.

While the position of Parliament and the political parties has declined for all these reasons, the significance of the major pressure groups has become evident and their reputation for getting what they want has grown. Anyone with a knowledge of these bodies, from the

Confederation of British Industry to the National Union of Teachers, may know that they are cumbrous and have internal problems of organisation. Their full-time officers may be accused of being 'out of touch' and they may often guess at, rather than have accurate methods of ascertaining, their members' views. Yet their standing has improved as their capacity to command their members' loyalty has been demonstrated and as their record of success has become more evident. Thus, members may have doubts about a pressure group's course of action but the key economic and professional groups can usually command more loyalty than the government of the day. There were many miners, for example, who were opposed to the overtime ban called by the National Union of Mineworkers in the autumn of 1973 but by the time the situation had deteriorated and a full strike was called, almost all were behind the NUM executive. Many non-militants in bodies as diverse as the Association of University Teachers, the Local Authority Associations and the British Medical Association may disagree with particular points pressed by their representatives but they appreciate the need to retain a united front and not to discredit the spokesmen of their interest.

Such groups have, therefore, been able to insist that the citizen's first loyalty is to them rather than to any concept of the national well-being as enunciated by the government. Also, the high degree of interdependence in the economy means that if such groups act together, they can inflict much greater damage on the society at large than their members may suffer. Indeed, the members may endure only mild discomfort as a result of pressure group action which, nevertheless, may have a serious effect on the economy, on fuel supplies or the provision of essential services.

Two further factors have aided pressure groups in asserting their case in this way. One is the nature of the laws or instructions they are asking their members to defy. In many cases, no laws may be broken. The actions may be refusals to perform rather than acts that defy the law. For instance, teachers may refuse extra but essential tasks, doctors may refuse to take on extra duties to let colleagues go on holiday, businessmen may refuse to invest more or train drivers may work to rule. None of these activities on its own is illegal. They are certainly not illegal if done by a single person so there is a reluctance to regard them as wrong when done by a large number of people belonging to a pressure group. For instance, any doctor may contract out of the Health Service. It is not illegal for all in an area to do so. But if the objective of a mass resignation is to force up salaries by more than a norm laid down by statute, then those giving and those receiving the higher pay may be acting in a manner forbidden by anti-inflationary legislation. For the public at large, to break the kind of laws enforced by the police where the individual act is morally wrong and socially destructive is clearly reprehensible. But it is less obviously wrong to act in a manner which is legitimate if done by an individual and is socially reprehensible only if committed simultaneously by a mass of people and even then is wrong only if the analysis of the situation and the remedial measures of the government are accepted as fair and appropriate. Increasingly, governments have been drawn into legislating and target setting in areas of social policy, to try and secure stable prices or full employment or regional development, where defiance or refusal to co-operate may be due to disagreement with the objectives or the mechanism of the policy and where it is arguable whether the government is on the right track. . . .

All these points have to be put together – the changed nature of much legislation, the diminished conviction that a law is a special kind of command, the increased power and capacity of pressure groups and the lower standing of Parliament – in order to appreciate the situation which has arisen in the last decade where the will of the government, as expressed in laws or explicit policies, has been successfully disregarded or defied by powerful pressure groups. This has happened both over things the government wanted done and over actions it had intended to prohibit, though clearly the effect is more startling if the conflict is over a refusal to obey a law or over a demand for its repeal than if the conflict arises over a failure to comply with certain policies. Thus, the 1970–74 Heath government and, to some extent, the previous Labour government called on industrialists to invest more. Mr Heath was particularly bitter when the investment upsurge he had hoped for in 1971 did not take place, but this was a failure to respond and was the result of a number of individual decisions rather than of any concerted policy by the CBI.

Much more startling was the way the trade unions were able, through their direct contacts and through trade union sponsored MPs, to persuade a majority of the Labour cabinet to desert Mr Wilson and Mrs Castle and thus force them to abandon their proposed legislation on industrial relations in 1969. The TUC then went on to show such opposition to the Labour government's incomes policy that it, too, was abandoned in the winter of 1969–70. The next June, the Conservatives were elected and among their policies a central place was given to a new law on industrial relations. This had been elaborately prepared while the party was in opposition and once Mr Heath came

to power, it was rapidly introduced without the normal careful consultation with the TUC. From the start, the unions declared their
adamant opposition. The vast majority obeyed a TUC recommendation to refuse to register, thus placing their organisations outside the
legal protections the Act still conferred on unions. They refused to
register, in part because they would not let the agencies set up by the
government examine and approve their rule books. A minority refused to appear before the Industrial Relations Court or to defend
themselves, the Engineering Workers thus incurring a number of
fines. The unions also encouraged individual workers to refuse to obey
injunctions issued by the Industrial Court. As a result of all this
opposition, by the end of 1973 large sections of the Act were rendered
inoperative while the Court and the government tacitly allowed other
sections to lie unused rather than face renewed industrial conflict. At
the same time the unions, with no real difficulty, had the total repeal
of the Act given pride of place in the Labour Party's election manifesto and the Act was repealed by the minority Wilson government in
the summer of 1974. By then, the Conservatives had come to accept
that though they still wanted to achieve the Act's objectives, legislation so totally unacceptable to the section of the community it was
designed to regulate either could not be enforced or the effort caused
more disruption than it was worth; and the Conservatives therefore
did not oppose the repeal of the bulk of the Act.

In 1972, the Conservative government turned away from its previous objection to statutory incomes policies and this time, after elaborate consultation with industry and the unions, it set up a system of
controls with a Pay Board and a Prices Commission. By the autumn of
1973, the policy had moved into what was called Stage III and six
million workers accepted wage settlements within the formula set out
by the orders made under the Act. But the National Union of Mineworkers demanded an increase well above this limit – having defeated
the government and obtained a high award only eighteen months earlier. Mr Heath and his government set their faces against any concessions, announced fuel economies and then put industry on a three day
week to conserve coal stocks. The miners moved towards and then
called a full scale strike while the Prime Minister decided to hold a
general election on the question of whether a pressure group should
be permitted to defy the government in this way. After a confused and
mixed campaign neither of the major parties had a clear majority but
the result was manifestly a defeat for the Conservatives and Mr Wilson took over with a minority government. Immediately, the miners'
pay rise was conceded and the Labour administration began the dis-

mantling of the incomes policy and the repeal of the Industrial Relations Act, both so disliked by the trade unions.

For its part, the Labour Party announced that it had reached 'a social contract' with the unions whereby they would voluntarily limit wage increases to a level which did not exacerbate inflation. The government, in return, promised the abandonment of the two policies mentioned, a rent freeze and an immediate rise in pensions. All these policies were enacted or adopted by the Labour government and it, in turn, called on the unions to fulfil their side of the contract by limiting wage demands to a level which would maintain but not increase real wages. At the same time, Mr Wedgwood Benn sought an arrangement by which industry would inform the government of its investment plans, respond to pressures to increase or alter these plans and obtain extra money from (or face purchase by) a National Enterprise Board.

A final, and perhaps the sharpest experience any government has had with a pressure group came in the early summer of 1974 when Protestant workers in Northern Ireland organised by the Ulster Workers' Council staged a quite overt political strike to force the Faulkner coalition government out of office and succeeded. It seems to be the case that the Labour government considered asking the army to break the strike but either there was reluctance on the part of the army or senior officers dissuaded the government or it changed its mind. Whatever the explanation, the Ulster Workers' Council won and the Faulkner government resigned.

In all these cases, except the last, where there was a direct challenge to the existence of the Northern Irish government, pressure groups were, in fact, asking or forcing the British government to change its policies or to legislate in a certain way. It was assumed that once industry and the unions had agreed on the form of an incomes policy or on a social contract or on changes in laws dealing with industrial relations, these changes would be obediently and speedily enacted by the House of Commons. The interesting development in this process of consultation as compared with the kinds of dealings with pressure groups that have already been described is two-fold. First, the discussions often included both sides of industry. Second, they took into consideration matters such as the level of pensions, rents and the incidence of taxation which were strictly outside the immediate concern of the pressure groups involved. In fact, in every case, attempts were being made to reach some kind of 'contract' between the groups concerned, a 'contract' which recognised that these groups do have considerable power – if largely a veto power – and which assumed that

Parliament had no effective role to play except to register and enact the contents of any contract.

This approach, to draw in the most powerful pressure groups on both sides of industry, has sometimes been called 'tripartitism'. It has a respectable history in this country and has been developed quite extensively elsewhere. It began in Britain as an attempt to work out joint plans between government, industry and the unions in a manner which would encourage mutual confidence, show up weak areas and commit all participants to a common objective of faster growth. The National Economic Development Council was set up in 1962 with a representative tripartite council to bring in the constituent elements and an economic staff to contribute professional expertise. It was made clear that the NEDC was an independent body and that its role was purely advisory; there were no sanctions to enforce its conclusions. But the idea was that all the three constituent parts shared the common objective of faster growth, if there was a general agreement that certain steps were necessary to further this objective, then all three elements would seek to take these steps or to aid in their achievement.

Early in its existence, the Council looked at growth targets, picked 4 per cent per annum and asked its office to work out the implications. The result was a report on the targets[1] and a study on *Conditions Favourable to Faster Growth*.[2] This study indicated actions needed to back up the growth programme in such fields as education and training, labour mobility, regional development, the balance of payments, taxation and prices and incomes policy. The contribution government, industry and the unions could make in these various fields was indicated in rather general terms. The 4 per cent target was accepted as official government policy and the 1963 Budget was framed in order to achieve this objective. The Chancellor of the Exchequer said he did so in 'the confident belief that as the government set the lead so management and unions as well will join in a national drive to achieve a national objective'. Economic Development Committees (little Neddies) were set up for particular industries.

When the Department of Economic Affairs was created in October 1964, some of the NEDC planning staff were moved to that Department but the NEDC Council was enlarged and in August 1965, the Prime Minister became Chairman. When the NEDC Plan was brought up to date and reissued in September 1965 as *The National*

---

[1] *Growth of the UK Economy to 1966*, NEDC, 1963
[2] NEDC, 1963

Plan[3] it had become a 'commitment and blueprint for action' on the part of the government. The NEDC was asked 'to review regularly the progress being made in each field, to see whether the various policies are proving effective... and whether further action is required'. When the NEDC drew so close to the government and the DEA absorbed so much of its staff, the original concept of an independent body 'under the aegis of but not in' the administration, as Mr Maudling had put it, could have been lost. But this was a time when George Brown had extracted the 'Declaration of Intent' from the TUC that they would keep incomes in line with the growth of productivity and when industry was still prepared to co-operate with the Labour government. This atmosphere came to an end with the financial crisis of July 1966 when the National Plan targets were abandoned, the DEA lost the main reason for its existence and the government began to move from co-operation in reasonable growth of incomes to positive restraint and an incomes policy.

The impressive feature of the NEDC experiment was that the Council, the top-level meetings of the three constituents, survived these set-backs and the growing tension between the government and both sides of industry. From January 1969 to the June 1970 election, the NEDC again looked at the conditions for overall growth though the resulting document, *The Task Ahead*, was much more tentative[4]. Then the Conservative government elected in June 1970 wondered whether the whole institution should be abandoned, but soon decided to leave it in existence. It slipped, in practice, into the void left by the government's early dislike of any prices and incomes policy. Sir Frank Figgures, the third Director-General, got the three 'parties', government, CBI and TUC to talk about the problems of inflation, employment levels and the rate of investment. In August 1971, the need for these three estates of the realm to work together became so pressing – with inflation increasing, no investment revival and unemployment rising towards one million – that a 'Group of Four' was set up. They were the Permanent Secretary of the Treasury, the General Secretary of the TUC, the Director-General of NEDC and the Director-General of the CBI. Their task was to prepare an agenda for full Council meetings but not merely in the sense of listing points for discussion. *The Times* said their activity 'consists of that delicate therapy... whereby a conception develops into a considered consensus ready to be embodied in a visible contract'.[5]

[3] Department of Economic Affairs, Cmnd 2764, September 1965
[4] Department of Economic Affairs, *The Task Ahead*, HMSO, 1969
[5] *The Times*, 9 August 1971

As part of this therapy, the TUC brought forward the idea of cost-of-living threshold clauses in pay settlements. The CBI contributed a self-denying ordinance for the top two hundred firms, which were voluntarily to limit price increases to 5 per cent a year. It was on this basis that the Chancellor of the Exchequer, Mr Barber, set off on his dash for 5 per cent growth per annum. As a result of the discussions and the problems, the government, though at loggerheads with the TUC over the Industrial Relations Act and disenchanted with industry because of its failure to raise the rate of investment, felt it had to keep in close touch. The Group of Four was supposed to go over the issues so that when the pressures on the three parties rendered them willing to consider a social contract (these words were used at that time) on pay, prices, employment and growth, all misunderstandings and obstacles to agreement would have been cleared away.

In a curious way, the participants managed to operate in a very different fashion at two distinct levels. On the top political level, the government was in conflict with the unions over wage increases and industrial relations legislation and with industry over its reluctance to invest. At a different, broader level, there was a recognition of the need for collaboration in isolating the problems and narrowing the areas of disagreement. Thus, the NEDC provided the forum in which extensive consultations took place as the government turned back to an incomes policy. There were meetings of the Group of Four and then a Co-ordinating Committee which paved the way for meetings with the Prime Minister at Chequers or 10 Downing Street. There the incomes policy was hammered out with its Stages one, two and three, the government offering certain formulae in return for non-enforcement of sections of the Industrial Relations Act and controls over prices on the part of industry. It is often forgotten that much of this was successful and that six million workers did settle under Stage III of the Conservative prices and incomes policy. However closely the unions allied themselves to the Labour Party during its seven months of minority government in 1974, many union leaders were willing to reach a kind of social contract with the Conservatives before the February 1974 election and were clear in their minds that they would have to try again if and when the Conservatives returned to power.

At the same time, on the more political level, the government and the unions clashed over wages and industrial relations policy till the National Union of Mineworkers decided to press its demand for a claim far in excess of the norm permitted under the prices and incomes policy. The NUM held out for this despite all the pressure the government could muster, including a three-day working week, and finally a general election in February 1974. Much to the surprise of most politicians, the voters refused to rally to Mr Heath's cry of 'Who governs the country?'. In a curious way, the result reinforced the deeper level of activity in the NEDC and the tripartite discussions in that it showed that neither industry, the government nor the unions could easily over-rule the others; they had to work together if the country was to make reasonable progress.

So, in mid-1974, there has been the experience of two British governments, one Labour and one Conservative, each failing to get British industry to respond in the way they wanted and each taking on the unions over industrial relations policy and incomes policy and losing. On the other hand, neither of these pressure groups can operate without an effective government and both struggled at one political level to get the kind of government they wanted while at another level they sought to maintain good communications with whoever was the government.

Because of this, when any academics or commentators concerned about British problems have propounded solutions, they inevitably include these power blocs. Some of those writing on an incomes policy have wanted the share-out of wages determined by a kind of industrial parliament,[6] while others have advocated restoring industry by a £20 billion investment programme to be pushed through by a board representing unions, industry and the government[7]. These comments all recognise that in policy-making and legislation, those with power in the community have to be consulted and to concede a measure of agreement or the policy will not work.

The way the government approached this task in the 1960s and early 1970s meant that it descended into the ring and fought out a series of duels single-handed with these pressures groups. In the course of these bouts, the government had no method of rallying the other groups who had accepted its policies to its side. It was the government versus the miners while the six million workers who had accepted the policy and who had, therefore, a vested interest in seeing that the miners secured no special advantage over them were unable to bring their influence to bear. The public sometimes sympathised with the group which had taken on the government because they were unable to see what would happen if all unions (or industrialists) behaved

---

[6] See for example E. H. Phelps Brown, *Collective Bargaining Reconsidered*, Stamp Memorial Lecture, London School of Economics, 1971
[7] *The Times*, 19 December 1973

in the same way. Once the government committed itself to a trial of strength with a pressure group, it was in difficulties as the political leaders felt they would lose support if they were too adamant or 'abrasive' while the pressure group leaders knew they would be sacked by their members if they were not tough and did not insist on fighting to the last ditch.

Yet everyone knows that a country cannot be run in this way and the willingness of the pressure groups to go on talking through such bodies as the NEDC shows that they understand that such conduct ultimately harms everyone. So what can be done about this situation? How can the realities of policy and rule making in our society be incorporated in the machinery of government so as to recognise the legitimate interests of the various parties and, at the same time, restore the position of the government; that is restore it as a party above the battle, as the representative of the broader national interest, and give it a degree of authority different in kind from that of the pressure groups?

There are two areas in which it is possible to look for help. The one is previous attempts to solve this problem, for there have often been periods when governments have had to struggle to assert themselves against power blocs in the community. The second is to consider attempts made by other nations to tackle this same problem. On the first, the history of mediaeval parliaments is helpful. The problem for mediaeval monarchs was that the barons often had all the attributes of monarchs within their own areas. Indeed, as with the modern pressure group, some barons could obtain the prior allegiance of their tenants in any dispute with the Crown. If there was a dispute between the Crown and some powerful baron, the Crown would not wish to take on such an overmighty subject single-handed while the barons watched to see if it would be worth their while to engage in similar confrontations. So it was in the Crown's interest to draw these tenants-in-chief into a constant consultation on national policy. If this was achieved, the barons went on record in front of their peers and any subsequent refusals to observe laws that had been agreed were defiance not merely of the Crown but also of the other tenants-in-chief. This meant that the King could expect the other barons to join in putting pressure on any recalcitrant individual. It was this desire to legitimise policies and laws by getting the prior consent of the most powerful men in the country that led to the creation of Houses of Lords which were, in practice, the most important chambers in mediaeval parliaments.

The chief difficulty the Crown faced was to persuade the more powerful barons to attend as they knew that in doing so, they accepted the sovereignty of the King and the practical fact that if they agreed to policies, they had to help carry them out. If, afterwards, they went their own way, they were defying rules or requirements whose legitimacy they had explicitly accepted. Because the King wanted to establish this kind of social contract with all the powerful elements in the country, bishops and abbots were also included, sometimes in a separate house, while in a lower chamber, there were representatives of the Commons who were expected to indicate what their counterparts at home would accept. If any group of representatives objected, they had to be won over or be made to feel that they were in too small a minority to maintain an opposition. Once they had agreed, they had to explain the policies to which they had consented to their constituents.

All this is useful because it points to the fact that one reason why the Commons has lost power is because its members are partly nominees rather than the actual representatives of an area or a group. Few now think the votes of MPs indicate the positive assent of those they are held to represent which is why the acceptance of a law by the House of Commons is not now regarded as conveying sufficient legitimacy by itself. But it is of considerable help to the government if the contemporary equivalent of the barons give their assent – if the CBI, the unions or professional associations indicate their agreement – since they can then be held to account and can be expected to secure the co-operation of their members. And if, in the process of consultation, some of the power blocks agree but others do not, then the minority is struggling not merely with the governments but with the rest of its peers who are prepared to agree. The importance of this kind of pressure was seen when Mr Scanlon's AUEW did not wish to endorse the 'social contract' with the Labour government at the TUC conference in September, 1974. Probably no government could have forced the AUEW to give its official consent but the other unions were able to make the Engineers feel so isolated that they decided to conform. And once they have conformed, though this may not guarantee observance of the contract by subordinate branches of the union (just as mediaeval barons could not always ensure good conduct by all the minor lords in their territory), at least there can be no argument about the legitimacy of the contract and it is much harder for the union itself to countenance or promote blatant breaches.

Mediaeval parliaments were based on the sensible assumption that if there were powerful elements in the country whose understanding and agreement had to be obtained for any common policy to be enforced (and taxes raised), then it was far easier if these groups could be gathered together, the common problems examined, a certain unity obtained and then these elements could not avoid some responsibility for the rules and for their enforcement. In the late nineteenth century, the remnants of these Houses of Lords declined in importance partly because landed magnates wielded much less power, partly because the other powerful groups without land sought representation in the lower or elected houses. Now that power groups are not territorial and so do not fit a constituency pattern and since these groups also tend to neglect the elected houses and deal directly with the governments, it may make sense to try and bring those with power together in a chamber like the old upper houses of mediaeval parliaments. The object would be to obtain greater mutual understanding, to get in consequence some pressure by peer groups on recalcitrant authorities, to have an open record of any support that is conceded and to accord greater legitimacy to any rules or policies which have been endorsed by such a body.

It is for this reason that various modern countries have set up a modern range of bodies varying from advisory planning organisations of the NEDC type to virtual third chambers like the French Economic and Social Council whose composition and powers are set out in the Constitution. The latter consists of 200 (originally 205) members chosen for five years by the appropriate organisations. There are 45 representatives of manual and black-coated workers, 41 from the managerial side of private and nationalised industry, 40 from agriculture and 40 government nominees, with small numbers of representatives of social and cultural organisations. The Council is restricted to matters on which it is consulted by the government except for any suggestions it may make about social or economic reforms necessitated by technical changes. Its object is to bring together the representatives of the major social and economic pressure groups who either would not normally meet or would be summoned only at a time of crisis when their interests had come into sharp conflict. The Council breaks into 'sections' to study economic problems and to put forward reports to the government, but its success should be measured more in terms of the understanding that has developed among the leaders of interest groups, whose members' general ignorance of each other and mutual hostility is still very marked. It is difficult to be precise about the impact of the Council because so much of its work is in secret and it is essentially a consultative body. The French government itself stated in 1960 that 'In the field of agricultural policy the advice of the ESC on the agricultural bills has been substantially utilised by the government in the preparation of the legislation submitted to Parliament'.[8] In 1961, General de Gaulle congratulated the Council on its work over the Fourth Plan: 'Your participation in this vital matter ... has been both skilled and objective.' Then the Council wanted to go further than consultation and the proposal of amendments. Over the Fifth Plan, it wanted to set out a series of alternatives from which Parliament could choose while the government decided to make its own proposals without first submitting them to the ESC. As a result, the Council's reactions to the Plan were extremely critical and Parliament drew heavily on its report when criticising the Plan. In 1963 and 1964, the Council turned to an examination of the prerequisites of an incomes policy and one of the trade union representatives said 'Of all the institutions in which the social partners at present meet, we prefer the ESC to serve as the framework for an incomes policy'; but in early 1965 the draft proposals were defeated by 93 to 29 as the interest groups did not have enough confidence in the government to entrust it with the task of carrying through an incomes policy.

Although the ESC thus, in rejecting an incomes policy, ranged itself along with other 'factious obstructors' of Gaullist policy, the General said there was a larger role for the Council to fulfil and in 1964 he talked of merging it with the Senate or of the Council acquiring legislative powers. In France, the Senate embodies the old republican elite, the representatives of the many town councils throughout France, while the ESC represents the more recent pressure group leaders. There was therefore nothing very strange in suggesting that the latter might more appropriately exercise the legislative powers of the Senate. M. Mendès-France[9] pointed out that this would stop the groups merely presenting their own grievances. If they had to share responsibility for making the rules, they would have to consider the broader national interest. Others who have considered the role and composition of the Council have discussed whether interest group representatives should be elected or nominated by the groups, whether the weak or unorganised should be represented and whether consultation by the government on all economic questions should be made compulsory. The farmers' organisations have been most enthusiastic about the work of the Council, the businessmen somewhat reticent, while the trade unions are torn between a desire to influence decisions and a refusal to accept any responsibility for the working of 'the sys-

[8] This and the subsequent quotations on the French Economic and Social Council are taken from J. E. S. Hayward's *Private Interests and Public Policy: The Experience of the French Economic and Social Council*, Longman, 1966.
[9] *La République Moderne*, Paris, 1962.

tem'. The history of the Council certainly confirms Professor A. Sauvy's claim that it 'is a more or less conscious attempt to legalise the powers that be, the only serious attempt to modernise our political system'.

In Belgium, a Central Economic Council was created in 1948 and a National Council of Labour in 1952. The former has 50 members, 22 being nominated by the 'most representative organisations' of industry, agriculture, commerce and small business while the two largest trade union organisations have eight each, five come from consumer co-operatives, one from a small labour organisation, and the remaining six are chosen by the government on a three pro-labour, three pro-management basis. Below this, there are the equivalent of 'little Neddies' for the various industries. The Council prepares reports on economic questions, particularly in the period each year before the government produces its budget and then afterwards comments on the results. There is also the National Council of Labour which deals with 'social objectives' and which has been kept as a separate body to overcome Labour's fear that if there was an economic council only, economic efficiency would take priority over all other considerations.

One of the first issues in which the Central Economic Council played a decisive role was in persuading the government to set up a planning department in 1959, the Office for Economic Programming. This Office consults the Council when preparing plans and, when agreed, these become laws as far as the government is concerned. The plans or laws do not set out objectives for the private sector but there is an implicit obligation on employers' and union representatives to help the government carry out the plan, to sell its objectives to their members and to direct their organisations in a manner which fits in with the plan.

In the Netherlands, a Social and Economic Council consisting of employers, employees and public representatives was set up in 1950 and has proved useful. When relations broke down between government and the two sides of industry over a wages pause in 1971, the only way consultations could be resumed was by asking the Council for its opinion. When it unanimously recommended a restriction of government intervention in overall wage and price policies, the government agreed and turned instead to regular tripartite consultations over wage and price policies. It was because three of the original members of the European Community had bodies of this kind that the Treaty of Rome established an Economic and Social Committee of 121 members, appointed by the Council of Ministers as 'representatives of the various categories of economic and social life'. One third came from employers' organisations, one third from the unions, while the remainder represented 'the general interest'. In certain cases, the Council of Ministers has to seek the advice of this body while in others, consultation is optional. The advice does not have to be taken but some important interests (particularly in agriculture) are represented and their views are given due weight.

The question is, first, whether it would be useful to bring the pressure groups into an institution which emphasises the legislative character of the decisions that they and the government take. If so, the second question is: What would be the best form of institution?

On point one, part of the answer is evident. The relations between the major economic groups and the government are already arranged in and through the NEDC, while the other pressure groups have their conventional arrangements with Whitehall. If no more is needed, then all that is necessary is to develop these institutions and processes. During the October general election, Mr Heath addressed himself to this problem and wanted the NEDC arrangements to be extended, formalised and conducted before the media so that those participating could subsequently be held to what they had said and undertaken at the Council.

But this points to a feeling that the NEDC approach has not so far been entirely satisfactory. First, it has failed to put participants 'on the record'. The main decisions have still been taken at smaller, informal and totally private meetings. Secondly, the system excludes other, often equally important pressure groups. Thirdly, it still downgrades Parliament and encourages the pressure groups to look only to Whitehall. Fourthly, it fails to force the representatives of special interests to explain their case in front of other pressure groups competing for the same scarce resources. Finally, for the same reasons, public opinion is inadequately informed and roused about decisions which often seriously affect people as consumers, citizens and taxpayers.

If these disadvantages suggest that something more than an expanded or strengthened NEDC is necessary, should Britain contemplate the creation of a third chamber, an economic and social council? This would meet some of the deficiencies listed above in that it would include the other important groups and would be a chamber where discussions could be in public and cover broader issues than the bilateral relations between a single pressure group and the government. The weakness of the proposal is that it must be open to doubt whether such a chamber would ever be accepted as an integral part of Parliament, in the sense that the Lords and Commons are parts of Parliament. And part of the objective is to restore the position and prestige of Parliament and to restore a proper sense of legitimacy to its legislation.

As a result, it might be simpler to combine the creation of a new institution with the reform or transformation of the existing House of Lords. Some might feel diffident about calling pressure group leaders 'Lords' (though some strange creations have appeared in that Chamber). In this case, all existing peers could keep their titles but would no longer be members of parliament. The new members could be called 'Members of the Upper House'. A total of, say, 200 Members would be appointed for the duration of each Parliament, the trades unions and industry being asked to nominate 40 each; the government would appoint perhaps 20 ministers, officials and experts to put its case and the remaining 100 would be allocated among the existing pressure groups 'recognised' by Whitehall.

One convenient aspect of this solution is that the existing powers of the Upper House would be entirely suitable for the new chamber. It would continue to exercise the present very restricted powers to review legislation and to hold up measures for a maximum of six months but it would have no power over financial legislation. Also, it would have nothing to do with the political complexion of the government as the Prime Minister would still owe his position to his control of a majority in the House of Commons. In order to retain the consultative and fact-finding role of the NEDC and of the present secret negotiations between pressure groups and Whitehall, provision would have to be made for a select committee system in the Lords. Select committees on economic policy, agriculture, transport, trade and industry and so on, could continue to bring the various interests together, produce reports, find out government thinking on new legislation, put the pressure groups' case and prepare members for the broader debates in the House itself on policy matters.

There are many objections to such a radical proposal, but the issues are the same whether a third chamber is established or use is made of a reformed Upper House. It is perhaps better to consider these objections in sequence, first dealing with the 'will it work?' questions, then turning to possible dangers and finally to the advantages.

The first question is: Why should the pressure groups agree to take part? Almost all of them will feel it is better to negotiate on their own with the government; they can always make their special case look convincing if it is simply set against a very amorphous 'national interest' represented by the government. It is quite different and much harder for them (if they are, say, farmers) to convince the representatives of the consumers or, if they are miners, to convince postmen and dustmen or, if they are trade associations, to put their case across to a variety of other interests. Moreover, much or all of the discussions will be in public and the pressure group members will know what their spokesmen are saying. The answer is that the inducement to participate will be the same inducement that has kept both sides of industry going to the NEDC despite public confrontations, show-downs and the periodic collapse of communications; it is the desire to be consulted, to be in on the framing of policy. This is the desire that has kept the NFU going constantly to the Ministry of Agriculture whatever the level of disagreement the farmers and the government have had about particular policies. The government would simply need to insist that all consultation takes place through the committee system of the House of Lords so that those who do not come are excluded. This would, judging by the experience of all the countries that have adopted any system of consultation, ensure full participa-tion.

The second objection concerns the numbers and method of selec-tion of members. If the reconstituted Upper Chamber is to vote on issues, there could be serious disputes about the numbers. Why should 'Labour' have only 40 (or whatever) out of 200? But the other interest group representatives would not all fall on the other side in straight class divisions; the agricultural vote would include representa-tives of the agricultural workers and the teachers and other white col-lar professional groups might well join with the trade union repre-sentatives. Yet the real answer is that in a House of this kind, for a government to press on with a labour relations policy against the advice of the labour members or with an investment policy against the express wishes of the business interests would be to court defeat. Also, much more attention would have to be paid to the committees and an agricultural bill which was unanimously rejected by the agri-cultural committee or a health measure objected to by all the repre-sentatives of the Health Service would clearly be difficult to operate. Moreover, the objections of the interest groups would be seized on by the opposition in the House of Commons and it would be hard for a government to proceed unless it was prepared for a confron-tation.

There might be some argument as to whether the representatives of the groups should be directly elected by the members. How far, it could be asked, are the existing pressure group leaders really repre-sentative of their members? But there would be great resentment if the government tried to intervene in or lay down rules for the internal arrangements of the pressure groups. The value of the system being proposed depends very much on the participation of the recognised spokesmen for the interests and therefore it seems better to leave them to arrange the method of nomination. If all other modes of consultation were banned, then it is virtually certain that the existing office-bearers would nominate themselves or arrange for an election of the kind which chooses the members of the TUC from among the various unions.

Turning to the dangers which some might detect in such a system, there might be worries about the effect on the normal working of Parliament and whether the creation of a new chamber described as 'the Upper House' would in fact place it in a position superior to the Commons. There might even be suggestions that this would be a step towards a 'corporate state'. On the first, it might be thought that any such chamber should be purely consultative, but if so there is the danger that when proposals were really tendentious, the government would cease to consult (as the Conservatives did over the Industrial Relations Bill). Also, this kind of second or upper chamber would have a role to play in all forms of legislation except taxation and if it is thought that this would mean that many bills would pass without much discussion, it should be remembered that this is the situation now in the House of Lords. What matters is that issues closely affecting the powerful groups in the community would be properly studied in committee by all those affected and then their views would have to be taken into account in the actual legislative process. And as one of the objectives is to gain greater legitimacy for laws, there is no substitute for involving the groups who can confer such legitimacy not only, as at present, in the informal preparatory stages but also later in the formal legalising stage.

As to dangers to the House of Commons, these must be considered against the present reduced power and prestige of that body. The Commons would keep the existing chief source of its remaining authority: that it is out of the Commons majority that the government is formed, and it is to the Commons that the government would remain responsible. At the moment, the most serious challenge to the authority of the House lies in the periodic quasi-legislative yet informal meetings held between the government and the major pressure groups and it would help Parliament as a whole if this process was brought back within the Palace of Westminster.

Finally, some may look back to theories of the corporate state current in the 1930s and ask how far the recognition of the power of such groups is a denial of democracy. Clearly, in the sense that these pro-

133

posals recognise that legislative chambers based on 'one person one vote' are not enough in themselves either to contain all the necessary parties to negotiations or to legitimise all laws, this is true. But if power in a society is 'lumpy', then the lumps will remain and the only question is whether their position is to be regularised and institutionalised or left on an informal basis. There might be a claim that the representation of such groups should be counterbalanced in the Upper House by the inclusion of representatives of the public, of the weaker sections of society or of the unorganised. But this would really be open to serious objections as it would suggest that a genuine numerical balance could be achieved between the pressure groups and the public at large in one chamber. It is better to recognise that the upper house would be a rough and ready way of gathering the voices of the powerful and that precise numbers did not matter while the Commons remained the true voice of the people, the consumers and the taxpayers.

Lastly, some will say that this is all constitutional tinkering beloved of political scientists and of academic reformers steeped in the nineteenth century liberal tradition. But such a criticism neglects the crucial fact that in society, modern or ancient, only two ways have been found of getting people to work together. One is force. The other is the observance of laws based on consent. Recently, the British system of government has failed to generate an adequate sense of consent and powerful pressure groups have successfully defied successive governments. As a result, if the system of government is not to degenerate into chaos, either force must be applied or a new and better method of producing legitimacy must be evolved. Many people, because they have no idea how to produce the last of these situations and they shrink from physical force, are turning to the idea of nonphysical force: the fear and weakness caused by mass unemployment. Yet this solution brings as many or more problems than those it sets out to cure. So there is nothing cranky or academic in pointing out that there is a method of obtaining greater consent which has worked in previous historical periods and has begun to be tried in other countries: that is to draw the elements whose consent is required into institutionalised processes which encourage co-operation and help confer legitimacy on what is decided.

Nor are these proposals long term. They could be started at once with one simple Bill which would alter the composition of the present House of Lords and bring the bargaining process between the pressure groups and the government back inside Parliament. This new method of decision-making could be in operation within a reasonably short period. The only thing required is an agreement that it is better to try the institutional alternative rather than wait till the position deteriorates to a level where force becomes not merely the idle day-dream of retired colonels but the preferred solution for influential sections of the community.

2.6 'The declining respect for the law' (From Anthony King (ed.), *Why is Britain Becoming Harder to Govern?*, BBC Publications, 1976, pp. 74–95)

The evening before the writing of this chapter was started, the author attended a meeting in the village of Earlston in the Scottish borders. Three hundred people were present to protest at a 246 per cent increase in the local rates. Towards the end of the meeting, in what is a deeply traditional and conservative rural area, a well-dressed man arose to move that all those present should refuse to pay rates till certain points had been met. The motion was later withdrawn but that it was moved at all in such a community was amazing.

Yet MPs of all parties find themselves going from one meeting to another where forceful actions or breaches of the law are proposed. In recent months, the author has been asked to support the Scottish school teachers' strike, the blockade of ports by inshore fishermen and several suggested rate and rent strikes. Nor are MPs themselves immune from making such calls. Mr. Russell Johnston, the MP for Inverness, has urged the withholding of taxes till proportional representation is conceded. A majority of the Parliamentary Labour Party voted in their party meeting and then in the House of Commons for the retrospective withdrawal of the proper legal disqualification imposed on the councillors at Clay Cross who had refused to implement the Housing Finance Act of 1972, while other Labour MPs wanted to overturn the court's decision in the case of two men found guilty of intimidation while picketing a building site in Shrewsbury.

In addition to demands by local groups and similar suggestions by MPs, reputable pressure groups contemplate or carry through actions intended to break a law or defy the Government. Two successive Governments, one Labour, the other Conservative, attempted to alter the law dealing with industrial relations and to impose a statutory incomes policy, and in each case the policies had to be abandoned because of the opposition of powerful pressure groups. Over industrial relations,

135

the unions were able to swing round enough Labour MPs and then the Labour Cabinet to stop the introduction of a bill in 1969 based on the White Paper, *In Place of Strife*. The Conservatives were able to carry their bill into law but it was boycotted by the TUC and disobeyed by several unions. It largely ceased to be implemented while it was on the statute book and was finally repealed by the incoming Labour Government.

But Governments themselves act in a way outside the law and, in so doing, indicate their attitude towards laws and the process of law-making. In a Granada television programme on 'The State of the Nation', Sir William Armstrong, then still head of the civil service, said that when he had been a young official and a minister proposed certain actions, these were abandoned directly the official said, in effect, 'But, minister, you have no such powers.' Now it is common for the minister (in whatever party) to say, 'Very well, we will introduce the appropriate legislation and meanwhile I will announce my intention to enforce these proposals. The bill will give the Government retrospective authority.' At the time of writing, there is a letter in *The Times* pointing out that the Government is advertising posts in a new Welsh Land Authority which is proposed under legislation presently passing through the Commons. Actions are being taken to implement a law which cannot receive the royal assent for several months.

The question is why both Government and the governed, Members of Parliament and electors, pressure groups and civil servants, have come to take this view of the law, to remove it from the rather special reverence it had a century ago so that at times they contemplate breaking the law without any sense that this is a dangerous matter and is, in a strict sense, criminal activity.

If the question is put to ordinary members of the public, 'Why are you proposing to break the law?', the answer usually comes in two forms. The first is to explain the frustrations or governmental failures that have led to the situation. Fishermen explain soaring costs, sagging prices, voice their fears about a 'sell out in Brussels' or their alarms about foreign fishing fleets operating within the present fishing limits and their lack of confidence in the government's understanding of their problems. When trade unionists are asked why they are prepared to strike against an incomes policy that has been enacted by Parliament, they point to prices, to rents, to their general sense that their economic expectations have not been met. Their sense is of Governments that do not know or care about their case. Clearly this is not an explanation given by MPs, pressure group leaders or civil servants when they ignore, belittle or defy the law, so it is by no means a complete or adequate explanation. Nevertheless, it does seem to be true that, if post-war British Governments had been markedly more successful, if the British standard of living had shot up and if we were as much richer than the Germans and the French as we were in the period just after the war, and therefore more successful and self-confident, then there would be, if not a greater willingness to obey laws, at least far fewer occasions when there was any temptation to break them.

The second response, perhaps even more common than the first, but one which usually follows on the complaints about governmental policies and failures, is the observation that this is the only way to achieve anything. People at once say, 'It worked for the miners. Why not for us?' When striking school teachers were asked what example they thought they were giving to their pupils, the reply was always in terms of 'this is the only way to make the Government listen' or 'if you go according to the rules, you get nowhere'.

Several thoughts occur at once. The first is that this goes deeper as an explanation than mere complaints about governmental failures. After all, Governments failed to achieve their objectives long before recent decades and yet were able to secure obedience. Now this response indicates a lack of confidence in the democratic procedures for obtaining redress of grievances or changes in policy. Also, the response pinpoints a failure of democratic machinery, as many would regard this reply as reasonable in certain kinds of dictatorships. If citizens in a dictatorship said they had to demonstrate or riot or break laws, there would be little if any readiness to question the propriety of such action; the only issue would be whether this was a safe or sensible way to behave. But the traditional view in Western democracies is that because established procedures exist for pressing a point of view, for seeking to change policies, and because most voters have indicated their acceptance of these procedures by taking part in elections, it is wrong to go outside or defy the system. Just because there is a method of compromising between the demands of individuals and of majority and minority groups, it is assumed that, when a demand is not met, this is because it has not met with sufficient favour or won sufficient support to become the established policy of the whole community. Again, to break the rules to enforce conduct or views that have not been accepted in this way seems to be challenging the framework of the society; it seems to be insisting on the rule of force rather than the rule of law and, if every person or group acted in this way,

137

the society in its existing form would collapse.

When points of this kind are put to potential law-breakers, they elicit a variety of responses. (These are practical observations as the author has on four occasions attended protest meetings where such actions have been proposed and has opposed such suggestions.) The first response is the one already mentioned. It is a repetition of 'if it is all right for others, why not for us?' This only takes us back to square one.

A second response, which is often heard, is really a criticism of the system of communications. This is the assertion that direct action of some kind is the only way of bringing the issue to the attention of the decision-makers. The assumption is that if the representative or democratic system was working properly, then the policy being advocated would have been adopted. A further assumption is that, if the system could be seen to be working well and if the objectors' view was definitely and properly considered and rejected, then there would be no desire at that stage to go on and enforce the rejected view or policy by direct action. This is part of the case that the only way to get results is to press for them by means of disruption or law-breaking on the ground that the legislators or governors are too busy or ill-informed or insensitive to act on their own but in the belief that, when the matter is brought to their attention, they will accept the justice of the case.

Only a few go on and say that they would continue by direct action even if it was clear that, after full and proper consideration, their wishes were not those of the majority. But such groups do exist. These are the most consciously political elements. The extreme examples are the IRA, the Angry Brigade or the committed revolutionary groups who would persist whatever the reactions of the rest of the society. But it is interesting that these sections are a highly ideological minority. The vast bulk of those willing to break the law are deeply reluctant to accept that they are acting against the interests of the majority and indeed in a manner which, if universalised, would destroy the rule of law and civilised democratic society as it is known in the Western world.

Two further points are worth noting at a purely practical level. The first is that there is some validity in the claim that conduct of this kind does produce results. The wages of those groups who have challenged successive pay policies have improved more than those of docile groups who have accepted Government policy. The individuals who ruined the test match cricket pitch in order to draw attention to what they believed was the wrongful conviction of a Mr George Davis

138

obtained an immediate Home Office inquiry into the case. Whatever the final outcome, the fishermen never had such concern shown about their problems as was forthcoming when the blockade of the ports was undertaken.

The second practical point is the weakness of the Governments concerned. They have shown an extreme lack of self confidence in response to such pressure. They have half conceded the disruptors' argument by paying excessive attention to the pressure. This stretches from the view prevalent in large sections of both the Labour and Conservative parties not that an incomes policy is undesirable but that 'it will not work'. By this, what is meant is that, when challenged, Governments either cannot or will not rally the public, pass emergency laws or call out the troops, and in the end will cave in. Perhaps what underlies this belief is the fear, especially after Mr Heath took on the miners in February 1974 and lost, that the public will not back up the Government. However, this cannot be demonstrated, as the public might back up a vigorous, confident Government that knew what it wanted and showed that it was not going to be pushed around. But successive British Governments have only shown their weakness and, in this sense, they have half endorsed the objectors' case that Governments only respond to threats or violence and that, moreover, once these occur, the policies that have been pressed in this way are not only accepted but are accepted in a manner which shows that they are not unwelcome to the majority of the community. From this, it follows that certain questions must be asked. Is the democratic machinery sluggish and slow? Does it fail to bring genuine popular demands to the fore? Is there something wrong with the representative system as it is now practised in Britain and other Western countries? . . .

In trying to explain the situation, it may be best to look back at the classic period of British representative democracy when there was a much more positive feeling that laws passed by Parliament had received popular assent, that such laws were legitimate and should be obeyed. These laws were clearly set apart from the ordinary conventions of good behaviour, which could be ignored, abandoned or violated if this seemed to be in the interest of an individual or of an organized and determined group in the community.

How then is it possible to explain the efficacy and supremacy of law in the heyday of the nineteenth-century parliamentary system in Britain? If we look at the speeches of politicians and the standard texts from Bagehot to Lowell, certain points emerge. The main one is that the consent-giving model was clear and comprehensible and was positively enforced. The model that was explained to the public went

139

as follows. Electors choose an MP in each constituency. These MPs meet and choose a Prime Minister who, with the rest of the Cabinet, presents the Government's policies and measures to the House of Commons. These same MPs are able to, and do, reject or amend laws and are also able, by a more definite combination on what is clearly an issue of confidence, to get rid of the Government. But while the administration remains acceptable, most of its measures will be passed.

Once a law was passed, a minister responsible to the House of Commons and under its day-by-day supervision had the task of carrying out the law. His civil servants executed his commands. They did not make policy or advise on its content; they carried out the minister's instructions. As a result, the public were governed by laws made by ministers whom they had chosen, albeit indirectly. An interesting confirmatory point is that it was considered wrong for pressure groups to see civil servants. Pressure groups could only communicate with departmental officials in writing. If such groups wanted to exercise influence, they could only do so through the legitimate centre of political decision-making, the House of Commons, by dealing directly with ministers and MPs. This is why the original executive of the TUC, founded in 1868, was called 'the Parliamentary Committee', because its chief task was to lobby MPs. Other groups such as the East and West India trading interests, the Anti-Corn Law League, the railway company directors and even the nonconformist churches, either sought to elect a certain number of their members to Parliament or sought to keep the backing of a body of interested and sympathetic MPs.

So the 'consent model' was relatively simple and easily understood by the public. Everything was channelled through Parliament. All those wanting to influence policy worked on MPs. These representatives were relatively free from party control (though close to their constituents) and they voted as they thought proper. In consequence, the measures passed after long, probing debates, with amendments moved and accepted, were regarded as proper laws bearing the consent of the people. These were special commandments which it was assumed the public would accept as something requiring obedience.

What has happened to this concept? The basic change has been an elaboration of political and administrative life which has confused the old 'consent model' by introducing new forms of consent, of public endorsement of policies, so that it is no longer clear when a bill or act is fully legitimate. But the outcome is certainly to suggest that endorsement by a majority in the House of Commons is not any longer enough of itself.

The new forms of consent intrude at different points in the process of decison-making. One form is the assertion that policies or laws are not legitimate unless they have been included in the victorious party's election manifesto and have therefore received some kind of endorsement by the electorate. It was said again and again that the House of Commons' vote in favour of British membership of the EEC in 1971 was not sufficient because the then Conservative Government had stated in its previous election manifesto, 'Our commitment is to negotiate ... nothing more; nothing less.' According to this view, Governments can act to meet new and developing situations but may not carry out overall policies or enact important items of legislation unless these have been endorsed by the voters. Hence Mr Wilson's effort to demonstrate that the £6 limit in wage increases in 1975–76 was not a statutory incomes policy in the terms in which such a policy had been repudiated in this party's most recent election manifesto.

The peculiar feature of this new form of consent is that, while most Governments in Britain are elected on 40 to 45 per cent of the popular vote, the manifesto policies are often the work of small groups in the party or (in the case of Labour) of the National Executive Committee, and passage by the Annual Party Conference does not alter this fact. But the idea or force behind the effort to introduce some kind of popular mandate into British politics is fairly clear. The idea is that parties and MPs cannot be left to devise or adapt policies based on their general philosophies as new situations arise. Policies are not legitimate unless they have been put to and endorsed by the electorate. It is clearly impossible for all the things a Government may want to do in the last two years of a parliament to have been foreseen in the run up to a general election years earlier. Also, many Governments are forced to abandon policies on which they fought the last election (making U-turns as it is colloquially described). But all such new or reversed policies have the shadow cast over them that they are not fully legitimate. If there is a desire to repudiate these policies among the public or to resist the laws in which they are embodied, then the argument will be used that the Government has no mandate to act in this way or to call for obedience. The problem is not that this is a new and clear requirement for laws if they are to be legitimate, in addition to passage by the House of Commons (and the Lords). The difficulty is that this is a source of legitimacy which is only half accepted, sometimes used and sometimes disregarded, so that its existence leads to an element of confusion.

This confusion over the mandate leads to a similar confusion over the position of MPs and how they should behave. Most Members of

Parliament are used to being told that no one can have any respect for their judgement so long as they are mere lobby-fodder, being marshalled by the party whips to vote for measures which, though listed in the party manifesto, they have not considered and approved of themselves. But perhaps the very same person on the same occasion, given a different context, can ask the MP, 'Why did you vote for X when this is not part of the party's policy? We did not send you to Parliament to act in an élitist, eighteenth-century manner exercising your own judgement. We sent you there to put through Labour policies.' The lack of clarity (very marked compared with the late Victorian period) over the value and meaning of representative democracy tends to mean that MPs and Parliament lose or are blamed whatever they do. If ever there was an occasion when Parliament broke ranks and voted according to Members' views of the country's interest, it was in the 1971 vote of principle in favour of British membership of the EEC. Yet that this was so gave this 'free' act no greater validity than all the normal whipped votes where each MP votes his party ticket. And many MPs were attacked in their constituencies for making up their own minds (though only one, Mr Dick Taverne, was actually refused renomination because of this). But had all those Labour MPs who had voted for the application to join the EEC in 1967 and who were open and avowed Europeans changed their minds or at least their conduct and obeyed the party whip, there would have been a torrent of criticism of the two-faced invertebrates, the weak-kneed time-servers who were destroying the reputation of a once free and great Parliament.

Besides the weakening of Parliament's authority caused by this confusion over whether consent comes directly from the public in the form of a mandate for a party programme or whether it comes from the judgement exercised by those elected to represent the people, there is a further intrusion into the old simple consent model which adds further confusion and weakness. This is the role of the major pressure groups. Because Government does so much more and intervenes so much more than it did in the last century, the old doctrine that pressure groups can only reach the administration through MPs or ministers has long been abandoned. Part of the same process has been the end of the notion that civil servants merely execute policies decided on by ministers and authorised by Parliament. It is now accepted that officials do not merely advise on policy but, in many areas, actually make policy. As a result, pressure groups seek and gain direct access to Whitehall departments. . . .

So what has happened is that there has been introduced into the old, simple system of parliamentary consent-giving a further source of consent, the approval of the pressure groups. Not only does this raise the consequential issue of whether laws or policies are fully valid if this consent is refused, but it has two further effects. One is to raise the question in the public's mind of whether they are better represented through their pressure group or through their Member of Parliament. Secondly, the status and efficacy of MPs and of Parliament is further reduced. Many people organise themselves into groups in the belief that only in this way can they have an effective voice in matters concerning them. This is why there has been a flood of members to join an organisation for the self-employed. Facing extra insurance payments and taxes, the conclusion of the self-employed was not to see their MP or join a political party but to form a union. When a group of those organised in some body are contemplating direct action and are appealed to on the grounds that Britain is a democracy and that there is no need for them to go outside the normal procedures, their usual reply is that these procedures are too slow and achieve little or nothing. What is also significant is that those who vote against such direct action, if they are in a minority, usually decide that to refuse to go along with the majority would be to weaken the organised group and thus prevent it from working effectively for its members. Loyalty to the pressure group thus comes before loyalty to democratic procedures and institutions.

All this downgrades Parliament and gives people some justification when they contemplate refusing to obey a law passed by Parliament. It is evident that the leaders of industry, the professions and the unions prefer to work in their various organisations and to remain outside Parliament because they have more influence on decision-making and even on legislation in this way. Through the right to prior consultation they can play a larger and more effective part than the trade unionists or industrialists or professional men who get themselves elected to Parliament. . . .

So, for all these reasons, it is not surprising if the public do not consider mere passage by a majority in the Commons sufficient to confer a special moral authority on laws. They want to know whether their pressure groups have been consulted and have agreed, whether the proposal was in the party manifesto and whether the measure has evident public support. The old, straightforward parliamentary system of democracy has been added to and been confused by other concepts of legitimacy and other methods of obtaining and demonstrating support, the total result of which is to take away the automatic reverence for the process of law and to make people ask, 'Why should I?',

'What is in this for me?', 'How am I affected?', and 'Can I see the point of this regulation?'. ...

The phenomena being described have been commented on widely. Whether it is workers in a factory, students and their professors, children and school teachers or the public and the police, there is less readiness to accept orders or leadership. The explanations vary. Some have attributed this development to declining sanctions. They feel that, if corporal punishment were restored or heavier penalties (including the death penalty), then reasonable obedience would be restored. Others have blamed widespread education which, it is said, has taught people enough to put questions to those above them but not enough to realise the need for an element of hierarchy and responsibility.

The reasons why people are willing to obey or follow leaders are elaborate and difficult to analyse but it is not solely or even chiefly a matter of sanctions. One interesting situation is when all sanctions are removed. Authority has been examined in cases in which entire military units have been captured and when to obey the officers might be to encounter sanctions from the captors. In this situation, some units' internal authority collapsed, while in others from different nationalities discipline remained good or even better than usual.

Looking at the cases where authority declined, it would appear that the reason was lack of a sense of common purpose. In United States units, where there was a mixture of races, people of different pre-American backgrounds and considerable mutual suspicion and tension, discipline collapsed. Where order was best maintained was in units from traditional communities with long-standing loyalties and established social patterns. In universities, authority has been best maintained where there has been a sense of common respect for certain academic standards, the students desiring to obtain, and the staffs being willing to help them obtain, the best possible qualifications. Order has broken down in universities and among groups of students who have no longer shared values and had common purposes with the staff. Similarly, industrial authority has been maintained best in countries where recent experience and popular ideology accept that the interests of management and workers have much in common – that success for one benefits the other.

What has happened in Britain has been a decline in the sense of common purpose among the various sections of the society. This has been hastened by the governmental failures that have been so evident over the last two decades. It has been revealed and reinforced by the weakness of governments under pressure. As some groups, by the use of direct action, have won concessions at the expense of others, the sense of common purpose in the society has declined. At the same time, the weakness of Parliament is partly the result of the lack of a clear, popularly accepted doctrine of representative government. As each section can quote some form of democracy or participation that seems to support its case, the old unity in support of parliamentary government (and any clarity about what that concept implies) has declined. . . .

This is not the place to attempt to set out ways of reversing the decline in a sense of common purpose in the society and in the consequent increase in people's willingness to see society as an orange to be squeezed by those with the strength or the nerve to extract most juice for themselves. But the phenomenon exists and is serious. If it continues, there may be a descent into anarchy, or the public may find it so uncomfortable that they turn to a form of autocracy which will impose its authority, or matters may trickle on in much the same rather dispiriting way that they have done in recent years. But an awareness of the problem and a willingness to analyse it is at least a start in preparing for a solution which would, it is to be hoped, restore a greater degree of respect for authority without resorting to any restrictions of the liberties that used to be an integral part of a society based firmly on the rule of law.

2.7 'Select Committees and the House' (From *The Listener*, 6 July 1978, pp. 5–6)

Before I was elected to Parliament, I used to teach that the chief function of the House was to criticise and check the government; but any new backbencher soon gets this knocked out of him. One is told again and again that the main task of those on the majority side of the House is to support the government, while the main task of opposition backbenchers is to support their leaders in this constant conflict across the floor of the chamber – conflict designed to rouse support in the country and to set the scene for the next general election, however far off that might be.

Now, considering this, some very radical reformers have argued, possibly rightly, that the House will never be an effective critic of government till the executive is taken out of the legislature – that is, until the need for support of the government is no longer the primary

145

purpose of a majority in the House. Perhaps they are right, but such a drastic change, leading to the adoption of the American system, seems too much to expect in the current climate of opinion.

Given this basic purpose of the floor of the House – to continue the political struggle between the parties – the next question is whether anything can be done to reform the House of Commons. First, the concentration on the clashes on the floor of the House means that it is a totally unsuitable place for considering any matters of detail. Members of Parliament concentrate, on these occasions, on the broad political issues. There is no better evidence of this than the recent history of the Scottish devolution bill, where clause after clause of important, detailed matters went by undebated as members on each side repeated the overall case for and against devolution, one amendment after another, and irrespective of the precise points raised by the amendments.

This is why reformers have made the case that the only hope for detailed scrutiny of the many-sided activities of government, and the only hope of examining important issues on which both sides of the House are agreed, lies in the development of specialist or select committees.

On the other hand, the critics of a more comprehensive and effective committee system have always included some of the leading members of the House, those who have preferred the set-piece political clash of the kind I have described. They have argued, first, that committee work would detract from the floor of the House. Members would be in committee all the time and unable to come and listen to or take part in the major debates. A second criticism they make is that the task of Parliament is not to scrutinise detail – that is for people with a civil servant's cast of mind. The real task of an MP is to sniff out the hot political issue, to scent the wind of public opinion and then take a hold of the salient questions and hammer them again and again and again, until either the government gives way or, at least, the case is established as far as the public is concerned.

Another criticism made by these people is that no able men would go on the committees, as those with ambition want to be seen. The place to catch the prime minister's eye and the way to do it is to make able speeches on the floor of the House. This criticism was carried farther with the allegation that committee work breeds consensus attitudes, that cross-party liaisons are formed, that opposition MPs come to see the government's case or, conversely, that government MPs become a little unhappy about the case being made by their own side.

As a result, these MPs might act together, thus weakening and spoiling the normal two-party conflict.

An added motive now, incidentally, for ambitious MPs concentrating on the chamber, has come with the broadcasting of debates. For MPs go home each weekend and encounter their supporters saying: 'I listened all week and I never heard you, Bill.' If they work on committee, their activities may be lost.

Finally, the critics have objected to committee work by saying that there have been few opportunities to debate the reports of the committees. They also say that action is seldom taken as a result of these reports. Ronald Butt, for instance, wrote in *The Times* recently that, since the reports of the Select Committee on Nationalised Industries – and he was particularly dealing with the report on the British Steel Corporation – did not lead either to a dramatic change of government policy or the sacking of one or two of the ministers concerned, then the report was somehow worthless. He even argued that the work of this kind of committee strengthened the hand of the executive.

A further point that is made by critics is to say that if reports are debated on the floor of the House, then the committee members tend to dominate the debates. It is said that this creates first-class and second-class members.

I have gone through all the criticisms of select committee development, and I have tried to give their full strength and force. I want to examine them in detail, because those who argue, as I do, that these criticisms are wrong, have to establish not only that they are wrong but that they will not damage what happens on the floor of the House.

First, on the question of time and the actual attention of members: those who hold that there are not enough MPs to service the existing committees, and that to have more members in committee would clash with debates in the chamber, are making a mistake in simple factual terms. It is true that the whips have had difficulty in getting MPs to serve on committees, but the problem is really with standing legislative committees which are microcosms of the House, those committees that take the committee stage of most bills at present. The real point here is that MPs like working on select or investigatory committees, and they often use their service on such committees as an excuse, or a reason at least, for not going on to standing committees of the kind I have described.

Secondly, on the question of performance in the House, often people who visit the House say that only 20 or 30 MPs are in the chamber, and that this indicates lack of attention by the House. Now, the idea that these MPs would increase in number if there were no committees does not hold, and, in fact, if no committees were sitting, there is no evidence that a larger number of MPs would go into the chamber.

Consider the actual statistics of the situation. There are 635 MPs. Even when one takes away 85 ministers and 50 shadow ministers, there remain 500 MPs, who cannot possibly all take part in debates on the floor of the House. In most day-long debates, between the end of the frontbench introductory speeches at about 5 pm and the opening of the wind-up speeches at 9 pm, an average of only 16 backbench speeches can be made. Now, one of the great virtues of committee work is that it finds something useful for the bulk of members, otherwise excluded from all parliamentary activity, to do. One simply cannot expect large numbers of members to sit endlessly in the chamber listening to debates in which they cannot take part.

Also on this point, the public know that government nowadays touches them at a great many points, and there is evidence that they do get tired of what Professor S. E. Finer has stigmatised as 'adversary politics'. They do expect other aspects of governmental activity, which may not be in the limelight but which affect them, to be considered. For instance, the farmers expect their MPs to do more than have one or two rows a year about farm prices; there is the effect of EEC regulations in so many fields.

In addition, it is simply not true, nowadays, that debates on the floor of the House can bring out all the key issues. Even deeply experienced politicians such as Powell or Callaghan cannot conjure up the key issues without overlooking some vital aspects, if they have no means of extracting the relevant information. For instance, it may be possible, by skimming through a defence white paper, to detect flaws in the government's case. But it is also possible that serious shortages of military equipment or deficiencies in training may go undetected if there is no procedure by which generals and admirals can voice their worries.

To take another example, the Scottish Office has 11,000 civil servants and does the work of the equivalent of nine ministries in England. Yet it can get to the length of closing four colleges of education before a word of this policy leaks out to the public or to MPs. Continuing this example, below the Scottish Office, there are 204 ad hoc or nominated boards, bureaux, commissions and so on, with 5083 patronage places, whose accountability to the House of Commons or to anyone else is negligible. How is it possible for MPs to deduce or guess at which of these activities is legitimate or illegitimate, wasteful or sensible? And the public have no other recourse but Parliament when it comes to controlling these bodies. One has only to look at the recent reports of the Public Accounts Committee to see that what can be unearthed by an effective scrutinising committee with a proper staff is of the utmost importance. Once such a committee discloses faults in certain ministries or in certain programmes, these can then become the subject of one of these major political clashes on the floor of the House. But without the original discovery of the information by the committee, the matter would never have become public.

As to the effect on MPs taking part in debates on the floor of the House, nothing is more depressing that the present procedure, by which there is an audience for the ministerial speeches at the start of a debate, and for the concluding speeches, but, in between, no one (barring a handful who expect to speak) is present because not a word they say would make any difference to the outcome. But if a committee has been involved, there are several good effects. The first is that speeches are far better informed. This was very evident during the two-year lifetime of the Select Committee on Agriculture, between 1967 and 1969, when members who had no detailed knowledge of the subject had a store of information they could turn to in the reports of the evidence of the committee. The chairman, incidentally, also became a much more important figure than the average backbencher, and this development of some power centres other than merely those on the two front benches is highly desirable. Perhaps this is one reason why the government so rapidly abolished the committee.

As to the willingness of MPs to serve on these committees, select or specialist committees with investigatory powers, these committees are over-subscribed. There is a constant demand to serve on them because the committees allow them to develop a knowledge of the subject, a knowledge which may be of importance in constituency terms or just in general political terms.

On the question of the debating of reports, this misses the point of committee work. In the last century and the earlier part of the present century, select committees were used rather like royal commissions are today. When an especially difficult problem arose, a select committee was set up. It investigated the point at issue, heard evidence, deliberated and produced a report recommending certain actions. If this report went undebated and nothing was done, understandably the members felt that their time had been wasted. But the point of continuous select or specialist committees, of the kind talked about now, is quite different. Committees whose task is to watch over the work of given departments have their value, not in their reports (though these can be useful), but in their existence, in the publicity they bring to bear on the work of the department, and in the fact that a particular civil servant has to come and answer for those things for which he is responsible. Even if the Public Accounts Committee reports were never debated, this would detract very little from the impact of the committee on civil servants who are forced to explain their actions and face the wrath of their superiors if any deficiencies are disclosed.

If one had an effective committee system, it might be possible to treat the House in a more sensible fashion: to meet at 10.30 in the morning, to stop at seven or 7.30 in the evening, and to deal with all business according to an agreed timetable. However, I must admit that this is one of the least likely reforms, so long as three major groups of MPs continue to oppose it. There are ministers who want to work in their departments in the mornings, and there are private MPs with outside jobs and, of course, there are the many out-of-town MPs with no homes in London and nothing else to do in the evening. To get to normal hours of working would mean having full-time MPs, proper pay and the chance for those who represent far-away constituencies either to bring their families to London, or, at least, to set up a reasonable second home in town to which they could go in the evenings.

To return to the question of the floor of the House. It is hard to see how this activity in debating terms could be damaged if government was forced to become more open, if British governments – like the US administration – had to explain their policies, to reveal the bargains they were making with outside pressure groups and to account for their expenditure to a series of select committees. It is interesting that those opposed to reform fall back on the allegation that such knowledge must blunt the edge of political controversy; that it must lead to consensus politics, with potential critics on committees unable to attack on the floor of the House, because their teeth have already been drawn by commitments made on some committee.

This case comes dangerously close to accepting the criticisms of those who say that the House of Commons is so geared to adversary politics that it fights about foolish things; that it has conflicts where better knowledge would reveal that no conflict exists (and, conversely, as I have suggested, that it does not often fight over real conflicts because the factual information about them is unknown). To go back to the case of the short-lived Committee on Agriculture, it contained bitter anti-Marketeers and fervent pro-Europeans. For a year, it examined the implications for British agriculture of accepting the Common Agricultural Policy, and the result was not, as the critics would suggest, to produce a wishy-washy common ground. On the contrary, disagreements were as keen as ever, but they took place on real issues. Whereas, before, fights had taken place over misapprehensions, after the committee had been at work, there was a group of MPs who really comprehended the issues at stake and focused Parliament, the farming community and the public on the issues that mattered. It only does Parliament harm for the public to realise that often great battles take place on issues which are not fully understood, or where the real points that should be settled are not at the center of the debate.

Part 3

Social democracy

3.1 'Socialism or social democracy?' (From *The Political Quarterly*, Oct.–Dec. 1972, pp. 470–84)

There has never been a time in the history of the Labour Party when it would not have been appropriate to write an article on 'the current crisis', but there are features of the present situation which are both more peculiar and more serious than the old recurrent crises over leadership, doctrine and tactics.

A brief summary of the situation is that, for the first time since the early 1930s, a combination of forces including the Left has won the support of the non-doctrinal centre of the Party, but the peculiarity is that this has happened when the Left (and, as a result of its commanding position, the Party as a whole) stands for nothing except hostility to the measures of the present Conservative Government. Yet those normally labelled as the Right, who have provided most of the ideas since the late 1950s, have been so upset and thrown off balance by their recent defeats that they appear to be divided and somewhat demoralised and have managed only to fight rear-guard actions.

The oddity of the situation is brought out, for example, by looking at the Twelfth Annual Congress of the Second Socialist International held this July in Vienna. If the programmes and achievements of the many socialist parties represented at the Congress are examined, there is a great degree of similarity. All the parties have become reformist, in the sense that they accept the democratic system and free elections and, while all are prepared to intervene in economic affairs to promote social justice, none of them intend to replace capitalism by a totally different or 'socialist' economic system. Once in power these parties have followed similar policies introducing increased welfare benefits, a public housing programme, a health service, and they have all attempted to plan the economy of their own country, including taking control of certain industries. The principal objective has been greater social equality within each community. The Germans being very conscious of theory, spelt this out in their Bad Godesburg Programme of 1959. Hugh Gaitskell tried to do the same in the Clause Four controversy, but because the Labour Party is a non-theoretical and somewhat backward-looking or sentimental party, he lost, though his policies were adopted in practice both then and in the subsequent period in office under Harold Wilson. It is significant that, having won a large majority in 1966, Harold Wilson only completed the last remnant of the old nationalisation programmes by taking over the iron and steel industry. Though he shared a pragmatic readiness to take over docks or special industries that were failing, there was no nationalisation 'shopping list' of the kind the Labour Party had had in its manifesto in 1945, 1950 or 1951 each of which was intended as a step towards further, virtually total public ownership.

The peculiarity of current British politics is that at a time when all the socialist parties in the world are clearly reformist and even the French Communist Party has joined the French Socialists in an alliance based on a reformist programme, the Left are in a strong position in the Labour Party and have managed to suggest that to be a 'social democrat' is something undesirable and that a return to a purer, more fundamental socialism is possible.

It is hard to discover what is meant by this. In fact, the Left do not appear to want a return to the old Clause Four type of total public ownership. Although one or two Labour MPs still talk in this way and although there are elements in the constituency parties still moving resolutions on these lines at branch meetings (one such resolution is carried *nem con* every year at the conference of the Scottish Regional Council of the Labour Party), there are few who do in fact believe that this is the correct course for the Party. Most people realise that nationalisation was never an end in itself; it was always a means to several ends. The old theory was that by ending the payment of profits to rentiers in these industries, the class system would be weakened (the manager who took over from the former owners was just a better paid, specialised worker). Also, by removing those with an interest in exploitation, nationalisation was supposed to bring harmony into labour relations. In addition, by imposing public control, these industries could be fitted into a national plan and it was thought that with no profit motive, production could be designed to meet social needs rather than simply the demands of those with money.

Broadly speaking, nationalisation has not had any of these specifically socialistic effects here or in other countries, though it has permitted increased investment and concern about the impact of policy changes on the workers and on the public. But these improvements could equally well be achieved by other methods. As a result, few people think the Labour Party would recover its relevance and idealism if it simply proposed to take over one major industry after another in its next period of office.

So what is this more authentic socialism which is being proposed as an alternative to the social democracy of recent years? It cannot be a serious list of policy proposals because this is just what the Labour Party is lacking at the moment. (The recent 'Green Paper' published by the NEC does not come into this category.) No one could enumerate a series of positive commitments for change with which the Labour Party or any section of it, from the Tribune Group to the extreme Right, is presently identified.

The new socialist fundamentalism currently being advocated is more a mood or an approach to politics. It may be hard to pin down in policy terms, but it can be smelt. John Gyford and Stephen Haseler have made a serious attempt to identify it in their Fabian pamphlet, *Social Democracy: beyond revisionism.* They call it 'working class populism'. It derives from 'a mild, tolerant yet real class war' and 'has always had a feeling of the grass roots about it'. This populist-socialist approach, they say, has been a 'channel for the unwealthy, the uneducated and the unmetropolitan'. They accept that many of the socialists of this kind are well-off workers but the resentments are relative; what is taking place is 'a movement of the marginally well-heeled, the provincial, the regional, the unfashionable and the unimportant'.

The alternative group identified by Gyford and Haseler are the social democrats or 'left-wing liberals' as the 'true socialists' often call them. It is alleged that they are preponderantly middle class, impressed by technology and 'élitist' in their outlook. They do not respect working class culture and prefer to emphasise *classlessness*; group rights do not seem as important to them as *individual* rights.

This analysis has clearly fastened on to some of the current divisions in the Labour Party and has some relevance to recent social developments. Many on the traditional Left, from Michael Foot to Stan Orme, support populist class-orientated demands not because they derive from a socialist philosophy but because they come from 'their people'. This means that they can support car workers or dockers demanding wage increases far above national increases in productivity simply because they are made by a group of organised workers acting in a class-conscious way and united by a common feeling of alienation, boredom and resentment at the standards enjoyed by the university trained, white collar managerial staff. On the other hand, the social democrat is culpable of élitism and intellectualism because he looks at the consequences of granting such demands, sees that the result is to push up prices and thus cut the living standards of those who cannot win above the average pay awards; in other words, that the result is to increase inequality whereas he wants a criterion by which to support only those demands that do not damage other workers or those living on social security benefits. Gyford and Haseler point out that the difference of outlook highlighted by this example spreads far beyond the central issue of wages and equality. Because the social democrats are interested in individual rights and social justice, they will accept liberal legislation legalising homosexual relations or abortion when much of this is alien to working-class group feeling which thinks of liberty more in terms of what *groups* can do and of what status they have in society. For much the same reasons, the social democrats are keen to pay out money to the Arts Council and favour the BBC while the populist/ socialists would prefer to help provide facilities for football clubs and watch commercial TV since it talks their language. The social democrat is bothered about economic growth producing pollution and damaging 'natural ecological systems' while the populist/socialist wants rapid growth since it will provide more jobs, higher pay and better conditions in physical terms.

If this contrast is developed and widened to cover the full spectrum of current political issues, social democrats are internationalist and pro-Common Market while the populist/socialist is suspicious of foreigners and uninterested in foreign policy. For much the same motives, the former try to be liberal on immigration laws while the latter group is suspicious of coloured workers. Underlying all these specific reactions, the social democrat wants to end the class system (and can therefore be accused of wanting to make everyone middle class) while the socialist by instinct expects the class system to continue and this is comforting as he can then continue to resent the system. This kind of socialism is a deeply conservative outlook based upon fear of change; it expects that the inevitable burden of adjusting to modern methods will fall predominantly on the workers so that the first priority is to defend the positions already won by the Labour Movement.

It is obvious that to characterise these two approaches is at once to caricature, to impose a coherence which does not fully exist. It is easy to think of people who, though mainly in one category, have some opinions shared by the other side. For instance, some who are clearly 'socialist' by this set of criteria nevertheless are deeply involved in race issues, that is, in ensuring fair treatment for coloured immigrants and in getting immigration quotas relaxed. The Left in the House of Commons played a major and honourable part in resisting the Commonwealth Immigration (Kenyan Asians) Bill in 1968. On the other hand, there are those, of whom Tony Crosland is the most conspicuous example, who are archetypal social democrats, yet are strongly in favour of economic growth and regard most of the ecology-doomwatch case as alarmist nonsense whose practical effect, if implemented, would be to perpetuate inequality.

Yet it would appear to be true that this division between a populist/ socialism ready to back all demands from the working class and a perhaps older desire to pursue reformist left-wing principles on the merits of each case, does indeed exist. The division came out quite clearly on two occasions in the Dick Taverne case. The first was revealed on television, when it became clear that some of the activists in the Lincoln Constituency Party did not merely object to Taverne's pro-European views; they objected to his lack of a class-conscious approach to politics. It came out again when the NEC turned down his appeal on a twelve to eight vote which fell almost directly along the lines suggested. This decision set aside the recommendation of the Organisation Sub-Committee of the NEC that Taverne's appeal should be upheld on the grounds that the rules of natural justice had not been fully observed by the Lincoln Party.

This division also explains how former Right-Wingers, such as James Callaghan, Fred Peart and Willie Ross, have been able to work in an easy and comfortable alliance on the Shadow Cabinet with Left-Wingers such as Michael Foot and Peter Shore; they are united not just by hostility to the Common Market but by their common willingness to back all opposition to redundancies, to back all strikes and to reject all aspects of Conservative legislation, indeed all change of any kind. In this sense, the populist/socialist approach has moved away from what used to be known as Bevanism. The latter was a doctrinaire position ready to advocate new measures and ready to oppose working-class group demands if these, on analysis, proved to be contrary to socialist principles. Viewed in this way, Barbara Castle was the last of the Bevanites because, when she became convinced, as Minister of Employment, that certain aspects of trade union activity were contrary to the interests of the working class as a whole, she was prepared to argue this case and to introduce legislation to prevent such actions. Whether her proposals would have been effective or not, the point is that her whole approach was to judge the results of social actions according to her political principles, whereas the current populist/socialist approach is quite different; the major unions want to retain the 1968 legal *status quo* in industrial relations and that is enough. For them, to discuss the legislative framework surrounding British industrial relations and to examine the effects of certain types of group actions on other sections of the community is half-way to

159

becoming a Tory; none of the present 'genuine socialists' would contemplate such behaviour.

It is true that some of this reluctance springs from one of the traditional approaches to opposition; that the Opposition should not make constructive suggestions but just oppose. It is far easier to offer a blanket opposition. Nevertheless, there is a gap between this position and that of the more old fashioned socialists who believed they were creating a new fairer society and that the abuse of power by any group just because it had a stranglehold on a section of the economy was both anti-social and anti-socialist. The present populist/socialist position is not to raise such questions but simply to ask who is making the demand? If it is a group of workers, they must be supported and only those who are intellectuals, élitists and middle-class social democrats would pause to consider the effects of the conduct in question.

There are, however, some intractable difficulties for those taking the populist/socialist position. The first is that there is no method of solving conflicts between one group of workers and another. If dockers claim the right to 'strip and stuff' containers and thus threaten the jobs of packers dispersed around a number of factories, who is right? The support of the populist/socialist tends to go to the best organised and most defiant group, presumably because they are showing most working-class vigour, but this has no obvious relationship to socialism or to justice. Put in another way, to back those who shout loudest or press hardest is to neglect the weakest and worst paid groups who are often incapable of making a strong case. Another aspect of the problem is that the large general unions, realising that the worst paid workers excite public sympathy, often frame their demands in this light; but if they then also insist on keeping differentials, they are not in fact doing anything to decrease relative poverty. Yet, once again, the socialists who are pledged to support every trade union position have nothing to say about this.

These difficulties come to a head over the question of an incomes policy. Part of the doctrine of the socialists is that any incomes policy is undesirable simply because it is unacceptable to the larger, more powerful unions. But if all union demands are permitted, the result is to increase inequality in two ways. The first occurs simply because the better paid are the best organised. A recent analysis found that between January 1 and January 31 1970, the top ten working-class groups had wage settlements on average every ten months and had rises on average of 18 per cent. The ten poorest paid workers' groups had settlements on average every twenty months of an average of 7.7 per cent. This shows that the result of leaving the unions to battle for themselves is to increase inequality.

The second effect of extravagant wage increases on income differentials comes through the effect on prices. Professor Beckerman, in his book on *The Economic Record of the Labour Government, 1964– 70,* concludes that while the improved cash benefits provided by the Labour Government did reduce inequality, this narrowing of the gaps ceased in 1969–70 because excessive wage demands led to inflation, which in turn reduced the standard of living of the poor and those living on fixed incomes or social security benefits. He concludes that inflation damaged the position of the working class as a whole and that those union leaders responsible for the excessive wage demands are 'either incapable of understanding this or are guilty of cynical betrayal of the interests of their members'.

The point of raising these issues is that if the Labour Party has any purpose, whether under 'socialist' or 'social democratic' leadership, a major part of the purpose must be to promote social justice. And it is impossible to have social justice in a society where there are gross inequalities in income and in personal wealth. In other words, one of the fundamental purposes of the Labour Party is to reduce inequality. Yet there is irrefutable evidence that to permit free collective bargaining and to encourage inflationary wage demands runs directly counter to this basic objective. Thus a socialist party without an incomes policy is a contradiction in terms.

There is no 'real socialist' country in the world, from Yugoslavia to Sweden, from China to Rumania, that leaves wage bargaining to the free play of the power groups concerned. Those of the populist-socialist left who are prepared to discuss the issue, will feel embarrassed at this point and take refuge in the argument that they are prepared to contemplate an incomes policy, but only when all other social and taxation policies are entirely acceptable. This is a perfect get out, as the condition will never be fulfilled. It is clearly true that a government which was actively taxing the rich and helping to reduce poverty would be more acceptable to the unions, but it is quite another matter to suggest that all unions would voluntarily ask only for non-inflationary increases.

Certain things cannot be denied. The first is that it is the task of trade union leaders to seek the maximum benefit for their members and this may easily exceed the amount which would prevent further price rises and thus safeguard the interests of the weaker sections of the community. Secondly, a socially just policy nowadays may involve taxing the upper groups among the weekly wage-earners to help those who are at the bottom of the scale and this is bound to be unpopular with at least some of those affected. But thirdly, and even more to the point, it is surely wrong to argue that, given a government which redistributes income in a socialist way, this would have enough impact upon rank and file trade unionists to persuade them in all cases to moderate their own demands in such a way as to make a voluntary incomes policy feasible. After all, doctors and school teachers are no less socially responsible than miners or railway workers and most of these professional groups are quite uninterested in or positively opposed to a wealth tax or higher family allowances; and they have been putting in wage claims of the 22 per cent to 30 per cent level. The point is that organised groups seek their own interests and, as such groups have become more powerful in modern societies, there is more and more difficulty in persuading them to consider the well-being either of their class or of the community as a whole, whether or not the Government is, in its other policies, pursuing socially equitable policies.

The central defect in the current populist-socialist position is that they will not consider the overall principles involved. They are not far from the position of Enoch Powell who argues that the degree of intervention and paternalism involved in an incomes policy makes it inherently unworkable in a democracy. Powell would regulate total consumption (that is, he would have an incomes policy) by overall control of the money supply and a floating exchange rate. To devalue (or float downwards) is, after all, just a method of cutting everyone's standard of living by putting up prices. But, once again, it is grossly inequitable and it is amazing to find people who regard themselves as being on the Left in politics advocating what amounts to a Right-wing *laissez-faire* policy on wages. Yet to refuse to set out criteria for wage increases and to destroy machinery for enforcing such criteria is to admit that there is no way of pressing the case of the weakest, most poorly paid elements in the community.

Another problem for populist-socialism is that, being suspicious of any reservations about working-class demands and of any talk of reconciling interests among workers, there is a tendency among the Left to imagine and to say that the answers to current political problems are easy and obvious; that rank and file activists have solutions to policy problems at their finger tips, or rather in their instinctive responses, so that any failures by Labour Governments must be due to the pernicious refusal of social democratic leaders to enact these obvious policies. In fact, nothing could be further from the case. There is, for example, no issue which the Labour Party would like to solve more than the present rapid escalation in land prices. The inhibiting factor is not lack of 'socialist will-power' but lack of a viable solution. Two solutions have been tried, one being the development charges introduced by the Attlee Government and abandoned soon after the Conservatives took office in 1951 and the other being the Land Commission set up by Harold Wilson. Both solutions failed and, at present, no one in the Labour Party has produced a workable and equitable alternative. One thing is certain; there is no easy answer, much less one which is obvious to most party members. The same is true of such complex questions as a reduction of regional differentials or the abolition of poverty in a way which neither destroys incentives nor antagonises the section of the working class who are earning incomes which are just above the benefit level.

Anti-internationalism marks the populist-socialists, springing in part from the arguments of the anti-marketeers and in part from the mild but definite xenophobia which can easily be aroused among the working class. Yet it is clearly important for the next Labour Government to avoid the difficulties which the Wilson administration encountered because it kept trying to operate as a world power capable of standing on its own. It will be necessary to work with the European powers of much the same international standing as Britain to prevent more currency crises, to devise an industrial policy which will allow multi-national companies to develop in Europe while keeping them under proper supervision and to see that one country's regional policies do not undercut those of its neighbours. Yet it is still convenient for the Left to pretend that co-operation, particularly with the most relevant powers in Europe who are joined in the EEC, is either unnecessary or too geographically restricted, too ineffective or too dangerous to be accepted as a permanent feature of British foreign policy.

A final weakness of the populist-socialist position is its largely negative or conservative character. The almost conscious refusal to think through a socialist answer to the central problems facing Britain, the problems of inflation and a fair incomes policy, has encouraged a tendency to reject all attempts to work out relevant political policies as being middle-class, social democratic, élitist pastimes. A substitute has been found in the slogan that this is the worst Tory Government in modern times – a slogan which is not only of dubious truth but one which avoids the real problem that almost all the Government's policies have some sensible aspects which any future Labour Government would have to retain. To admit this would involve the Opposition in producing fair workable alternatives. The activists and far-left groups in some constituency parties and some unions encourage a negative approach, because they call for a blanket rejection of the entire Industrial Relations Act, the entire policy of joining the EEC, the entire Housing Finance Bill and so on, a policy which would leave the next Labour Government committed only to a return to the 1968–70 status quo.

The paradox is that the Left, who prided themselves on being the most persistent critics of the last Wilson Government, are now in practice working hard to ensure that the next Labour Government is as like its predecessor as possible.

It is symptomatic of the curious reversal of roles not only between the parties but inside the Labour Party that it is Roy Jenkins and his social democratic supporters who have been rethinking socialist policy in terms of how the next Labour Government should tackle poverty, relative deprivation in the cities, the need for increased aid to the underdeveloped countries, and so on. They accept that the Labour Party must be a party of change. They also accept that, in a highly complex society, government intervention to diminish class barriers in education or to end homelessness has to be carefully thought out if the desired results are to be obtained. They are prepared to face the reality of Britain's declining position as a nation state and our greater dependence on other countries, facts which mean that to achieve the maximum control of our own affairs, it is necessary to share sovereignty with and thus influence those powers whose policies most closely affect this country. It is also symptomatic that the Left have not met these arguments with counter-arguments; they have not developed a policy or a position but have proposed changes in the Labour Party's constitution whose practical effect would be to strengthen the power of those external activist groups in the Party which in turn would vote for and bolster the position of the left inside the Parliamentary Labour Party.

The only important pamphlet produced recently by the Tribune Group, or rather by Frank Allaun, Ian Mikardo and Jim Sillars on behalf of the Group (called *Labour: Party or Puppet? Making the Labour Party fit for Democrats*), does not deal with policy questions but proposes four changes in the Party's constitution or procedures. The first is that constituency selection conferences for parliamentary candidates should be narrower groups than at present, delegates only being allowed to attend if they have been present at a certain proportion of management committee meetings over the previous two years. Secondly, there should be no women's section on the National Executive Committee, the five women's places being allocated to the constituency parties (making twelve in all), but the constituency parties would then elect six MPs and six rank-and-file delegates to the NEC. Thirdly, MPs would be expected to 'sign an undertaking to carry out the programme and policy of the party as decided by Conference'. Finally, the Leader of the Party would be elected not by the Parliamentary Party but by the annual conference.

Two aspects of these proposals are interesting and reveal the attitudes underlying them. The first is the assumption that there is some kind of gap between the Parliamentary Labour Party, the bulk of the MPs and 'the real Labour Party' in the constituency management committees and among shop stewards and trade union officials. In fact, MPs are usually selected by the biggest and most representative gatherings that ever take place in the constituency parties. Yet this is just what the Tribune pamphlet objects to; it wants to cut out the delegates who represent the large number of party members with broader interests than simply sitting on management committees: these are the people who turn out at elections to do the work, but who have other calls on their time as well as the Labour Party between elections. This broader, more representative group of committed party members do such unforgivable things as vote for candidates who are articulate, who have some training in problems of public policy and who can put across a good case from a platform (all qualities, according to the Tribune pamphlets, which are apparently barely desirable in MPs). And this proposal to narrow the group who in fact choose the bulk of MPs is made in the name of democracy! There is the further point that because MPs then have to deal with the community at large, to meet, help and represent non-party members and to put up a case which carries conviction outside the confines of party executive meetings, it is alleged that these MPs somehow become less representative and increasingly out of touch with the mass of Labour voters.

In fact, the situation is the opposite. It is the small group of constant party activists who spend their entire lives inside the party with few other interests or conversation, who become less representative even of the bulk of Labour voters. On the other hand, MPs who have to have wide-spread contacts and who have to be re-elected, do keep in touch with these wider groups. It is fantastic to suggest that such MPs are less in contact with Labour voters than are trade union leaders who are often elected for life on grounds which

165

have no relation to their knowledge of or capacity to represent the public at large. The second important and revealing aspect of these proposals is the idea that the Labour Party and its parliamentary wing should not represent the mass of Labour voters but should be tied tightly to the interests of certain producer groups, namely, the larger unions. In practice, the Tribune Group's proposals would mean that the leader of the party would be chosen not on his capacity as revealed in parliament, but on his ability to meet the demands of a small number of trade union leaders.

As the pamphlet admits, the unions have ten times the votes of the constituency parties at the annual conference and, if they selected the leader and if MPs had to sign promises to follow all conference decisions, this small group of union leaders, in no way responsible to or elected by the public, would determine the entire policy of any Labour Government.

The objections to any such idea have to be stressed. First, there is no conceivable democratic defence for the block vote. The block votes of the unions bear no relation to the numbers of committed Labour voters in their ranks; the relationship is solely to the numbers for which the unions choose to pay affiliation fees. Union leaders at their own conferences deal largely with industrial matters and are often left a free hand or are only given broad guidance over political questions. This is why the change from a Right-Wing general secretary to a Left-Wing one (probably each elected on the quite different and, in the context, entirely proper grounds of their ability as wage bargainers) can mean that a million votes at the Labour Party Conference are switched from supporting Right Wing resolutions to supporting Left Wing ones. Aneurin Bevan, who belonged to the Left Wing in former days when its chief interest was in specific socialist policies and in campaigning to win over popular support for these political principles, strongly criticised the block vote as anti-democratic.

A second objection is that the conference, because it is union dominated, lays more stress on the interests of producer pressure groups than on the interests of consumers, citizens, taxpayers or the public at large. Yet the task of a parliamentary party is to represent these unorganised elements in the community. The best example is that it would be quite intolerable and contrary to the principles of parliamentary democracy for a Labour Government to decide to try and limit inflation by restraining wage increases above a certain level, only to find that some of the unions could, by a majority on the National Executive and at Conference, force a Labour Prime Minister to abandon this policy; a policy which had been adopted because it was in the interests of the nation as a whole and especially of the poorer rank-and-file workers. Although there was no such direct reversal of the Wilson Government's policies, it is clear that trade union opposition was the main reason for the abandonment of the Prices and Incomes Policy in 1969–70. This led both to the inflation, which was a major cause of the Conservative victory at the polls, and to the redistribution of income away from those dependent on social security benefits and low wages, which undid the tendency to greater equality of incomes achieved by the Labour Government between 1964 and 1968.

The task for those Labour Party leaders who are labelled social democrats is now clear. They must preach the principles of socialism on which the Labour Party was founded and explain the application of these principles to current social, economic and international conditions. This means a primary emphasis on putting the needs of the mass of the community before the interests of those with a monopoly-hold on economic power, be they financiers, multi-national corporations or unions controlling key sectors of the labour force. The first task for the Party is to produce a social welfare, taxation and incomes policy which will reduce income gaps and the class system that derives from these gaps. This policy, aimed at eroding the class system, needs to be reinforced by Government intervention to remove inequities in education and to end not only homelessness and slums but to prevent the growth of massive one-class estates in our cities. Urban development, with the serious problem of land and house prices, requires elaborate and careful government policies to create reasonable standards for all who live in built-up areas. Public transport and regional policies are needed to remove other forms of inequity. More resources should be devoted to the prevention of pollution and to aiding the underdeveloped world. A social democratic government that has come to terms with Britain's place in the world in the 1970s should pursue international policies designed to maximise our influence in those areas where Britain's interests and security are involved thus maximising our control over our own internal policies. These objectives will be achieved by a sharing of control over trade, investment and monetary policies in Europe rather than by the succession of attempts to act on our own followed by periods of being 'blown off course' that marked the last Labour Government.

Social democratic policies of this kind must be backed by a renewed emphasis on parliamentary democracy and debate. The current drift to government by sit-in, confrontation and defiance of the law only aids those with special positions of power in the community and is utterly at variance with the social democratic belief that priority goes to those with a just case established by open debate and the process of representative government. As part of this, the Labour Party should try to eliminate any position of special power accorded to pressure groups within its own constitution and should give each citizen who joins the Labour Party an equal chance of influencing its policies.

If these objectives are not successfully pursued and if the Labour Party drifts further towards the position where it has no ideology or idealism, it will become merely the puppet party of those powerful union leaders whose first interest is not socialism or social justice but simply the well-being of the particular groups of weekly wage-earners whom they represent. Then the Party will not only suffer further electoral defeats but it will deserve them.

3.2 'Is Labour facing catastrophe?' (From *Encounter*, Jan. 1977, pp. 47–54)

The Labour Party, like the nation of which it is a part, seems to have lost its way.

It has to be admitted that though it has been in office for eight of the last twelve years, Labour Governments have not had any impact on the pattern of British society. Their chief theme has been carrying further the policies of the 1945–50 Attlee Government by expanding the public sector but even this policy has been subject to continual cutbacks. The only new feature has been the rapid decline in the confidence of the private sector, the need to borrow abroad to maintain internal living standards and the slump in the value of sterling. There have also been new trends peculiar both in British history and among nations of a similar size and social composition. All the industrial countries, in 1974–76, faced heavier unemployment than in other post-War recessions and serious inflation; but in Britain there has been a relative fall in productivity per man-hour and a decline in the percentage of the work-force employed in manufacturing industry. The consequence of periodic economic crises, of regular cuts in public expenditure targets, and (after 1974) of two years of falling real wages has been a serious public loss of confidence in the political system. The Labour Party (like the Conservative Party) has seen its individual membership drop by a half, so that in many constituencies there is only a handful of members and very few young people see anything in mainstream politics to attract them.

Standing back a little from this immediate catalogue of problems, I have to ask: what should be the objective of the Labour Party? There is still much wrong with British society at two levels. One is the overall sense of failure which grips the country and makes it look inwards with little time for external issues, with declining concern for those overseas who are far worse off than the British. The Labour Party ought to seek to lift Britain out of this gloom by providing reasonable growth and successful economic management with a return to full employment and stable prices but without constant balance of payments crises, a sinking currency and cutbacks in the public sector.

Within this framework, at a second level, the Labour Party should try and remove injustices, most of which spring from the fact that among the developed countries Britain still has one of the most class-divided societies. No one thinks that drab uniformity is desirable, and it is taken for granted that people will prefer different types of houses, they will have different levels of pay, and some children will have more spent by the state on their education than others. What *is* unfair is that being at the bottom of one hierarchy, having, for example, a badly-paid dead-end job, often means that that person also lives in the poorest housing, his children have the least satisfactory schooling, and those in authority give him least time and sympathy. What the Labour Party should try to do is to bias society in favour of the underprivileged, to ensure that if they get the worst of some sides of life, they get the best of others. Also, while no socialist (well, hardly any) nowadays believes in total equality of incomes, in a society which lays so much emphasis on the enjoyment of material goods a wide gap between average income-levels and those of the poorest segments of society does bring real hardship. Is it fair if significant numbers of children are denied the standard of life that they constantly see presented as normal on television? It is also important to maintain equality of treatment of people by those with any form of power or authority; people must be treated with respect and the widest area of freedom to choose and to express themselves must be created and maintained.

Given these objectives for the Labour Party, two reservations should be made. The first is that the Party must not confuse ends and means. Historically, the Left advocated 'public ownership' as a means to achieve a variety of ends. These were a reduction of the *rentier* class who live on profits, production not solely based on market criteria, better labour relations, and higher investment. Public ownership can be a method of achieving some of these ends; but it must be judged as a technique and must be rejected if it is less effective than other techniques.

Also, a very wide extension of public ownership can produce limitations of freedom in a way which had not been appreciated by the early Socialists. If there is only one employer, freedoms to change jobs or to strike may be threatened (as Polish workers have demonstrated, and strikes in their publicly-owned economy become revolts against the state). If there is only one landlord, tenants can become the victims of petty bureaucrats or of rules designed to make life easy for administrators. (There are modern council-house estates where 'landlordism' is worse in this respect than in the old privately-owned tenements, e.g., rules banning dogs or prohibiting all sub-letting.) So public ownership should be advocated not for its own sake but only if its adoption does demonstrably materially improve people's standard of life and scope to live free from direction by others who are in positions of power.

For example, for many years landlords in the highlands of Scotland bought land for holidays and for sport and drove off the tenants or prohibited the residents from developing the area. It is quite clear that the state would be rather better than these highland landlords, and so there is a case for nationalisation of the land in this area. But, on the other hand, in small towns where all the houses are council houses – where there are enough houses for everyone wanting to live there and no waiting list – it would add enormously to people's sense of independence and freedom if the local authority simply gave all the houses to the tenants and everyone became an owner-occupier.

One other aspect of the refusal to think about ends is the recent assumption that everything demanded by each and every trade union is correct and must be supported by the Labour Party. Sometimes legitimate attempts by a union to protect or improve the position of its members can be damaging to the majority of working people or to the nation as a whole.

A second reservation is that there can never be a time when social development stops and a party of the Left can say 'our political objectives have been achieved . . . we have reached our Utopia'. Every change that is made and each new generation that takes over will produce new problems; and this is why today, as so often before, it is necessary to pause, draw the distinction between ends and means once again, look at methods and machinery, and then set off to tackle the new problems. Too often in politics, programmes are designed to solve the problems of the previous twenty years by methods devised after much trial-and-error by which time the problems have changed and the techniques have become counter-productive.

To take another example from the housing field, it was absolutely right to build local-authority houses of good quality to replace or supplement the slums of 19th-century cities. But in recent years, the points systems by which people became tenants of the local public authorities have had the effect of leaving only the poorest, the most hopeless, the vagrant, the sick and elderly, or the defenceless immigrant groups in the slums. Then these houses deteriorated further, and so the end effect of new council-house schemes has been to intensify segregation and the problems of the underprivileged.

The task of the Labour Party should be to restore national confidence and the sense that people can control their own affairs. At the same time, the Party must improve the degree of social justice by modifying and finally removing the class structure and insisting on equality of respect for all individuals. But it is one thing to set out the objectives; quite another to begin to achieve them.

What has gone wrong?

One common response is to ignore these discussions about ends or objectives and to concentrate on a sweeping critique of current society. And this critique usually fails to distinguish between British problems and the rather different situation say in Germany, Sweden or France, treating them all simply and mechanically as examples of 'the Crisis of Capitalism'. The argument is that if there is anything special about Britain, it is not that this country lags behind others but that it is a particularly advanced case of late-capitalist collapse. Is this a satisfactory account of the situation?

There is only one line of analysis which backs up this slogan about the 'collapse of Capitalism' with a coherent account of recent developments. Put at its simplest, this account says that there has been a tremendous concentration of industrial and commercial activities in the hands of a relatively small number of huge corporations. These corporations operate in many states; they are therefore able to avoid Keynesian methods of national economic control and regulation, the

171

only solution being to take them over so that all national and social progress depends on a massive extension of public ownership. Stuart Holland sets out this case in its most complete form,[1] and it has become the basis of the thinking of the Left in the Labour Party (apart from that of the pure dogmatic Marxists). However, as an account of recent economic, social and political history, it has a number of serious weaknesses.

First, it is true that there has been a concentration of economic activity in the hands of a smaller number of multinational firms, but this does not explain why the British economy dominated by these firms does so much worse than similar economies in other countries. Moreover, while firms of this size can fix their markets and determine many of the prices they charge, they cannot totally avoid the market mechanism, i.e., the judgment of the consumer. Why do so many Britons prefer foreign cars, Japanese TV sets, or Italian refrigerators? Why are British car-manufacturers howling for import controls while the German Automobile Association awards Leyland 'the silver lemon' for the most undesirable and unsaleable car on the German market?

One overall point has to be accepted by the Labour Movement. This country cannot set up a wall of 'import controls' and live autarchically off its own. We import a great deal of the necessities of life and cannot maintain our standards of life if we cannot sell enough on the international market to pay for these imports. This would be true whether this country was socialist, communist, or capitalist. Nor can the situation be the product of a 'conspiracy by the multinationals.' They can have no reason for wanting their German or their French sectors to succeed at the expense of the sectors (and the capital invested) in Britain. Whatever the explanation of this relative failure, it is rooted in British society and not in the corporate structure or intentions of the large firms which dominate our economy and the economies of the other industrial states of Western Europe.

Secondly, there is very little evidence that these firms dictate to or dominate successive British Governments. No doubt some of them try to dodge taxes and go in for dubious financial practices, but they give every evidence of fear when any government rounds on them. The big steel bosses tried to boycott the Board of the British Steel Corporation to no avail. A few months ago Lord Watkinson said his Confederation of British Industries would not send out a letter urging its members to

---

[1] *The Socialist Challenge*, Stuart Holland, Quartet Books

invest more, but very few industrialists take a whit of notice what the CBI says. It is true that British industry has not responded adequately to recent tax incentives to invest (introduced by both Conservative and Labour Governments), but this has not been due to combined action motivated by political considerations, rather to a genuine lack of confidence in the rate of profit that will be earned and in the continuance of government policies designed to encourage investment. If British governments have been open to pressure by external agencies in recent years, the trade unions have proved far more potent than the multinationals and have defeated or obtained the withdrawal of industrial-relations and incomes policies which both the Wilson and the Heath Governments tried to enact or in fact did enact and then had to abandon. No companies individually or collectively have managed anything of this kind or have even tried to operate directly in this way at a national political level. If the huge corporations had anything like the power attributed to them, they would force the Government to restrict unofficial strikes and other forms of industrial pressure on them. In practice, all the pressure has come from the other direction and unions can demand and get anti-industry policies enacted when industry cannot (and has barely even tried) to get anti-union policies put forward.

Thirdly, if the Stuart Holland type of argument were correct, there would be a dramatic change in the conduct and performance of industries once they were nationalised and, accordingly, liberated from the quasi-political objectives of the privately-owned multinationals. In fact there is no evidence that the nationalised industries have done much better than the private sector either in terms of investment, of support for government policies, or of better industrial relations. Mr Richard Pryke argued that the investment record of the nationalised industries was better in the 1950s and early 1960s but now thinks this advantage has gone due to political interference. What is clear is that large public corporations do fall victim to problems of bureaucratic control while the remaining market pressures which do, to some extent, discipline the private conglomerates have less effect on them. This is why the British public, which has little confidence in the present economic system (for good reason), equally shows no enthusiasm for the extension of public ownership. Not only is the performance of such industry no better than that of the private sector but there is a genuine and justified conviction that, in the face of public monopolies, the consumer counts for even less. The problems for consumers and for employees – indeed for the public at large – if the vast bulk of the economy was under public ownership would not be dissimilar from the situation in certain other countries where this is already the case.

If, then, this Marxist-type analysis neither explains why Britain has had this period of relative economic decline nor propounds solutions which look like producing either more rapid growth or more freedom of choice and more social justice, what is the explanation of these problems and what are the lines along which solutions could be attempted?

Consider, first, the relative failure of the British economy. The central feature is the decline in British productivity. In 1955, after ten years of post-War reconstruction, British productivity was 15% above that of Germany and France, and 40% above that of Italy. Since 1973 all industrialised European countries have been ahead of Britain: the Netherlands being 54% higher, Belgium 40% higher, with France and Germany each 30% above the British rate. Given the presence of much the same package of multinationals with much the same motives in each of these countries, why should this dramatic reversal have taken place?

It is correct that British finance is not as closely allied to British industry as in the case of some of these countries (as the Labour Party's NEC paper on nationalising the banks and insurance companies argues). But it is not the case that viable, profitable ventures are starved of capital. Indeed, the whole theory of the dominance of a few vast firms invalidates this as internal financing is usually possible in these multinationals. The problem is lack of confidence in the profitability – that is the productivity – of British industry, and this is due to the cumulative effect of British political institutions, taxation policies, social habits, and businessmen's experiences in recent years.

As has so often been contended, management in Britain is weak, relatively badly trained and lacks dynamism and self-confidence. It must have an effect that the first preference of the ablest in our universities is to go into academic life, the next group prefers to enter the professions, the third choice is the civil service and the fourth local government; industry and commerce come at the bottom of the list. Then there is the effect of the class system which does inhibit any kind of easy and understanding relations between management and workers.[2] The sense of a common interest is too often lacking. The

---

[2] See the essay by Goronwy Rees, 'Amateurs and Gentlemen', which was published by *Encounter* as long ago as July 1963 in Arthur Koestler's special issue, 'Suicide of a Nation'.

result, added to the disappointing economic experience of the last fifteen years, is to make trade unions defensive and resistant to change. The argument that, whatever happens, 'any change is likely to be for the worse' and that the workers have to 'carry the heavy end of the stick' has been true too often to allow a confident, forward-looking approach to technical innovation.

In general, British society is conservative with a small 'c': reluctant to try new ideas, lacking impatience over bad service and unsatisfactory products, while weak management and poor labour relations only make matters worse.

Finally, Government is to blame. Successive governments have wanted marked improvements in investment and in productivity and have brought in new policies. They have tried carrots and sticks, have talked of 'restructuring' in little Neddies or of compulsion through a National Enterprise Board. Each policy was brought in and dropped before the last policy had had time to produce results, time in the literal sense of time to take on staff, train them, put in the machines, obtain finished products, get orders and arrange sales. In these same years, taxation has been heavy and profit levels have steadily declined. As a result, British industry is bewildered, feels threatened and has largely stopped reacting to these goals, preferring simply to settle for something low-level, for a quiet life.

It will, I know, take years to get British industry back to a rate of investment, of competence and confidence which will put British productivity back up to the level of the best of our rivals – back to a level which would create real confidence in the pound, prevent balance of payments crises and let everyone, both politicians and the public, take their eyes off the monthly economic indicators. But suppose that Britain's relative prosperity could be restored overnight. Suppose that this had happened yesterday, would the Labour Party's problems be solved and its sense of idealism restored? Would 'the Movement' feel that it knew what was needed to improve British society and to achieve the objectives that have been outlined?

The answer clearly is 'no'. It would help electorally if a Labour Government was clearly responsible for such a transformation; but the Left is in no great shape in countries like Germany where there has been economic success, or in Sweden where the Left has just been defeated after 44 years in power and a long record of economic success.

Aside from Britain's special economic problems, what are the difficulties the Labour Party has to overcome in evolving means to achieve its general goals?

The first is to give up the outmoded obsession over ownership. The idea that to change the ownership of a company or an industry is to alter its whole approach and capacity has been proved wrong time and again. Yet arguments over ownership still absorb the energies of the Left (and the Right). It would be so easy and simple if extensions of public ownership did make the 'fundamental' difference claimed by the Left. But the class structure remains unaltered as the new managers buy better houses and private education for their children. As for disagreeable political interference, there is certainly more of it in nationalised industry and bureaucracy is a shade worse. But in general there is little 'fundamental' difference.

The first task for the Labour Party is to evolve criteria for running a successful mixed economy where both the public and the private sectors feel they are useful. There must be a positive theoretical defence of such a system on grounds of freedom and of economic performance. It must not be regarded simply as a stage on the road to full public ownership (or on the way back to full private enterprise). Methods have to be found of manning and supervising both the public and the private sectors and of protecting the interests of consumers.

A second problem is that the Labour movement and the trade unions no longer include virtually all the underprivileged in British society and no one else. Thus, a social policy which is egalitarian – which really seeks to help the underprivileged and the poor – has to be paid for (in part) by some within the ranks of the Labour movement. The biggest cause of inequality is income differentials, but to narrow these (by flat-rate income increases) horrifies certain Unions. To push up child-welfare benefits leads to more taxation and nowadays many workers pay a considerable rate of tax (which is the main reason why the recent child welfare scheme was shelved). To eradicate poverty means considerable expenditure on limited groups which can be deeply resented by those just above the cut-off point, i.e., by those whose incomes may be no higher after tax but who do work often for long hours and at the least pleasant jobs.

Some of these weaknesses, or problems, are built into the structure of the Labour Party in that the unions have a commanding voice through the block vote at the annual Conference and in the elections for the National Executive Committee. As a result, it is difficult for the Party to say, 'We represent the bulk of the people and it is in their interests to prevent the kind of restrictive practices that impoverish the nation. We also intend to redistribute income to the poor (many of whom are not represented in unions), to single-parent families and to the sick (even if it means less in the pay-packet of large and powerful groups who hold key positions in our Party). ...' The Labour Party today is not sure whether it represents the less privileged or whether it represents certain powerful producer groups. In the last few months, introduction of the unpopular Dock Work Bill largely to please the Transport and General Workers Union and the postponement of the child-benefit scheme to please the TUC both show where power lies within the Party.

Lastly, there is a problem about *participation*. The Labour Movement has governed Britain for half the post-War period. In many local areas, it has been 'the Establishment' for years on end. When Labour gets power, it tends to be very reluctant to share it, to consult its own members, or to set up machinery for participation. Labour Governments have done nothing to restore the power of the Commons or its capacity to watch over civil servants and to make them explain their policies. It has clung to official secrecy. The resistance to devolution for Scotland and Wales comes from the Left's traditional view that once a policy has been approved, it must be imposed throughout the country. Local preferences or choices are seen as essentially particularist, selfish and reactionary.

What, then, should be the programme of a revitalised Labour Party? The programme has to fulfil two separate but connected objectives. It has to restore the British economy and show how our society could be made fairer, more open, more responsive to the needs of the underprivileged. The first task is to shake loose of the restrictions of special interests. Any Labour Party must rely on the votes and the backing of the bulk of trade unionists and work in close cooperation with the unions. But it must be made clear that the Party is bigger than these groups, that it also represents those who are unorganised and have no voice. For example, it is in everyone's interest to get exports and imports cheaply in and out of this country. If this damages dockers' interests, they must be helped but not at the permanent expense of the rest of the community. (It is worth noting that dockers in Amsterdam – where new methods come in more easily and more rapidly – are better paid than dockers in London.)

The Labour Party must have policies that give industry stability and continuity and it must explain to all its members, the university students, and the unions that we have to live by our efforts in the world market, and that it is of the highest value to society to do a good job in trade, commerce or industry.

Then the Party must produce a coherent anti-poverty programme designed to channel resources to those sectors of our society in need while excluding blanket benefits and subsidies to those on adequate incomes. All the Party's education, housing, and social policies must be geared to removing Britain's debilitating and degrading class distinctions, and this may require new techniques very different from those which served a useful purpose when there was widespread poverty and deprivation.

The task is to create a programme which is realistic but will revive optimism and confidence in the future of the United Kingdom and in the possibility of achieving significant reforms, economic success, and social justice.

3.3 'A passion for tolerance' (From *The Listener*, 17 Feb. 1977, pp. 217–18. Review of *Utopia and Revolution*, by Melvin Lasky, Macmillan, 1978)

At the height of Senator Joseph McCarthy's attack on American liberals and academics, when he announced his next target was the Ivy League University in which I was studying, I recall the reaction of a distinguished professor who was clearly going to be involved. 'How', he said, 'can one build up a passionate support for tolerance? How does one preach a crusade for understanding, for diversity, for the right to be wrong?' This is possibly the major dilemma which Melvin Lasky is exploring in his monumental book, *Utopia and Revolution*.

One says 'possibly', because there is such a torrent of ideas, such an outpouring of illustration, revealing insights and unexpected analogies, that it is sometimes hard to distinguish the themes. Nevertheless, the main argument that I detected was exciting and original. Melvin Lasky is really offering a theory of historical development. It is the opposite of Marxism, in that the theory of history worked out by Marx and his disciplines located the chief force for change in economic developments. Probably there was an underlying psychological assumption (redolent of the 19th-century economists) that men were determined to better themselves. So they worked away in a class system till new forms of production were discovered and

178

became sufficiently prevalent to create a new class structure, which broke through the constraints of the old system.

Melvin Lasky goes back to the Hegelian insistence on the supremacy, not of economic forces, but of ideas. But he does not return to the zigzag of the dialectic. Rather, he substitutes a continual circle. First, men turn to ideas of perfection. They construct utopias. In a brilliant chapter, he looks at all the different forms these ideas take. It can be paradise for the religious, an ideal world for Platonists, an ant-heap for the orderly or a new world over the seas for Columbus and his followers. For some, it is a reconstruction of existing society; it may be begun in a small way at New Lanark by Robert Owen, or at special settlements in the United States; or the utopia may be created by the sudden transformation of man and his existing society.

The second stage is that this transformation requires some form of revolution. Here the book becomes almost autobiographical, for Lasky has been through all this in his own lifetime. Some utopians become revolutionaries. Others take on revolution for its own sake. There is a most perceptive section in which some of the strength of Marxism is shown to come from Marx's constant refusal to specify the utopia at which he was aiming. As Lenin said in 1918: 'What socialism will be we just don't know.' So Marxism was able to rest on its great strength, its insights into social structure and its rejection of a class society. All who followed these ideas were, by definition, revolutionaries, but they could then write in their own immediate conditions and objectives; they could dream up their own utopias.

After a careful look at all forms of revolution, the analysis turns to stage three, which is the descent of successful revolutions into dogmatism. As no one can be sure when a revolution is successful, those who come to doubt the results are doubly damned. This is why the heretic is hated and feared so much more than the unbeliever. All who have been through left-wing revolutionary politics will know that special bitterness reserved for those who say 'This is not the utopia we wanted' or 'Was the revolution worth while?' All at once, the doubter or the deviant is found to have been a secret agent since his youth, a constant subversive, corrupt and wicked, deserving only elimination.

The tendency to dogmatism, to the insistence on conformity, is there from the start of the process. One cannot build multiple utopias. No utopia has stood on the need to create diversity, to admit alternative visions. Similarly, the drive to achieve the new order, the

179

revolutionary commitment, cannot be a commitment to the kind of freedom that permits alternative goals or the denial of any goal. So when the utopia fails to achieve the intended state of bliss, when either the reality does not come up to the ideal or the ideal itself is found to be incapable of meeting man's great talent for self-expression, then the only reaction to the dogma is to become a heretic. So many men from Dubcek to Djilas, from Gomulka to Gorky, hover on the verge of being great minds who carry the vision and the revolution a stage further, but, if they slip a centimetre or two, can immediately become renegades.

But then heresy, in time, demands tolerance. Voltaire was the first to use the word in 1733, and the English were the first to build it into their system of government. While all this could be the basis of a late 19th-century belief in progress, in the development of mankind, stage by stage, towards a more liberal, tolerant society, this is not Lasky's view. After a spell of tolerance, those enjoying their liberty feel dissatisfied and, when the penalties of dogmatism and the risks of being a heretic are forgotten, they start on the utopia-constructing process all over again. For some reason, though toleration and freedom do represent the fundamental spirit of man, societies embodying these values are inherently unstable; they are a prey to ideologists and utopia-builders who soon start the whole cycle going again.

Now why should this be? Why cannot the truth not merely prevail at one phase in the cycle, but become established? This is where Melvin Lasky produces an unexpected twist. It is all the fault of certain words. 'There is ... in every century a generation of men for whom things are no longer things and words no longer their names.' This pull of words about class, expropriation, struggle and so on is a devastating disease, and drives men back onto the utopian treadmill. Against this, there is only the indefensible nature of Western society. Although there is a great measure of tolerance in modern Europe and America, the intellectuals who enjoy this freedom have not, as my American professor said, been able to produce a vital and satisfying defence of the system. Either they are complacent, smugly anti-totalitarian, or they are weak and constantly conceding the presence of imperfections. In either case, they cannot stand up to, or win back, the younger generation seduced by and armed with 'bug words' which demand new utopian visions.

Melvin Lasky has so much material with which to illustrate his thesis that he goes round the cycle (dealing chiefly with England in the 17th and early 19th centuries) so that the analysis can sink in and be seen to have general validity. Like all good theories of history, it can also apply to the experience or development of a single individual. There are the visions of the youth reacting to his social environment, the ardent desire of the young man to give up all in the pursuit of change, the intolerance of the man who has committed so much and who knows all the answers but is beginning to suspect (perish the thought) that there may be facets of the truth that he has overlooked, the vigour of his reaction declining into recognition of heresy among his children and then into a tolerant old age. The whole cycle could be autobiographical, as well as fit so much of what Melvin Lasky has read and absorbed.

But the weakness, to me, is the trigger mechanism which sets off the cycle once again. I do not believe in the autonomous force of words. They must mean something, in the sense of relating to people's experience. To produce the 'bug words' of utopias or revolutions for some people would lead only to incomprehension or apathy; they produce excitement, action and belief only if there is something in their moral force which is contradicted by the experience of the hearers.

This is where Lasky's book fits the analogy of the ageing man but not the history of society. For the weary ex-revolutionary who has seen it all, who has learnt of the dangers of dogmatism, who has the toleration of experience, the wisdom of unbelief, certain words that galvanised him in his youth no longer have the same effect. But he sees the young shouting the old slogans, saying 'Yes, but it *is* exploitation', 'There *is* a class struggle', and he is puzzled. Why doesn't he react? Why does a great weariness overtake him? He sighs and feels with Sir James Mackintosh that 'melancholy experience has undeceived me on many subjects in which I was the dupe of my own enthusiasm'. But there are the young, reacting to what are for him mere words.

This proves that it is not the words alone that have force – the drive comes from what he has lost. The missing element is the simple moral imperatives which are passed on or reappear from generation to generation, and seem to arise out of the nature of man. However different the societies, however contrary their philosophies, however some, like Hobbes or Nietzsche, may seek to deny or to eliminate such factors, some ways of treating people will seem to those, of whatever age, who view the world with a fresh, youthful, optimistic eye, to be intolerable. Out of this springs their desire to reconstruct the world, and their belief that a better way of living, of treating each other, is possible. It is out of this urge that the utopians of each new cycle are born. Nor can the process be stopped, as we will never have a totally just society, a situation which will not arouse the potential idealist in all fresh generations to contemplate reconstruction.

Melvin Lasky has written a superb, deeply civilised and knowledgeable book. He is scarcely to be blamed for perhaps (I must employ the tolerance we both want) missing out one stage in his cycle. It is also the most difficult and philosophical stage which has puzzled writers and thinkers over the centuries – what is the nature of man, and why is there this recurrent sense not only of what is, but what ought to be? Why, after periods when experience has calmed people, and tolerance taught them to accept situations, does the cry ring out once again: 'This is unfair, this is untrue to the better, the perfectible nature of, man and we must now reconstruct society and build the New Jerusalem'?

3.4 'Liberty and equality: getting the balance right'
(Unpublished MS, probably written some time in 1977 or 1978)

Over the past century those on the left in British politics who have struggled for greater equality have never felt that this objective was incompatible with personal liberty; indeed, the assumption has always been that the two aims were complimentary. Equality for British reformers has always meant equality of treatment, of respect for the individual, equality in the sense of the same chance to develop one's personality and to live a full and free life. For this reason, it has never been thought likely that to increase an under-privileged person's chance of a comfortable house, an adequate education, a good job or a satisfactory pension could do anything except increase the freedom of that person to have a satisfactory existence.

But the mechanism by which this equality of treatment is induced is the intervention of the state, either by central or by local government action which can involve some loss of liberty. This may happen if activities leading to inequality have to be prohibited or penalised but it also can occur if people are dealt with in broad categories, irrespective of the merits of particular cases; if there is an insensitive bureaucracy which does not see or is not strong enough to adapt rules when the particular application of the rule is producing undesirable results. In either situation the application of laws designed to produce greater equality can so inhibit liberty as to raise the question of whether the total freedom of the individual is in fact enhanced. It would seem to be the case that in a number of aspects of British life this position has been reached.

Consider the impact of the current levels of taxation. It was George Bernard Shaw who pointed out the egalitarian implications of Marshall's marginal theory of value. If, as Marshall argued, each extra pound a rich man earned mattered less to him in terms of what he could buy, then there was the strongest possible case for progressive taxation. To be able to buy or rent one house and enough to eat was a necessity of life. To have a country cottage and large meals was enjoyable and pleased one's children. To add on a London flat and suppers at expensive restaurants was a luxury but a fourth house and double dinners became pointless or even nauseating. If progressive taxation took this last slice of income and gave it, through pensions or unemployment relief, to those with no home and a starvation diet, this was a clear gain in terms of both equality and the freedom to live a reasonable life.

Now, in the 1970s, taxation cuts deeply into the incomes of many weekly wage–earners. Denis Healey had to spell out the situation clearly to the recent Labour Party Conference and he stressed that any increase in public expenditure will have to be paid for out of taxation. It is much less clear now than it was in Bernard Shaw's time that there are gains in all the transfers of income that are taking place. For example, £60 million have been given to keep Harland and Wolff's shipyard going, £42 million was allocated to Upper Clyde Shipbuilders, £265 million was made available to support British Leyland and in September £175 million was set aside to try and prevent a further increase in unemployment. It can be asked whether the jobs created or saved by this expenditure mean more or less in terms of the freedom of the persons concerned to work and earn wages than the freedom lost by the taxpayers who have to pay extra in order to meet these costs.

This choice has become particularly evident in local government. The reformed system introduced in England in 1974 and in Scotland in 1975 has led to increases in staff and in their salaries and a consequent huge increase in rates. To take an example from Scotland; a range of hills over which the local people have walked happily for generations has now become a Regional Park. The post of Director of the Pentland Hills Regional Park has been advertised at a salary of £6909 to £7632 and it is reasonable to ask whether the equality of the citizenry in terms of access to the hills or their enjoyment of the landscape will be enhanced by more than the diminution of freedom to dispose of this income which they will suffer in consequence of the increased rate burden. There is no intention here to question the value of regional parks or of the new local authority departments of recreation and leisure. The point is simply that it is no longer self-evident, as it was before 1914 or even before the 1930's, that extra taxation clearly diminished the freedom of the rich less than it enhanced both the equal chance of the poor to live a fuller and therefore a more free existence.

Another example is in education. There is a powerful argument that the segregation of children into secondary modern, secondary, grammar schools, direct grant schools and public schools militated against equality of treatment for the children, both during their education and in subsequent life. At school, some had over-crowded classes, poor facilities and a constant turnover among their teachers, while others got stability and careful, almost personal tuition. Moreover, the whole effect was to produce different types of accent and patterns of behaviour which did much to reinforce the class divisions in British society; divisions which clearly make equality of opportunity for those involved and equality of respect by officials and from those supposed to serve the public, much harder to obtain.

It would be argued with great force that equality would be served if the system which did, and does still exist in the small towns of the Scottish highlands and borders, could be spread over the whole country. These were areas with no private (or 'public') schools where the existing town school had a long tradition, a reputation for good work and it was taken for granted that everyone from the well-off farmer, the clergyman and the doctor, down to the unskilled labourers, sent their children to the same school.

But if, particularly in cities, many secondary schools came into this broad category, would liberty not be enhanced if the maximum parental choice was allowed, provided this did not have an adverse effect on the school system? When parents have two or three schools within reach, and given that these schools all have room to take pupils from outside their immediate area, and if one has a reputation for athletics, another for a more permissive style of education, while a third is known to have a good music department, why not let parents choose the school they want their children to attend? This question of the school environment is accepted as being of vital importance in moulding the behaviour and outlook of the young. To permit segregation according to ability is held to be damaging, as is segregation on class lines, and for this reason the kind of freedom of choice that would produce these results is prohibited to parents. Yet many local authorities go on to assume and assert that it follows that all freedom of choice (except one) should be prohibited.

The single permitted exception is that if Catholic parents want a separate education for their children, and if there are enough for them to permit the maintenance of a separate Catholic school at no greater cost to the ratepayer, then this is allowed. In reality, the merits of this degree of choice rest on the outcome. If, in areas of strong communal tension, it could be demonstrated that separate schools led to intensified antagonism, then there would be the same case for prohibiting this choice as there is for prohibiting the kind of choice that derived from class background or private wealth.

But it is hard to imagine subsequent antagonisms lasting through adult life and marring the relationships of former pupils which derived from the fact that in certain years school X was known to have a specially good art or classics section or that the headmaster at that time placed strong emphasis on modern methods of learning. Yet all choice on these lines is denied; sometimes it is said that to allow choice would be 'administratively awkward'. In other cases the argument is that children would flood towards the schools with a reputation for good teaching, sometimes it is alleged that class preferences would reappear. In any case, it is argued, as all the schools must provide the same basic curriculum, there is no reason for preferring one to another; the choice is unreal.

The replies are obvious. Grounds for choice do exist, as the parents in the area of Summerfield School in Aberdeen or William Tyndale School in Islington have shown. In my own constituency, the atmosphere in the (all very good) secondary schools in the six main towns is markedly different. The administrative argument only applies if a preferred school is physically full up and, if so, this is a different ground for refusing choice. As to any drift towards 'good schools' – that is those schools desired by parents who are prepared to take this degree of interest in their children's education, why not? This is how preferences should be recorded and is the only real check against bad or pernicious teaching. If all preference is forbidden, it just means that the wealthy can still choose by selling their houses and moving to live in the catchment area of the desirable school. It is the children of those who cannot afford to move who are stuck where they are and who have no redress if the teaching at the local school is unacceptable.

All this would seem to be fairly clear, yet the means to achieving equality – the prohibition of certain kinds of preference for fee–

paying schools – has so obscured the end objective (and the prohibition of all choice is so convenient for the educational bureaucracy) that the limitation of liberty is held by some reformers to be desirable in itself and to be a hallmark of a progressive system. To allow parents and children to vote with their feet in certain circumstances would be to restore freedom of choice in one of the most important and long-lasting aspects of a person's life.

Some of the same issues arise in housing. When one considers housing conditions in many of the poorer industrial areas before local authorities began building houses in the 1920s, the existence of a large stock of public authority housing is a great step towards one essential kind of equality. But, compared with owner-occupiers, the tenants of council houses suffer many restrictions on their liberty. In many cases, they are not allowed to paint, repair or adapt the houses as they see fit. They are usually forbidden to sublet. And movement to new jobs or to be near relatives is much harder as to transfer to an area under the jurisdiction of another local authority involves going to the bottom of the local queue of applicants – a process which may mean several years in sub-standard property before a council house can be obtained. This compares adversely with the owner occupier's relative freedom to sell and buy again in another area.

While the opportunity to rent a council house of a reasonable standard was a great step forward in terms of equality, at the same time the existence of the two broad categories of housing owner occupiers and council house tenants, is now one of the main perpetuators of all the inequalities that spring from class divisions. Political agents are accustomed to surveying an area and writing down all in one category as 'ours' and all in the other as 'theirs'. An owner-occupier who has financial problems becomes a case for help from his bank manager, or longer credit from the shops or for an addition to his mortgage, when similar problems befalling a person in a council house often means that they become a 'case' on the books of the local social worker.

The difference in treatment of the two groups and the restrictions imposed on the freedom of council house tenants came out in the recent drive for the modernisation of old council houses. Owner occupiers naturally decide for themselves whether they wish to pay for any improvements to their houses. But when there is only one landlord, the local council, and when the central government offers a large grant towards modernisation for a limited number of months, then no choice is permitted. While central heating, better bathrooms and rewiring are all desirable, many elderly couples were happy with their houses and did not want to be disturbed. Some asked if the job could be done after they died or left but this was impossible.

These people were forced to have over £4000 of public money spent on their houses (which had often cost between £300 and £800 to build forty years ago). Then they were forced to have the modernisation exactly as specified and appeals to have a plug moved a foot to the right to accommodate a favourite cabinet or a built-in wardrobe were usually refused. Finally, having had a forced modernisation which left some elderly tenants unhappy and faced with exhausting and expensive redecoration, the rents were then put up to meet part of the cost they had not wanted to incur.

One cannot help wondering whether equality and liberty would not both have been better served (and public money saved in the long run) if these vast sums spent on modernisation had not been used to wipe off the remaining debt on the older council houses and those houses that had been continuously occupied for 20 years had been given to the tenants.

Other examples of this problem are more straightforward as they arise over the more traditional boundaries of freedom. It has been said that one of the freedoms that ought to be respected is a man's right to refuse to work with people he finds unacceptable. This could mean just that there is a right to leave a job; but this is not contested. The problem becomes greater when the objector has no intention of leaving but insists that the person to whom he objects has to go. Again, this may have little effect but if the bulk of the work force threaten not to leave but to strike if an unacceptable person is employed (that is the essence of the closed shop), then the claims to liberty are much more finely balanced.

At present, it is illegal to refuse to work with someone on racial grounds but it is permitted to refuse to accept as fellow employees those who are not members of the prevalent trade union. Then the matter may go further as once the closed shop is established, then the union can deprive a man of that old bastion of both liberty and equality, his right to seek work, if the union refuses to accept him as a member. There may be little infringement if the grounds of rejection are offences such as refusal to pay union dues. But will penalties always be restricted just to anti-social rule breaking? This issue arose recently in the debate over the Trade Union and Labour Relations (Amendment) Bill and especially over the clauses permitting the enforcement of a closed shop in the press.

Mr Michael Foot contended that it was a proper freedom to be able to insist on union membership for all employees. And if this was a

187

proper freedom, it was contrary to equality to single out the press or any part of the communications industry and deny this section alone the right to enforce a closed shop. But there is the other side. If the closed shop means either that no non-union members can contribute articles to the press or that such persons can, from time to time, be excluded if the local union chapel dislikes what they have written, then this would appear to be such an extreme version of the freedom of employees as to deny an important area of freedom to other persons (both to the part-time contributor and to the public who may want to read the contributions). What makes the position worse is that local union branches can not only deny access to the press on the grounds that they are entitled to exclude non-union members but they can also refuse to admit to the union anyone who does not earn the bulk of their income by journalism. Carried to these lengths, a struggle for certain freedoms of association (or non-association) ends up by becoming a dangerous and pernicious limitation of the freedom of other individuals and of the reading public; a limitation which may spring from certain ideologies or simply from a desire to preserve jobs and pay for those already in possession of these advantages.

The same issues are raised in a more general way by the role that organised groups have achieved, or has been conceded to them in dealing with government and in the formation of policy. The dispute about the freedom of the press is a good example in that the original drafts of the Trade Union and Labour Relations (Amendment) Bill made no mention of the press; the situation in that industry was so special that it was excluded and this was with the consent both of the National Union of Journalists and of the editors and proprietors. But apparently when this exclusion was reported to the TUC, its negotiators objected and said the press must be included. So this was done by the Government, with all the difficulties and disputes that have sprung from a quite unnecessary concession to the TUC. It has been increasingly the policy of both Conservative and Labour Governments to cultivate good relations with powerful unions, professional associations and the organised leaders of industry and to make concessions to those bodies which would certainly not be contemplated if the pressure was coming from the elected representatives of the people in the House of Commons. One of the arguments advanced by Mr Foot in the House of Commons when opposing any hint by the House that a denial of the freedom of the press might be contrary to public policy and that this point could be made in a court of law was that if Parliament took such a line, it might upset the National Union of Journalists; it might irritate them and this would be counter-productive. But Mr Foot had no similar qualms about irritating or upsetting the many MPs who were worried about restrictions on press freedom. They were subjected to the full weight of his oratorical denunciations and he gave way a little only when it was clear that total intransigence might lead to a defeat in the lobbies.

The relevance of this whole issue of the power of these groups is that originally, banding together in order to increase bargaining power, was designed to produce some equality between a mass of individuals and an employer or a minister, who had wealth in the first case and authority in both cases, and could otherwise have an unfair bargaining advantage. Yet the balance has tilted so far in the other direction that now small organised groups can act in a manner which, because of their power, gives them considerable advantages over a mass of unorganised citizens and often accords the views of their spokesmen (elected often by under 10% of their membership) more weight than the views of MPs who were only chosen by individual voters at a general election. Thus the public have the widespread and largely correct view that to get a hearing or to win a case, to be right or persuasive, does not matter. What matters is to be part of a group, and preferably of a group which has the capacity to inflict real damage on the rest of the society. If this is the case, the government is likely, not merely to listen, but to fall over itself in a desire to conciliate and to meet any request almost before it is formulated.

The conclusion being drawn from all these rather mixed examples and trends is that though extremist politics are out of fashion in Britain – no threat of overt right wing or communist coups is evident – there is a real danger that individual liberty is being eroded. This kind of liberty cannot survive unless there is a mixed economy with alternative employers, with places to go if one is dissatisfied, unless there is some choice in housing or in education. Liberty is limited if the big battalions get first consideration, not only in the sense that individual cases (especially if they do not fit the categories set up by the standard conflicts accepted by the pressure groups) tend to be ignored but there may also be a little consideration of the individual within the big battalions. The drive for equality used to be fired by a desire to increase individual liberty but there is now evidence that the means used can go to an extent where liberty is being undermined or reduced and in a modern, relatively affluent society, the stage may have been reached where the average person now would prefer a renewed emphasis on his liberty; equality may have gone far enough to be subsumed or accepted and now the next drive should be to reassert the value of the freedom of the individual.

3.5 'Liberals and Social Democrats' (From *The Scotsman*, 28 March 1977)

Face to face with political events, it is hard to assess their precise significance but it is difficult to escape the feeling that the agreement between the Government and the Liberals has made a major change in the shape of British politics.

For the Government, it has staved off an immediate General Election. No-one can be sure what would have happened in such an election and Mr Callaghan is a formidable campaigner, but the odds were on a Conservative victory. Nevertheless, the arrangement has done much more than that.

On a series of issues, the Government was committed to act, but was uncertain. It kept looking over its shoulder at the National Executive Committee and its own Left Wing. Now, David Steel and his colleagues have insisted that a much more positive attempt is made to move forward on these issues. Clearly, the Government cannot deliver on devolution. The forty or more opponents are still there. But now it cannot let the matter slide or slip into oblivion. One way forward would be to have separate Bills for Scotland and Wales, to redraft them on much more clear-cut and satisfactory lines (for the devolvers) and then to try again.

Similarly, the Government promised the electorate and its partners in the European Community that it would introduce a Bill providing for direct elections to the European Parliament. Opposition from the Left had led to a slowdown, a White Paper 'with green edges' and no sign of actual action. The agreement with the Liberals requires a positive effort on this question also, there is now a commitment to legislate this session and to include proportional representation as one of the options.

Other, smaller gains, are Government time for a Bill on homelessness, the sillier parts of the Bill on local authority direct labour schemes are dropped and (though it was not explicitly mentioned), it is hard to see any Bill to emasculate David Steel's Abortion Act being given much of a chance.

All these are great gains for the social democratic wing of the Labour Party. Whereas before, it was often the Left-wing tail that wagged the dog, there is now another tail at the other end, if such a curious beast can be imagined. But the Liberal influence is far more formidable as they can leave and thus bring down the Government. The Left have nowhere else to go. They will fume and fuss but they are held captive.

For the Liberals, there is an immediate great gain apart from any list of specific issues. The party, despite having only 13 MPs, has been treated as an equal by the Government; it is in a sense 'in power' for the first time and David Steel (who made the best speech of all the party leaders) played his hand with the utmost coolness and maturity. He knows that, in fact, Mr Callaghan cannot deliver on any of these issues. All the Prime Minister has done is to promise to try harder. David Steel also knows that if, at any time, the electoral climate for the Labour Party changes, he and his little group of MPs will be cast aside and the Government will call an election in the hope of winning an outright majority. But the polls are not likely to change in any substantial way till well into 1978.

The dangers for the Liberals are in their own constituencies. Only Cyril Smith holds what is basically a Labour seat. The other Liberals all sit for areas which are fundamentally conservative. Liberal MPs exist on their own talents and on the argument that they are a radical non-Labour alternative to Conservativism. For them now to maintain a Labour Government in power could cause them real trouble. After all, if the result of voting Liberal is to preserve Mr Callaghan, it might be more sensible either to vote for the genuine Labour candidate or, if the voter deeply dislikes the Labour Party, to vote Conservative. Either way, the Liberal loses.

David Steel faced this point in his speech and said that he was prepared to carry that particular can for the sake of getting continuity for essentially radical but not Tribune-type Left-wing policies; for the sake of maintaining continuity in economic policy. In this, he was making a very valuable point. He was forcing the Labour Party to recognise something it had rejected since the Ramsay Macdonald era: namely that arrangements with other parties need not be debilitating: that there are radicals outside the Labour Party and that to work with them might actually increase Labour's effectiveness. In this case, he has simply applied some pressure to get the Cabinet moving on policies it had already, a little half-heartedly, espoused.

The corollary of bringing the radical centre over to the Government is that the Conservatives have suddenly been pushed into an isolated corner on the Right. Mrs Thatcher, by the time she spoke, knew that her bid for an election had failed but she made no attempt to address herself to moderate opinion, to look at the outstanding problems facing the nation and to explain how a Conservative victory would be of help to the nation. She behaved like the extreme Left, quoting her party's manifesto as if it was the gospel, proclaiming her belief in freedom and in capitalism and saying not a word about incomes policy, industrial problems, investment, devolution or foreign policy issues such as direct elections to the European Parliament.

In fact, she simply reinforced David Steel's claim that it would not be in the country's interest to have an outright victory for such a partisan party which had slogans but no specific solutions to offer.

The important question which remains to be considered is whether this arrangement will last beyond the autumn. Is it the precursor of the long anticipated (but always remote) realignment of politics? Will it lead to Liberals joining the Government as Ministers? Will the Labour Left rebel if this kind of liaison grows closer, and leave, or will the agreement be subject to increasing strain and die either this year or when the next election returns one party with a clear majority over all its opponents?

No-one can say. Pressure will come from the party purists on both sides. Some Liberals will say that it is not their intention to prop up the party of the closed shop, the party of nationalisation, the party of Clay Cross. The Labour Left will be out in force at the next annual conference in October to reject direct elections, to urge the nationalisation of banks and insurance companies and to demand a wealth tax, all of which would have the added virtue of forcing the Liberals to swallow full-blooded socialist policies or give up the working agreement.

But, at the same time, cooperation can be habit-forming. Mr Callaghan may find the need to rely on Liberal votes a wonderful reason for rejecting policies he never wanted anyway (like the takeover of banks and insurance companies). It is true that he was never very keen on devolution or direct elections but pushing a little harder (and losing?) on those points is a small price to pay for a majority in the House and a perfect antidote to the pressures of the Left in the annual conference and on the National Executive.

Just as in Germany, the Liberals have, after years of alliance with the Social Democrats, become fairly closely wedded to that party, so the Liberal-Labour arrangement might be of long-term value to both parties. To the Liberals, it gives a share in responsibility, in policy-formation and in power which is so important for any political party. To Labour, it gives a way of keeping radicals and progressives away from the Conservatives and allied to or associated with a party which has recently tended to lose the support of these elements. It gives a counter-weight to the Left and puts Labour in touch with the five million voters who, in 1974, rejected both the traditional main parties.

There are two other great gains. The first is that it concentrates the minds of the politicians and the public on issues. It is no longer enough to say 'it was in the manifesto' or 'I'll back whatever my party does.' Now, the parties have to consider which issues matter in terms of their impact on people, that is they have to consider the merits of the case and not just who put it forward. Is the point essential or can it be modified or postponed in the interests of the agreement with the Liberals (or, in their case, with the Labour party)?

Secondly, it is a great gain for Parliament. A Government's survival has no longer depended solely on its deals with outside groups such as the IMF or the unions. It has, for once, depended on its arrangements with MPs and on the balance of forces within the Commons and therefore on the relations of the MPs concerned with their supporters in the constituencies. It is amazing how electoral necessity can break down old inhibitions. To make deals with or work with other MPs or parties was always regarded as unspeakable in the Labour Party.

One great objection to proportional representation was that it would lead to alliances or coalitions of precisely the type that has now been arranged with the Liberals. If this works for a period of time, that old objection to the formation of Governments by seeking agreements among groups of MPs will have to be revised in the light of actual experience.

All one can do is to wish this experiment well, to try to make it work and to hope that it does herald a new flexibility in our political system and a revival of confidence in our politicians and in parliamentary government.

3.6 'The case for a realignment of the Left' (From *The Times*, 22 July 1977)

Amid all the accusations and counter-accusations about this summer's political arrangements, there has been the steady, if muted, theme that the Lib-Lab pact could help towards a realignment in British politics. Some people have always wanted such a change. I recall, after Hugh Gaitskell had addressed a meeting in Edinburgh in the late 1950s, an earnest young student saying 'If that is the authentic voice of the Labour Party, I will join'. The student was David Steel and unfortunately he soon heard some other Labour voices.

Apart from all the problems of moving towards a realignment, what would the political situation look like after such a change had taken place? The object would be to produce a major left-of-centre party which would be tied neither to Marxist dogma nor to the trade unions.

The TUC would have no built-in position with a block vote at the annual conference, a dominant influence in electing the national executive, the right to sponsor candidates and perhaps, after this October's conference, a major voice in the choice of the leader of the party.

Such a radical party would expect to win the votes of many trade unionists but it would be free to press for what it saw as the national interest. Consider the difference such a party would have made to recent political history.

Without the built-in veto of the union leaders, Harold Wilson and Barbara Castle would have been able to carry their 1969 attempt to legislate on industrial relations. While Mr Heath might have wanted to amend or improve the result, the whole confrontation over the 1971 Industrial Relations Act and the current assumption that no British government can legislate on such matters without TUC approval would not have arisen.

Secondly, when Mr Heath ran into difficulties over his incomes policy in late 1973, there would have been far less temptation for Labour leaders to argue that the whole concept of regulating wages was wicked or counter-productive.

Then there might have been no 1974–75 wages explosion and no need for these same Labour leaders to come slowly round to an advocacy first of a voluntary and now a 'go-it-alone' (does this mean compulsory?) incomes policy. We might by now have reached a reasonable modus vivendi between unions which did their job of looking after their members' interests and governments which set and enforced guidelines according to what the economy could afford without fuelling inflation.

A realigned left-of-centre party free of institutional ties to the unions and without the hard left in its ideological make-up could also be far more radical on many issues. One thing Marxists and union militants now have in common is a mixture of English nationalism and a deeply conservative desire (so evident at Grunwicks) to go on fighting the battles of the 1930s and 1940s. Hence the desire to stop direct elections and resume the attack on British membership of the European Community.

Hence the present aridity of housing policy where Labour has to be 'for tenants' and 'against landlords', the result being to dry up the availability of property for rent, to make mobility harder and to make rational policies over the future of council housing so hard to pursue.

But the most important single consequence of a realigned left would be that the ambivalence over the value of a mixed economy would cease, and those who want to replace such an economy by a totally state-owned and controlled system would have to make their case to the electorate.

Because the Labour Party has never fully made up its mind whether a mixed economy is desirable in itself or is a stage on the road to a better, alternative system, it has never settled down to work out sensible rules for running the public sector. Nor has it decided whether the private sector is to be encouraged as a major source of growth and as an essential way of maintaining competition and free choice or whether it is to be sat on, taxed, regulated, pushed and pulled till it drops dead.

Finally, a realigned party could shed the desperate constitutional orthodoxy of the left and accept that the development of democratic controls over government, from Parliament downwards, has lagged behind the powers of the bureaucracy and that much needs to be done to restore the public's faith in the notion that democratic involvement can make a difference to what government does.

If this is what realignment means, does the Lib-Lab pact help? Mr Callaghan has astutely given the impression that to please his allies, he is stressing direct elections and devolution (though he would have done so anyway for other political reasons). With or without the Liberals, he would have insisted on some kind of incomes policy.

But Mr Callaghan is a very orthodox politician; he is a real product of the Labour Party and is utterly opposed to any notion of realignment. What is wrong, in his view, is not the relationship with the unions but the fact that in the late 1960s, a number of these positions of power fell into the hands of the left. If people of his outlook resumed control of the annual conference and the national executive, all would be well.

In Mr Callaghan's eyes, the Lib-Lab pact is a device to enable him to get the Labour Party, in its existing structure, through to a general election which he might win. If his best hopes come off, inflation will recede, with an oil buttressed balance of payments reflation can commence and the Government's popularity will revive. Then he will call an election, but will he beam from the box at the voters and say 'Thanks to the Liberals, who I hope will continue to work with us, I have been able to shed a lot of left-wing rubbish and push radical policies which would otherwise have been hard to put over. Please vote Labour, but if the Liberal is the chief threat to the sitting Tory, do remember what the pact has made possible in the past two years'?

Will he? On the contrary, he will say, with some truth, 'I have done nothing I would not have done had Labour had a solid majority. Support from other quarters? Of course, we had various people in our lobby from time to time; nationalists, Ulster unionists and others – people voted with us on the merits of our policies. But now the choice lies with you. Do you want this Government to continue or do you want a dose of the dreaded Thatcher?' Somewhere in the wings will be a small group of Liberals saying, 'Yes, the Labour Government has been a success and we helped.'

I have never doubted the deep desire among many Liberals for realignment and I am sure that this is a highly desirable objective only I now think that whatever the other effects of the Lib–Lab pact, in this respect it is a positive hindrance.

3.7 'Why the parties are losing members' (From *The Times*, 26 Sept. 1977)

Most of those interested in public affairs talk and write as if the existing political parties were constant features of the democratic landscape, as if they will always be there. Yet the evidence is of a steady decline in membership. One constantly encounters individuals who have 'torn up their cards'. It is customary, when this happens in the Labour Party, to say that the party makes its members what they are, not vice versa, and we are all well off without Mr X, but is there never a point at which such losses become damaging?

The Labour Party Conference next week is to be asked to look at the fall off in membership, the official figures indicating a fairly steady decline since 1952. The last recorded numbers show a drop from 674,905 individual members in 1975 to 659,058 in 1976. But this figure is achieved by counting all the members in constituency parties of over 1000 (as dues are paid on all of them) and then adding the remaining 523 parties at 1000 each, as this is the smallest number on which they are permitted to affiliate. Actual investigation indicates that many of these parties have far fewer than 1000 members, Lord Houghton's report estimating Labour's actual membership at 300,000 – while a PEP survey put it at 250,000.

The Conservative Party does not publish figures but surveys by outside bodies indicate that it also was at a peak in the early 1950s and that it has now dropped by about a half. The Liberals, quite apart from any special problems at the moment, have also fallen in membership and the only party that seems to be gaining members is the Scottish (and perhaps the Welsh) National Party.

The same tendencies naturally affect the quality of the intake into the House of Commons. In practice, the parties depend on blocks of talent which come in after periods when that party or its beliefs have flourished. The Conservatives are still living on the 1950–55 intakes which produced, among others, Mrs Thatcher, Mr Heath and Mr Maudling as well as Mr Powell. The Labour Party's last similar infusion was in 1964–66 but since then, neither side has gained much.

All this does not mean a declining interest in politics. The level of commentary and the concern shown by those in other walks of life remain high; what has happened is a retreat from commitment to work within the parties. To illustrate the point, how would one persuade an able, active young person to join a party today? There appears to be a rightward drift in the country and there may be people who would be prepared to follow this through into overt political action.

The kind of programme set out by the Headmaster of Westminster, Dr John Rae (I know nothing of his political allegiances) might well appeal. He advocated the revival of a competitive spirit, reduced taxation, the subordination of the unions to the state and proportional representation, all to restore Britain's level of performance and national pride.

Instead of putting forward such a coherent programme, the Conservative Party is deep in a controversy over its relations with the unions which reveals not only fear of being defeated once again by industrial conflicts but also a deep sense of doubt about the party's capacity to handle these problems. Some realize that if there is a confrontation, it must be won. Others feel that this fear cannot be openly discussed either because of electoral repercussions or because they doubt whether they could win (probably the reason why Mrs Thatcher has taken refuge in a referendum). The result is that Conservative propaganda has no prevailing theme and what emerges is a rather querulous complaint that life is not what it used to be for the middle classes. Quite so, but the party's appeal will always be limited if it cannot strike a broader, national note and if it cannot give its ideas at least a tinge of idealism.

Supposing that one is appealing to someone whose inclinations are on the left, could he or she be persuaded to join the Labour Party? Apart from the deadly boredom of most constituency party meetings, if the matter is kept at an ideological level, which Labour Party will

197

the person join? If he or she is on the socialist left, there can be little appeal about a Callaghan Government.

Presumably the hope would be that if Labour loses the forthcoming election, the party will swing further left, the next leader will be chosen by party activists and will be a 'real socialist'. But anyone with a knowledge of the party and its history must suspect that even with such a leader and a more left-wing programme, another period of office would be bound to see a return to moderation.

Soon after returning to power the value of staying in the EEC, the need to restore confidence in sterling and to revive investment in the private sector would all have their usual effect. In short, the left would be sold out again.

If the person is a social democrat, he or she will see that many of this group have already left the party. Those that remain, who are mostly in office, will be jockeying for prominence whether the next election is won, or lost.

If a left-winger is elected leader, they will decide that the chap is not so bad after all and will come to terms. But it will be difficult for a Labour Government to make a real success of the mixed economy and of membership of the community when large sections of the party are deeply opposed to both policies.

A third aspect of the Labour Party, the one in the ascendant at the moment, is the trade union connexion. The trouble with this (very conservative) arm of the party is that it cannot be joined. Like Mr Moss Evans, the new leader of the T&GWU, one is born into this section and evolved through time.

I believe that the bulk of those who might be active in British politics do not consider that either the Conservative or Labour Parties, as at present so constituted, adequately express their feelings. These are the people who want to tackle the structural defects, industrial and political, in our society from a radical viewpoint, discarding the old ideological divisions of the inter-war years and the stereotyped reactions of the bundles of vested interests which are the chief remaining components of the major parties.

David Steel has worked hard to try to draw such persons towards the Liberal Party. His original decision to make a pact with Labour showed his nose for power and his maturity in handling situations. Now, alas, the chief effect of the pact is to maintain the present party structure. If he succeeds, he will have kept the coalition which constitutes the Labour Party intact and, as a result, the Liberals are not being regarded as an alternative by those unhappy with the present political system.

198

Anyone in Scotland who is politically interested but unattached is bound to look seriously at the Nationalists. Their great appeal is that with British politics stuck in old conflicts, with people leaving the parties, with inaction always triumphing over radical solutions, it is tempting to say all would be different if one could make a clean start in an independent Scotland. The only trouble is that most Scots are also British and want the whole United Kingdom to overcome its difficulties. It is an admission of defeat, in this sense, to settle for going it alone, even if a separate Scotland could escape all the limitations and frustrations that have bedevilled British politics.

Despite all these reasons for avoiding political commitment, some commentators say there is no cause for alarm. The Americans get on well enough with no organized party system. But the weakness of repeating that situation here in Britain is that ministers can only be chosen from among MPs and MPs are only selected after serving for considerable periods as rank and file members of the political parties.

If the intake declines in quantity and quality, so does the output. Perhaps the real point of the recent left-wing attack on the senior Civil Service is the realization that many ministers do not match up to their officials.

Democratic theory is right in that the final options in this country are left to the politicians and without adequate capacity at this level the system will decline even further.

3.8 'Should government be limited?' (From *The Times*, 15 May 1978)

There is a campaign just now to revive the idea of limits within which British government should operate; to point out that there are many things governments simply cannot do.

Lord Hailsham in his recent book *The Dilemma of Democracy* attacks what he calls an 'elective dictatorship, an over-centralized and top heavy state possessing absolute powers in theory, but unable to exercise them in practice'. He is certainly right in drawing attention to the paradox that government now is expected to do far more than it did in previous periods but also – and perhaps in consequence – that sometimes its powers are not so decisive.

When Keir Hardie was first elected in 1896 and spoke about the plight of the unemployed, his speech was greeted with laughter. Modern students often assume that this was evidence of the callousness of Liberal and Conservative MPs at that time. But this was not so.

The laughter was because MPs thought it was ridiculous to suggest that Parliament or government could do anything about unemployment. How could a government create jobs? It was the kind of laughter which would greet an MP today if he made a speech asking the Government what it proposed to do about the weather.

It is also true that the doctrine of parliamentary sovereignty, the belief in a capacity, as John Stuart Mill said, 'to do anything except make a man into a woman' was prevalent in the late nineteenth century precisely at a time when parliaments and governments did, by convention, restrict themselves to a very narrow area of activity.

This area was one which did not seek to achieve complicated responses in incomes, prices or investment policies but where simple prohibitions were effective. Ships loaded above the Plimsoll Line could not go to sea. Women and children could not be employed in the mines and all children had to have primary education.

It is noticeable that at present the countries that retain the strongest belief in parliamentary sovereignty are the small countries such as Denmark and the Republic of Ireland, where no one imagines that islands of full employment can be established during a worldwide recession or that prices can be held stable if there is general inflation.

As a result, there is no attempt to claim that such things can be done, but the governments and parliaments concentrate on matters which they can affect, such as the internal distribution of resources, welfare policy and the control of the environment.

The question is whether it is possible or desirable to restore this concept of a limited government and therefore reinstate a convention or belief that there are areas in which Parliament ought not to legislate. There are two reason why attempts to do this might not be as good an idea as Lord Hailsham thinks.

The first is that it is very difficult to draw back, to sound a retreat, especially when sometimes some governments have acted in these matters with what appears to be success.

Supposing a party in Britain said it is nonsense to try and increase the level of investment and, if elected, would not try to do so. Other politicians could fairly say that this was ridiculous because at least the government could require more investment in the public sector which it controls and it could offer inducements in the private sector.

The same point arises over wages. Mrs Thatcher and her advisers might like to copy Michael Foot in the 1973–75 period and say that any incomes policy is undesirable, immoral and unworkable. But Mr

Callaghan has made a better attempt at maintaining such a policy than many thought was possible and it has had some beneficial effects. Any incoming government may be driven to do likewise.

The second reason is that in some cases it is positively desirable that the government should assert itself because it is the only authority capable of giving a lead.

One good example is the question of low productivity in Britain. If the remedy was a simple matter of cutting taxes on managers or of new incentives on the shop floor, then there would be no problem. All the evidence of the last 15 years suggests that this is a structural problem in that much of British management lacks the self-confidence, skill and assertiveness to give a strong lead and that concessions are too readily made which permit bad work practices.

But to alter this requires a long-term programme combining changes in educational policy, in rewards, in aspects of industrial law and in the whole social atmosphere. It requires a shift of attention from the distribution of wealth to the production of wealth and an increase in the prestige of those in industry above that of people in academic work, administration or the professions.

Now it may be precisely this kind of social engineering or atmosphere-changing which critics such as Lord Hailsham, drawing on conservative traditions since the time of Burke, say is impossible. Such changes, they insist, cannot be done by law, they can only occur through the normal development of the nation in response to new needs and circumstances.

The trouble is that if such a change is really necessary then it may never happen if no lead is given. Also, while it is true that no legislation called the 'Industrial Management Restoration of Morale Bill' could, if passed, immediately alter attitudes, much can be done to help in this direction.

There are at present a large number of factors in pay, pensions, conditions of service and in governmental and educational attitudes that are not neutral on this issue but are positively prejudicial and these could at least be altered and the bias be shifted in favour of an emphasis on the value of productive industry.

Another example is the current notion, dramatically confirmed in a recent report in *The Times* that no party can alter the legislation affecting industrial relations without the prior consent of the TUC and, indeed, that if there was any 'confrontation', a Conservative government would not have the strength to assert itself.

The doctrine of a limitation on the powers of government and Parliament would confirm these fears and would be disastrous because, if true, it would mean that sectional interests could always triumph over the only bodies entitled to speak for the general interest.

It might be that some people would object to the industrial relations policies pursued by a Conservative government (as some would object to those of a Labour government) but it is quite a different matter to say that no government should try to carry through policies for which there is widespread support among the electorate.

It is important to be clear what is being said. This is no argument that a precarious government, lacking a coherent policy which mishandles situations and loses the support of public opinion, should then be sure it can get its way whatever it does.

But if governments are elected with clearly stated and elaborated policies in these areas, then parliamentary democracy is weakened, not strengthened, by any act of renunciation; and the statement that these are fields in which nothing can be done.

Perhaps some institutional changes are needed to strengthen governments, to be sure they have a larger measure of support and that if one pressure group holds out, the support of others can be mobilised.

But so long as the major questions of policy are openly debated and most of the public come to one opinion rather than another, to say that there ought to be limits on the competence of governments which would prevent these policies being carried through by the normal process of enactment and enforcement damages rather than reinforces our democratic system.

3.9 'Britain's malaise: political or economic?' (From *The Scottish Banker's Magazine*, May 1978, pp. 7–27)

As long ago as 1964, I recall buying Allan Flanders' book *The Fawley Productivity Agreements*. It described the unprecedented departure from the usual form of collective bargaining by which, in 1960, the Esso Petroleum Company offered its employees large increases in wages in return for certain changes in working practices which included the reduction of overtime, fewer job demarcations and the redeployment of some underemployed workers. In the following two years, the productiviy of maintenance workers rose by 50 per cent, while their pay rose by 45 per cent. Trade union activity did not lose its vigour and, indeed, bargaining between shop stewards and management became even keener. But it was a daring and successful experiment in terms of productivity, the firm's profits and the men's pay.

I came back to this problem of productivity some years later and I want to trace the stages under the heading of this article, 'Britain's Malaise: Political or Economic?' Part of my problem has been that any new ideas have come to me slowly and by dint of struggling with actual situations, as they have occurred in practice or in the world of ideas.

By 1976, I had come to accept that something had gone wrong with the assumptions on which I had stood for Parliament in 1959 and 1964 and which I had held at the time of my election in 1966. In the early 1960's, I, like other Labour candidates, had attacked the low growth of the 1950's under the slogan of 'Thirteen Wasted Years'. In these years, unemployment had averaged around 2 per cent, inflation had been running at about 4 per cent a year and the gross domestic product had grown by 3 per cent a year. All this was most unsatisfactory, we claimed. Had anyone told me (or any of the other Labour candidates) that in 1977 a Labour Government would be presiding, somewhat complacently, over an inflation rate of 14 per cent (which had been up above 20 per cent), with 6 per cent or 1.5 million unemployed and a growth rate of about 1 per cent a year, I would not have believed that this was possible.

Moreover, having not anticipated any such developments, I had not thought about or appreciated how far the views of what is now called the social democratic section which was then dominant in the Labour Party depended on the kind of growth we had claimed was possible once the Tories were out of office. The Gaitskell-Crosland philosophy (shared for that matter by Harold Wilson, though he used different phrases) was that given suitable conditions and modern, efficient government, the mixed economy in Britain would grow at a rate which would equal or exceed R. A. Butler's 1954 forecast of a doubling of the standard of living in twenty-five years. This growth could then be used to eradicate not merely inefficiency and old, out-dated production methods but the extra wealth would allow higher real wages and greater public expenditure, both of which would reduce class differences and class indicators and therefore spell the end of class discrimination. Britain would become a richer, happier, more egalitarian society, while preserving and enhancing personal freedoms.

Looking back, I now realise that we had no adequate theory of how the mixed economy should work. We assumed that the public sector would get on with its mixed economic and social objectives, that the private sector, though a little suspect because of undue emphasis on private gain, would do its bit. If it seemed necessary, industries with special problems might be nationalised, but the public-private balance would remain at somewhere near its existing proportions. Perhaps we were to blame for making these assumptions but if they had worked, no one would have raised awkward questions. The German SPD had taken the same view when it drafted the Godesburg programme in the late 1950s and drove out its left wing but because the German economy had gone from strength to strength, these assumptions were still acceptable and still underlay the campaign fought by Helmut Schmidt in the general election of 1976.

So the problem began to come clear. Why had this reformist, egalitarian approach worked in Germany but not in Britain? The results of the failure have certainly had a profound effect on our political life. In a sense, these ideas were shared by the moderate wings of both the Labour and the Conservative Parties and both were discredited by the experience of the 1963–77 period. Leaders of both Parties had told the electorate that all would be well and that disappointments were due to the follies, incompetence or ideological obsessions of the other side.

In 1964, Mr Wilson planned 100 days of dramatic activity which would transform the scene. It would be all go. As he told me once during these days, 'No. 10, Downing Street has always been a powerhouse but what matters is the voltage running through it'. George Brown made a Declaration of Intent with the unions and published his National Plan which was based on an annual growth rate of 4¼%. But in July 1966, there was a sterling crisis and cutbacks were instituted which made the National Plan targets impossible. Further balance of payments weaknesses led to devaluation in November 1967, a loan from the International Monetary Fund and a major effort to rectify the balance of payments deficit at the cost of virtual stagnation and rising prices.

Meanwhile, Mr Wilson embarked on the restructuring of industry through the NEDC and 'Little Neddies' for each trade, through productivity conferences and 'shakeouts' of surplus labour. Every now and then, though with less frequency, the economic indicators improved for a few months and there would be further speeches about 'economic miracles', but each of these respites proved in turn to be a false dawn. Mr Heath, for his part, blamed the whole sorry record on government intervention, undue taxation and a destruction of business confidence leading to low investment and low growth. All would be remedied under a Conservative Government.

After his surprise victory in June 1970, Mr Heath's Government set about the pursuit of these policies. Mr (now Lord) Barber cut taxes, the pound was floated, subsidies were reduced and every effort was made to restore confidence in the private sector. But in 1971 unemployment rose to a million, Rolls Royce and Upper Clyde Shipbuilders went bankrupt and the Heath Government turned back to a statutory incomes policy, a consumer boom to stimulate employment, and subsidies to ailing industries. In neither phase did the private sector respond with increased investment and by the end of his period in office, the Prime Minister was making speeches about 'the unacceptable face of capitalism' and was on very bad terms with many in the City.

The Labour Government which came to office in February and October 1974, first began to try to manage the economy through a social contract with the unions, by increasing demand and by pushing public ownership as a method of inducing greater investment. The consequence was an unprecedented rise in the rate of inflation, economic stagnation, a colossal balance of payments deficit, mounting unemployment and a sag in the value of the pound. Then, in 1976, the Government had, after various measures of its own, to turn to the International Monetary Fund. This, heavy cuts in public expenditure, a tight hold on the money supply and some balance of payments benefits from North Sea oil helped to restore the situation. But the economy was still stagnant, there was a million and a half unemployed and the rate of inflation remained above 10 per cent.

The point of this very brief economic history of the 1964–77 period is to show that though governments of the moderate wings of both major Parties twisted and turned, though both blamed their opponents and struggled to find new policies to remedy the situation, there was no long-term revival and no fulfilment of the hopes that electors had entertained. These hopes were based not just on the competitive promises of politicians but on the actual experience of the 1950–1964 period.

The effect of this series of events and of the disappointments of the last fourteen years has been profound. Within the two major Parties there has been a drift towards the extremes. This has happened despite the fact that Britain is not seething with ideology. The electorate in this country when it is forced to realise that its expectations will not be achieved, does not react by adopting tough political positions. While many think that in some sense British industry has let them down, very few consider that a large-scale extension of public ownership would be anything except a disaster. If a Socialist who believed in a totally publicly-owned economy stood at an election on such a ticket, no one supposes that he or she would get more than a handful of votes. On the other side, however, most Conservatives also lack any conviction that a return to unfettered private enterprise would solve the country's problems or that all that is wrong is the cancer of socialism which, once cut out, would leave the body healthy.

Though the electorate are not turning to extreme solutions but are merely deeply unhappy about what they have been offered by the leading politicians, the two main Parties do seem to be drifting to left and to right. The Tribune Group in the Labour Party has had its setbacks but now it numbers about eighty MPs and dominates the National Executive of the Party. Its strength will probably grow after the next election, given the outlook of the candidates that have been adopted in safe seats and it may well be that after Callaghan retires, the next leader will be chosen by some group wider and more left wing than the current Parliamentary Party.

In the Conservative Party, extreme right wing populists are gaining ground, Sir Keith Joseph, Mr Teddy Taylor, Mr Heseltine and Dr Rhodes Boyson are preferred, while Mr Peter Walker and Mr Nicholas Scott are left outside and Mr Timothy Raison is dismissed. For the first time since the war, Conservatives can be heard saying that the whole experiment initiated by the Beveridge Report was a mistake and should be abandoned. It is significant and sad that the two most impressive men in politics in the early 1970s, Mr Heath and Mr Jenkins, were both too moderate, too near the centre, and both have been frozen out.

The reason for these developments is that economic failures have undermined the case made by the moderates – they have been in power and have tried their solutions without success. Thus in any debate inside the Labour Party, if the question is 'How will you get the private sector to respond to your sticks, carrots, incentives, aids and exhortations?' there is no answer. The left is getting stronger because, however improbable its techniques of far more detailed and widespread state control, at least it has a distinctive, non-Tory solution to offer.

And the same weakness saps the moderate Conservatives. They can say little in response to attacks from their own right over the failure of the mixed economy. However improbable it may be that a revival of industrial investment and of productivity would be a necessary consequence of a Friedmanite policy of monetarism and of making people pay for their health and education, at least it is a distinctive, non-left-wing answer to the central issue of the decline in productivity, in investment and in the numbers employed in the manufacturing industry.

Though the electorate have not followed suit and swung to either extreme, they have shown strong signs of dissatisfaction with the records of successive governments and both major Parties. During the 1950s, with a growth rate of 3 per cent and three consecutive Conservative election victories, it was often thought that any reasonably competent government could so manage the economy as to create a pre-electoral boom and be returned with enhanced popularity. But Mr Wilson lost his huge majority of 1964 and 1966 and Mr Heath then lost in the two elections of 1974. But these defeats were not because voters turned with increasing confidence from the government and towards the opposition. Instead, voters turned to third and fourth Parties. While 97 per cent of the electorate voted for the two major Parties in 1950 and 1951, by 1974 this was down to 75 per cent. As a result, whereas it had taken 49 per cent to 44 per cent electoral support to win elections in the 1950s, in October 1974 Mr Wilson came back to office on 39 per cent of the public's votes.

Much of the support for the Scottish and Welsh National Parties springs from the same feeling of disappointment over and consequent distaste for what these Parties describe as 'London Government'. While English voters feel frustrated or vote Liberal or even National Front, in Scotland and Wales there is another way of registering disapprobation and a feeling that things could not be much worse; that is by voting Nationalist.

Finally, the public scepticism over politicians, Parties, officials, Parliament, indeed all the apparatus of government, has grown. When the public know their own local MP and think of him as their spokesman against those in power, they tend to approve of him. But when he is viewed as a politician, as one of 'them' who does things to us, who taxes us, rules us, makes promises and fails to keep them, then there is a very different feeling which includes cynicism, scepticism and at times even a dash of real hostility.

If these are the consequence of the performance of recent governments, what is the cause? What explanations are given for this sequence of disappointments? The first in order of time and the one made most often in accounts of this period, from Sir Harold Wilson's own book *The Labour Government of 1964–70; A Personal Record* to Michael Stewart's *The Jekyll and Hyde Years; Political and Economic Policy Since 1964*, may be summarised as the 'blown off course' explanation. This is put forward by politicians responsible for government in these years and by their economic advisers who were, almost without exception, orthodox Keynesians. According to this theory, the Labour Government's economic strategy after 1964 would have worked from the outset but for the uncontrolled boom organised by Mr Maudling with its legacy of an £800 million balance of payments deficit. The Labour Government could then have managed matters, had the economists' advice been taken and the pound devalued in 1964 or 1966 but when Mr Wilson was 'blown off course' in July 1966, he preferred to deflate. His aversion for devaluation prevented a rectification of the balance of payments problem till the necessary measures had to be drastic. Mr Heath inherited a better position but his over-reaction to the general depression of 1971 led to an uncontrolled expansion. Just as he was getting over this phase, restoring growth and working a sensible incomes policy he, in his turn, was 'blown off course' by the oil embargo and then by the quadrupling of the price of oil in 1973. This theory is still held by many politicians and civil servants and they help write the speeches, formerly used by Mr Wilson and Mr Heath, and now used by Mr Callaghan, in which he prophesies that 'if only X is achieved . . . (at present if the income policy targets are adhered to) . . .', Britain faces a golden period ahead of unprecedented prosperity.

The trouble with these theories is that one can understand fortuitous factors spoiling one set of policies but not the policies of three successive governments. Moreover, the oil price rise affected the whole of Western Europe yet since it happened in 1973, British manufacturing productivity has risen 3 per cent over three years while in the same period, productivity in the USA and France has gone up by 10 per cent, in Italy by 12 per cent, in Japan by 14 per cent and in Germany by 15 per cent (*National Institute Economic Review*, No. 81, August 1977). Some have said that all this proves is that Keynesian demand management no longer works. Perhaps Keynes did neglect the power of the unions to push up wages costs in conditions of near full employment. Perhaps the price of energy was artificially low before 1973. But it is hard to believe that the root of the difference between the economic performances of Britain and of such countries as Germany, France, Italy and Japan was that their economic and political managers had better luck, using the same macro-economic techniques of demand management, than our leaders enjoyed in Britain.

If the 'blown off course' argument is rejected, what are the other possible explanations? One point which is sometimes made is that there is nothing new in all this. Britain's growth rate has been relatively low since 1870; the whole process has been going on for a century. There are two problems here. The first is that this, if true, only makes the necessary explanation one which covers the last century for it does not explain why these other countries' growth rates should have been rising more rapidly than Britain's in recent years nor does it explain why the British rate has been as low as 1 or 1½% a year for a century. But, in any case, restricting the argument to the post-war period, it is still not accurate. It does not explain why in the 1949–1963 period of fourteen years, the growth rate should have run at an average of 3 per cent in Britain but in the subsequent fourteen years of 1963 to 1977 the rate should have dropped to 1½%. There has been a strikingly poorer performance in this second period.

One or two other minor points can also be disposed of here. The curious argument that Britain suffered by not losing the war can be put aside. Why, except in some psychological terms, it should be a help for a country to have its capital shock and much of its infrastructure destroyed is hard to understand but, in any case, the significant contrast occurs in the period since 1955 when, by any standards, post-war recovery was over. In 1955, British productivity per man hour was 15 per cent ahead of that of France and Germany and 40 per cent ahead of Italy (*National Institute Economic Review*, No. 77, August 1976) whereas by 1973 Italy had overtaken Britain, France and Germany were 30 per cent ahead, while Belgium and the Netherlands were 40 per cent and 54 per cent higher. If the response is that what matters is the quality of life and why should there be all this emphasis on wealth creation, this may be fine for the individual who is happy with little or no growth in his or her standard of living over the years, someone who believes that life in Britain is better because of this. But this is not the reaction of the bulk of the electorate and it is their sense of disappointment or even of relative failure (which is true in terms of relative performance) that is the phenomenon that is being examined. Moreover, in any democracy a widespread lack of confidence in successive governments and therefore in the machinery of government can have the serious political consequences already described.

There remain two major explanations of this phenomenon. The first is that the root cause is what Professor Finer has called 'adversarial politics' or what other political scientists have described as 'overload'. The second is that it is an error to look at the demand side of the economic management – the problem is the supply side. The assumption on which Keynesian economics, like both classical and Marxist economics, has operated has been that individuals involved in all levels of the private and public sectors of the economy are all constantly eager to perform, to increase investment, output and sales so that they will respond at once to any turning on of the tap, to any incentives given by the economic planners. Thus all that is needed is to provide the correct demand management. The alternative considered here is that there are structural problems peculiar to British society which, it is argued, mean that whatever the alterations in demand, production hangs back because of a number of limiting factors on the supply side.

To take these points in turn, the political argument has two sides. One is that politicians, in order to win elections, have pushed public expectations up further than the economic system can meet. And the other side is to explain this failure to reach what may not have been unreasonable targets by saying that public and private business has been hampered by constant changes in policy, by torrents of legislation and by endless, harmful interference by governments. This damage has stretched from incomes policies, through over-heavy and elaborate taxation, to endless reversals of specific policies.

On the question of targets, the question is whether politicians should have guessed that the economy was going to grow so much more slowly in the 1960s and 1970s than it had done in the 1950s, and it is hard to see why they should have indulged in such pessimism (for there was no factual evidence which should have produced such a forecast). Indeed, R. A. Butler (now Lord Butler) was not far off the mark when he said, in 1954, that Britain's standard of living could double in twenty-five years. This would have needed a growth rate of only a little over 3 per cent and his forecast was on target for the next decade. Then again, it is hard to blame politicians for blaming each other when so many of their economic advisers belonged to the 'blown off course' school of thought. It is only natural that rival captains for the ships of state should take the view that if the man at the wheel is thus easily caught unawares, he should give way to another captain and crew. It is the case that hopes and forecasts have been scaled down recently as a result of the poor performance of the economy but there seems to be no good reason why, before this happened, our politicians should not have hoped for and therefore promised levels of increased real wages and of social services equivalent to those being achieved by other similar industrial nations.

Turning to the argument about policy changes, the evidence is formidable. From Mr (now Lord) Selwyn Lloyd's pay pause of the early 1960s, successive governments have set up and dismantled each other's machinery for conducting incomes policies. Regional incentives have moved from direct grants to tax relief on profits and back to direct grants till few industrialists have any clear picture of the financial assistance available if they move to development areas. Any rebates or grants or employment premiums tend to be accepted as bonuses or windfalls which occur after the key decisions have been taken. There have been similar changes in what have been alleged to be the long-term pension plans of successive governments. On industrial relations, Harold Wilson and Mrs Barbara Castle accepted that frequent unpredictable stoppages were a serious handicap to British industry and proposed strike ballots and restrictions on unofficial strikes to try to remedy this situation. But when they were defeated by their colleagues and by the TUC in 1969, there was no attempt to achieve the same objectives by other methods. Indeed, the Labour Party did everything it could to condemn the Conservatives' effort to remedy the same problem. As a result, it is now widely held that this kind of party conflict renders any attempt to improve the law on industrial relations impossible.

In general, it has been argued that the political and industrial time scales are out of phase. It takes a number of years to build a modern steel works or a nuclear power station or to develop, make and market a successful car and yet in this same period, ministers in charge of industrial policy will have changed, governments may have changed and policies pursued by the same or by different governments are likely to have altered. The CBI were sufficiently disturbed by this phenomenon to set up a working party which has asked 300 firms about their investment time scales. How long, after a given government policy directed towards or affecting industry is announced, do the results take to emerge? The Hansard Society for Parliamentary Government has appointed a working party under Sir Richard Marsh to see whether the political time scale fits that of industry. While it would be wrong to try to pre-empt the results of these two studies, it is fair to forecast that they certainly support those who say that government policies are seriously out of phase with and often hamper industrial development.

The response of many in industry, in public and in academic life, who take this view is that various changes are needed to remove these defects from our political system. They propose, for instance, proportional representation in order to get coalition governments which will, they think (and as David Steel claims), give more weight to the centre in British politics, thus emphasising continuity in policy.

Other proposals include primaries for candidates for Parliament in order to exclude the more extreme figures which, it is held, tend to be selected when there are small, unrepresentative groups of extremists in control of local parties. There are other proposals such as those for a stronger second chamber but the main objective of all of them is to undo or counteract the tendency noted earlier in this article for an increase in the strength of the left wing of the Labour and the right wing of the Conservative Party. A second objective is to discourage parties from promising radical changes of direction in the hope of producing clearcut benefits which are not forthcoming. Proportional representation and constant coalition government would, it is argued, lead to much greater continuity of industrial, financial and labour policies. Such a system would weaken the hold of the big pressure groups since centre party support would matter more than the agreement of the TUC or CBI and in general there would be steadier and more positive backing for the present form of mixed economy which would, in time, restore business confidence.

The difficulty about accepting the argument that political weaknesses – which undoubtedly exist – are a primary cause of this country's problems, is simply that the British political system has been in existence for a long time and there is no good reason why it should have permitted the industrialisation of Britain but should now suddenly become a disastrous handicap. Indeed, it is much easier to see these phenomena of governments rejecting the policies of their predecessors in office, of twisting and turning to try and produce results, as a consequence rather than as a cause of a poor economic performance. When the economic record has been more or less satisfactory as has happened here in the past and currently in other countries, the parties have gone on arguing over future policy developments but have accepted each other's legislation and major policy decisions.

For instance, it was in the relatively successful period of the 1950s that the Labour Party was in the hands of its moderates or reformers and the Conservative Party developed good relations with the unions that commentators used to talk about Butskellism. This certainly allowed for continuity of policy towards industry and in other fields of the kind which has been evident in Germany and in the United States in recent years where the 1976 Kohl-Schmidt election campaign and even the Ford-Carter campaign revealed large areas of common ground on essential questions of how the economy should be managed. Democracy is, after all, the process of making four or five yearly adjustments to priorities, to the direction of change and to the social atmosphere. Democracy is not a machinery for conducting abrupt about-turns and if drastic changes are demanded, then long-term planning and confidence will be damaged, but if this does happen, it is evidence that all is not well with the economic performance of the society.

If then blaming the political system as the basic cause of our difficulties is not entirely convincing, though current political practice may well have contributory or secondary effects, this leaves the structural explanation which points to the supply side of the economy as the main cause. William Rees-Mogg, the Editor of *The Times*, has put his finger on one central aspect of the problem in two recent articles (28th September 1977 and 5th October 1977) in his paper. He said that 'the British disease is low manpower productivity' and that this 'is an underlying cause of *all* other weaknesses in our economy'. Drawing on the same statistics in the *National Institute Economic Review*, No. 77, August 1976, he showed how far Britain had fallen behind other nations:

The Increase in Productivity 1955–74

(Gross value added per man hour in manufacturing)

	Level 1974 UK = 100	Rise 1955–74 per cent	Rate of increase UK = 100
Netherlands	196	228	248
Belgium	179	210	228
France	167	166	180
Germany	162	171	186
Italy	103	185	201
United Kingdom	100	92	100

Based on Chart 2 of A. T. Jones's 'Output, Employment and Labour Productivity in Europe since 1955', *National Institute Economic Review*, August 1976.

Taking the specific case of current performance in the steel industry, the figures are:

Productivity in Steel 1976–77

	000 Metric tons	000 Workers	Tons per man year
US	116,300	471	247
Japan	107,400	316	340
W. Germany	42,000	264	161
Italy	23,200	147	158
UK	22,500	363	62

The qualification has to be made that this is not true of all British industries – electronics and chemicals are better and I began the article by referring to the break-through achieved by the 1960 Fawley productivity agreements. Some foreign multinationals report productivity rates in their UK subsidiaries as high as those in factories in other countries such as Germany or the United States. But these overall figures represent an average. On the supply side there are clearly acute problems in Britain. Productivity in the mines is falling and the British car industry has produced 440,000 fewer cars last year than in 1973 so that almost a half of the domestic car market has gone to foreign producers. Output per man in British Airways is 35 per cent of that in Pan American Airways, 47 per cent of Japanese Airways, 60 per cent of KLM and 76 per cent of Air France (Michael Beckett, *Daily Telegraph*, 19th September 1977). Low productivity has led the shipbuilding industry to fall from a dominant position where it built 38 per cent of world output after the war to a mere 4 per cent.

If it is agreed that low productivity is the measure of Britain's economic weakness, the problem is how this has come about and it is here that the arguments of most commentators become a little obscure. Mr William Rees-Mogg says that 'almost throughout British industry managers have lost the most essential power of management. They cannot decide how many people they will employ to carry out a particular job'. If he is correct that in Britain there are a mass of restrictive practices leading to overmanning and that these practices do not occur to anything like the same extent among our competitors, there can be only two explanations. The first is that the unions are inherently more aggressive, capable and effective in forcing British managers to accept these damaging concessions and the second is that British managers are less willing to resist these encroachments than their opposite numbers in other countries. Rees-Mogg notes that British managers do as well as their competitors when they are managing firms located abroad and that they are as effective as their rivals in running multinationals. They do not waste labour when they are free not to do so. Labour is underused (or wasted) in Britain because this is forced on British management. But he recognises that the national trade union leadership is unhappy about over-manning (though it will not make any effort to stop it) and therefore the conclusion must be that the root of the problem is the greater power of shop floor militancy which forces managers to concede restrictive practices and over-manning which they know will wreck the business. But why are British workers so much tougher and more capable of pinning down their bosses than workers in Japan, Germany, France or Italy? The Editor of *The Times* is deeply involved in the problem as Fleet Street is one of the worst examples of over-manning and consequent low productivity in this country. And the one obvious explanation of this situation which he cannot bring himself to admit is that the management, however able in terms of other aspects of their jobs, have been willing to concede ground, bit by bit on these issues, till they have lost control. After all, there is no inherent reason why this, as he says 'the most essential power of management' should be lost in Britain but not elsewhere unless British managers had come to accept this situation.

The other person who has addressed himself to this problem is Sir Keith Joseph. Speaking in the debate on the Queen's Speech on 8th November, he accepted all the points so far advanced about low productivity and came to the opposite conclusion to Rees-Mogg. He said that 'management must take the responsibility' and he did go on to try and explain this weakness. He blamed 'the wet blanket of high taxation' which 'has stifled initiative and effort, risk-taking and enterprise at every level of responsibility, from the boardroom through to the floor cleaner in industry' (*Hansard*, 8th November 1977, Col. 507). If the argument is that British managers are willing to accept restrictive practices and over-manning because they are heavily taxed, it seems surprising. Why should they give up this area of authority which has little to do with their level of pay but a great deal to do with their capacity to perform and with their job satisfaction just because the marginal rate of taxation is higher than in some other countries (and some evidence on tax rates does not support this contention)? Is there, conversely, a point at which tax cuts would suddenly restore managements' morale and make them begin to assert control once again?

This theory may be useful for Conservative political propaganda but it seems a highly implausible explanation. The theory I want to advance to explain low productivity and the acceptance by managers of a mass of restrictive practices is that the whole social, political and industrial atmosphere in Britain leads managers to believe that they will lose any confrontations and indeed that this is not only inevitable but may also be almost correct; it may be a part of modern life. One aspect of this is that we in Britain have always rated the professions, research and administration higher than manufacturing and selling. Those who go into industry have tended to be the less able, less socially confident

215

men and women. They have felt that they lack glamour and prestige. Also there has been no clear-cut theory which justifies the objectives of the private sector. Money-making has appeared to be a little sordid. Again, while the unions may not be stronger in Britain than elsewhere, the old class battle lines have not disappeared. While labour is full of its rights, ready to go on television and make its case, while students, left wing papers and some of the media rally to its side, management is embarrassed, reluctant to fight, half-beaten before it starts and gets no support from any third parties.

It is hard to separate out these strands but some evidence can be collected to add to general impressions and it is worth examining, in contrast, the position in the one industry in Britain that has beaten all rivals in other countries for productivity. The separate strands are first the quality of people going into engineering, technology and business management. In July 1977, the Department of Industry issued a discussion paper entitled 'Industry, Education and Management' which showed that 'the proportion of graduates entering home employment who go into manufacturing has fallen from 35 per cent to 40 per cent up to 1970 to only 26 per cent in 1975'. The paper also showed that students going into engineering and technology had lower school qualifications than those entering other subjects. While the numbers studying other disciplines had increased steadily, the number of vacant places in engineering was between 7000 and 4000. Section VIII of the paper argued that production management is a particularly weak area in the UK, and that the percentage working in this field who had appropriate degrees had fallen from 9.4 per cent in 1966 to 6.2 per cent in 1975.

In a brilliant article in *Encounter* (Autumn 1977), Mr John Rae, Headmaster of Westminster School, points out that till well into the last century the chief British characteristics were being aggressive, successful and enterprising. Then our imperial role disguised the fact that if this advantage was lost, Britain would revert to being a small trading state which would have to live off its wits. During this period, administration expanded as Britain ruled so many parts of the world. Trade and manufactures were downgraded but this did not produce disaster as the Empire was also a market specially open to British products. But when the Empire was finally dismantled in the 1950s, instead of turning back to earning our living in an intensively competitive world, the attitudes of the 1960s continued to downgrade competition. Profit and capitalism were suspect words and labour was, on the whole, pushing for advantages which were held to be its due. The new comprehensive schools and expanded universities shared with the old public schools and Oxbridge a contempt for trade and industry and for the kind of individuality needed in commerce. Public service in the Empire was replaced by what Noel Annan has called 'the new bureaucracy of higher education, broadcasting, journalism, research organisations, social welfare [and] planning'.

All this confirms the impression I have gained in my combination of academic and political life. The pursuit of social justice, while admirable, has so downgraded the role of industrialists and of businessmen in this country that they are on the defensive. I have been fascinated by the way in which the very able men in British journalism have watched the collapse of their livelihoods as restrictive practices have destroyed the economic viability of their papers. To visit the boardroom of one of these journals is to engage in high level discussions of foreign affairs and of politics, but when one asks about the crucial issues of 'break-even points', over-manning, advertising revenue and distribution costs, an air of ennui immediately appears. These low level matters are left to the second echelon of executives who are not considered suitable persons to have to boardroom lunches. Time and again, in local industrial disputes, I have been called in by management and asked not 'are we behaving sensibly?' or 'should we win?', but 'how can we give way gracefully to defeat?' In my experience, unions always expect to win most of what they want in disputes. When Glasgow Corporation had a strike of refuse truck drivers and not only refused to give way but called in troops and drove the men back to work at their former level of pay, a shock went through Clydeside. This, I was told by one of the men's leaders, was totally without precedent. One could certainly not have imagined any private industrialists behaving in this way. While one may not accept all the stands made by Mr George Ward of Grunwick's, it is true that his determination to run his own factory the way he wants is not in line with the attitude of most British industrialists.

This weakness of British management, its lack of a coherent theory on which to base a defence of its work and attitudes, its defensiveness, its sense that public opinion is not on its side, all come out in its handling of the media. When any industrial issue arises, television companies and papers can always get union leaders, politicians and academics to comment, but will any industrialist stand up and put the case of the managers? Time and again, this side of the argument goes by default and industrialists excuse themselves by saying they speak only for themselves or they will not come and be pushed around by some TV interviewer. As a result, if school leavers are asked to name trade unionists, most can list four or five but they can think of no

217

industrialists and the only names that are ever mentioned are those of men such as Poulson or of firms such as Slater-Walker where there have been inquiries or allegations. This imbalance was underlined recently when 54 per cent of a poll said they thought Mr Jack Jones was more important than the Prime Minister.

To bring out the points being made, it is worth looking at the one British industry which has a better record than its rivals in Europe – agriculture. In the period between 1969 and 1973 productivity in British farming grew 1 per cent per annum faster than on the continent. This certainly comes as no surprise to someone like myself who represents an agricultural constituency. I know that when I go, once a year, to the local branches of the NFU to meet farmers, I have to be fully informed of all the latest prices and statistics. Almost all farmers follow the news in the specialist farming press, they do their sums and can quote chapter and verse about the last price review here or in Brussels. Most of them can give the break-even points on each product on their own farm. Looking for an explanation of this level of expertise and of confidence, one gets the impression that farming is an 'all right' occupation and that able boys are eager to follow their fathers while the industrialist talks of the success of his son by explaining that the boy is now a surgeon or a research scientist. Also the value of training is recognised and most farmers have been through the colleges of agriculture. All the factors necessary to build up and maintain competence in a group are present. Agriculture has a specialist press, sections in the major newspapers and programmes on the radio, all of which sustain the level of information and the application of new ideas. Farming has its expert gatherings. At one of these, the Oxford Farming Conference, Sir Frederick Catherwood pointed out that after five years of dealing with over thirty organisations representing various industries, he had no hesitation in naming the National Farmers' Union as 'by far and away the best organised, most competent and most effective of all such bodies'. Finally, it is clear that there is competition. This is not of the take-over kind but simply that anyone can look over the hedge and see how the farmer is doing and his near neighbours are all working away on the same products so that everyone knows who is not coming up to scratch. It may be argued that one important factor is that agriculture does not have militant unions. But this can be an effect of farmers' attitudes as well as a cause of higher productivity and few farmers fail to work alongside their men or take a turn on the tractor.

In my constituency, besides farming, there is another instructive contrast. There are three subsidiaries of foreign firms, two American

and one Norwegian, with executives drawn from their home
countries. All three claim that productivity is as high as in their other
branch factories. Going round with these able young men from
institutions like the Harvard Business School, one hears them call
workers by their first names in a way which might arouse suspicion, a
sense of being patronised, if it was done by a Briton but is acceptable
coming from someone outside the British class system. These
managers are full of confidence, they refuse to look at restrictive
practices, they have dealt with over-manning by doubling production
with the same labour force and, as in the Fawley Agreements, wages
have followed suit and nearly doubled. This would also explain why
British managers do better overseas when they too can step outside
the restrictions of the current British intellectual climate and respond
like other executives in the countries where they are working.

Coming, finally, to some conclusions, I find William Rees-Mogg and
Sir Keith Joseph's solutions unacceptable because their analyses seem
to be faulty. Rees-Mogg thinks all restrictive practices could be
registered with and annulled by a suitable court or tribunal. But why
should workers who have insisted on these restrictive practices and
industrialists who have already caved into these demands, agree
voluntarily to either register them or abolish them at the suggestion of
a court or tribunal?

Similarly, I see no evidence that lighter taxation – tried by
Anthony, now Lord, Barber – would, though welcome, change the
spirit and atmosphere in British management. Indeed, the agricultural
countercase is instructive for farmers have faced not only the same
income taxes but a penal capital transfer tax and yet this has not
weakened their capacity for innovation or diminished their
achievement in terms of productivity.

These two remedies are also too easy and too simple. If the diag-
nosis in this article is correct, the task is far harder because it is necessary to change the social atmosphere and values. This may be
beginning to happen. There is more questioning now of the rejection
of competition by many schools and school teachers. But it will be
necessary to push this further and faster by mounting a board programme to raise the prestige of industry and commerce and to pub-
licise its personalities and achievements. The curriculum in schools
and universities must lay emphasis on these skills while careers
in administration, academic work and social welfare should be given
less prominence. Our theorists must produce an ideological defence
of the mixed economy which is convincing and which gives the pri-

vate sector its proper place. Above all, it must be repeated again and again that we can only enjoy wealth which we have created and that to buy a holiday abroad requires that we produce goods and services of equal value which foreigners want to purchase. Now we have to recover those old characteristics of determination, drive and self-confidence which are essential if this country is to earn the standard of living which the bulk of people want to enjoy.

3.10 'Mrs Thatcher is a Leftie' (From *The Listener*, 13 July 1978)

This volume of *Conservative Essays* is unusual in that it seeks to establish an intellectual case for a conservatism far to the right of anything now contemplated by the bulk of the Conservative Party. For all the essayists, liberalism is the enemy. Several explicitly reject the market economy and monetarist policies of the Institute of Economic Affairs – and, therefore, much of what Mrs Thatcher and Sir Keith Joseph have to say.

The problem comes when one tries to discover precisely what the essayists are saying. First, they want an open and confident advocacy of more inequality which must somehow be based on 'a unity of national sentiment transcending the divisions of the classes'. Disraeli is no guide to this kind of Conservatism, as he was an alien opportunist. Churchill is rejected, since he was a Whig. One acceptable father figure is Lord Salisbury, for whom the real criminals were those 'falsifying the purpose of politics by treating it as a branch of ethics and seeking . . . through legislation to propagate doctrine, embody "principle" or recognise some "social ideal". The other hero is Baldwin, for whom 'blood and soil were . . . central' and 'it was a matter of identifying soil as the womb of the true self'. 'After all,' as he said, 'the English stock is a true stock.'

Several of the authors observe that Marxism is better than liberalism, with the latter's talk of abstract rights and of principles of justice, because Marxism shows that people can only be understood in a given historical and social context – the trouble is that the Marxists have put the wrong emphasis on who matters in such a context, and on the forces at work. What is needed is a respect for tradition, and a piety towards existing institutions. As Peregrine Worsthorne puts it, 'in any society, at any time, there are some citizens who have more to contribute than others, and it is in everybody's interest that this outstanding minority should exercise more influence over public affairs than the untalented majority . . . This country . . . has become much too compassionate, much too concerned about the weak, the sick, the poor and the miserable.' 'Conservatism has no choice but to admit the truth – that it is about satisfying the needs of the strong.'

This, then, is the message of the book. But it took some effort to cull any clear or coherent assertions from amid the mass of vague reactionary phrases, and it has seemed best to omit many of the more ominous remarks (such as the one by Cowling that 'if the price paid for parliamentary government is too high, there will be those who will want parliamentary arrangements superseded'). But the weakness of the essays, perhaps inherent in the mental approach of the authors, is that they seem to see no need to make a rational argument for their views. They have not spotted the obvious inconsistencies, or realised the import of what they are saying if it is translated into different political contexts.

For instance, Cowling says that 'the Conservative conception of a social structure not only assumes that marked inequalities are inevitable, but also declines to justify them because their inevitability makes justification unnecessary'. So the existence of a state of affairs is its own justification. Then the book goes on to rail at methods of reducing inequality. But can these be attacked on Cowling's own criteria if they exist and work? Again, it is said that increased inequality is desirable. But how can this be possible, when what is is justified by its current existence? Certainly, no case is explicitly made for more or less equality, because this is to join battle with the wicked liberals on their own treacherous ground of what does or does not constitute social justice.

Then, Edwin Norman claims that Christianity has nothing to do with such social concepts or with inter-personal relations, but solely with such individual's relationship with God or Christ. So the guard and the victim standing at the door of the Auschwitz gas chamber are similar in that both represent, in different ways and in different degrees, the sinfulness of man, and both have to come to terms with their Creator. Such terms apparently do not include their immediate attitudes, conduct or relations to each other, the one as gasser and the other as gassee.

Again, Peregrine Worsthorne, if he so chooses, has a wonderful career ahead of him as leader-writer for *Pravda*. President Carter is clearly wicked and foolish to go on about human rights because there is (the title of Worsthorne's chapter) 'too much freedom'. Mr

Brezhnev would certainly agree that 'in any society, under any system, the majority has no choice but to be ruled by the minority... Any change in the nature of the minority is likely to be a change for the worse and...therefore the public must accept its subordinate role without any false promises about there being an Utopian escape from this fate.' This would merit the Order of Lenin first class.

So there it is. An undefended, unargued, almost deliberately irrational right-wingism, which eschews all 19th-century liberalism and has grave doubts about democracy. Perhaps the most interesting feature of the book is that it could have been written and published at all.

3.11 'Has social democracy failed in Britain?' (From *The Political Quarterly*, July–Sept. 1978, pp. 259–70)

It has often been said that the Labour Party in recent years has lacked books, theories, ideas of what it should be seeking in politics. The last major attempt to produce a theory of socialism appropriate to the post-war period was the late Tony Crosland's *The Future of Socialism* published in 1956.[1] He shared these ideas with his close friend, Hugh Gaitskell. Although Gaitskell was replaced as leader of the Labour Party by an opponent from the Left, Harold Wilson, for practical purposes Crosland's ideas continued to be almost unchallenged and dominated the Labour Governments of 1964–1970. After the 1970 defeat, there were attacks from a revived Left, though apart from Stuart Holland's book *The Socialist Challenge* (1975), these lacked a theoretical base. Much of the struggle was involved with pragmatic arguments over the Common Market. Yet despite this revival of a left-wing critique, the Labour Government which came into office in 1974 edged back towards a Croslandite position. By this time these views were being described as 'social democratic' in contrast to the unqualified socialism of the Left. When Mr Callaghan succeeded Mr Wilson in 1976, the social democrats felt discouraged and defeated. Their leader, Roy Jenkins, left British politics, but at the same time, if any ideas or policies could be said to have characterised Mr Callaghan's very matter-of-fact and cautious government, they were

---

[1] Crosland's views were set out over a period of time in the *New Fabian Essays*, ed. R H. S. Crossman (Hogarth Press, 1952), in this book and in *The Conservative Enemy*(Cape, 1962), and in *Socialism Now* (Cape, 1974), but this discussion concentrates on his views as set out in *The Future of Socialism* (Cape, 1956).

the continuation of an approach which Tony Crosland had set out in 1956. So any reappraisal of the theoretical basis in which the Labour Party has rested in the past 20 years must begin with and focus on a critique of Crosland's position.

Crosland had two objectives in his book, a negative and a positive. The negative one was to bring out the widespread but rather vague Marxist ideas which underlay much thinking in the Labour Party and to refute these ideas or rather to argue that they were totally out of date. The positive idea was to assert rather than demonstrate the moral objections to a class-divided society, to identify the root causes of these social evils and to indicate the kind of programme a Labour Government could pursue in order to remove these defects.

On the negative analysis, Crosland argued that the idea that capitalism was about to collapse was nonsense. He was writing at a time when the average annual growth rate was 3 per cent and when Mr R. A. Butler, speaking in 1954, could confidently forecast that the standard of living in Britain would double in 25 years. He said that the Marxist doctrine that the rich would get richer and the bulk of the population poorer till a crisis took place was manifest rubbish. He pointed out that public ownership, which was supposed to cut down the number of those living on profits and thus diminish the class system, did not have this effect whatever its other merits. In general, capitalism no longer had the confidence and the political power it had enjoyed before the Second World War. The climate of opinion had altered. Keynes had shown how a mixed economy could be changed in the public interest, trade union power had grown at the expense of the management, and industry knew it had to justify its conduct in terms that the public could appreciate or it would be subjected to increasing public regulation. This was basically the old doctrine that political democracy gave the people enough power to ensure that private industry met public needs together with the point that public ownership of itself did not alter class attitudes and divisions in a society which had these divisions built into its attitudes and institutions.

So the achievements of the 1945–51 Labour Government had had real value because they had demonstrated the power of democracy, its capacity to overcome private capitalism and to set up welfare schemes, a national health service and other forms of redistribution which reduced poverty and increased equality of opportunity. But all this had not ended class divisions in Britain. The society, though more egalitarian and more inclined to produce social justice, still contained gaps in people's understanding of each other which did not occur in more social democratic societies such as those in Scandinavia or even in the United States. Crosland says relatively little about this, but his main objective was to produce a situation where professors and plumbers, bankers and bakers, lived on the same street, could mix freely and unselfconsciously and enjoy the same holidays and sports, and have the same pensions while their children mixed freely in the same schools.

When he turned to the reason why the Attlee Government's nationalisation measures had not produced bigger strides in this direction and why, even in the United States, class divisions were not so pronounced, Crosland focused on social rather than economic causes. He concentrated on what he calls 'distance factors'. The four main ones were the education system in Britain, the differences in income and therefore in patterns of consumption, the unequal ownership of wealth and the different treatment of workers and of managers in industry. Of these, the most important was education. He wrote that 'the school system in Britain remains the most divisive, unjust and wasteful of all the aspects of social inequality'. Also he developed the old doctrine of marginal utility and pointed out that for a few to have cars and for the bulk of the community to be without creates much greater gaps than for all people to have cars but for some to have two cars. As he put it, 'the higher the level of average income, the more equal is the visible pattern of consumption' and this matters in societies where consumption is an indicator of social status and of personal happiness. Not only must visible consumption patterns be made more equal, but one of the root causes of differences which must be tackled is the unequal distribution of wealth. Crosland argues that further attempts to redistribute income from work will have relatively little effect in terms of well-being and could damage incentives, but there is no similar argument in favour of gross differences in the ownership of wealth. Finally, he focuses on differences of treatment in industry. He considers that this is not easily influenced by legislation but much more can be done by trade union action and he wants the unions to press for 'the equalisation of non-wage privileges, the spread of effective consultation, and high-level democracy at the national and industry level'.

This, then, is the revisionist or Croslandite programme for the Labour Party. Hugh Gaitskell carried it to an extreme and explicit level when he sought to cut Clause Four, the commitment to the public ownership of the means of production, distribution and exchange out of the Labour Party's constitution and when he even contemplated ending class war overtones by removing the word 'Labour' from the title of the Party. But the idea that public ownership, while a useful technique in particular cases, was no longer an effective overall solvent of both economic failings and of social divisions was, in effect, adopted by the Party. Harold Wilson lunching with John Janov of the *Daily Express* in the late 1950s said that Harold Macmillan was brilliant, for he talked about Empire while leading the Tories away from any commitment to imperial policies. Wilson said, 'It is my ambition to do the same for the Labour Party over public ownership'; and Labour went into the 1964 and 1966 General Elections with only one measure of nationalisation in its programme and that was the old one, left over from the Attlee Government, the commitment to take over the iron and steel industry.

So this philosophy produced the programme on which Labour fought the 1964 and 1966 elections. There was to be a small increase in public ownership but the attack on class injustices was to come from comprehensive schools, progressive attempts to equalise wealth, better working conditions and a higher social usage. Here Professor Galbraith's work, *The Affluent Society*, added emphasis to Crosland's analysis that increased public expenditure could build up the social wage of the less privileged and make a major difference in reducing inequality. All this rested on the assumption that a successful mixed economy would produce a level of growth which would facilitate these changes in that increasing public expenditure and the real wages of the less well-off would be possible without the acute tension involved in reducing the standard of living of other groups.

This, then, was the programme which the subsequent Labour Governments tried to carry through. Without going into elaborate details, it is clear that in some senses the programme was a failure. Fourteen years later, the kind of class divisions that Crosland objected to may have diminished a little but no more, and his ideal of a more egalitarian society is not markedly nearer. The Wilson administrations of 1964–70 and 1974–76 have not left behind a change in British society to match the achievements of the two previous left-of-centre governments of this century: the Liberal Government elected in 1906 or the Labour Government of 1945. The question is, why should this be? Was there a failing in Crosland's analysis?

The criticisms of his views have come from three directions. There has been a left-wing criticism of his position which argues that the original socialist or Marxist analysis was correct. Anthony Arblaster has set out this case in his article 'Anthony Crosland: Labour's Last

Revisionist?'[2] and similar arguments are put in Stuart Holland's book.[3] Then there is the right-wing attack, not so much on Crosland's objectives but on the possibility of carrying out his programme without crippling the economy or producing both a disastrous inflation and a lapse into authoritarian policies.[4] Finally, there is the cogent criticism of the actual experience of recent years: that the programme does not appear to have worked. So, all in all, Crosland's adherents are on the defensive in the Labour Party, some have left politics, and those who remain are unclear about which way to turn.

Taking the Marxist criticism first, the core of the case is that Crosland underestimated the power of capitalism. His thesis that it could be curbed and altered by the modern democratic state machine backed by public opinion was wrong. Stuart Holland argues that the multi-national corporations bend governments to their will and make nonsense of their economic policies. Anthony Arblaster recalls that the 1965 National Plan did not *order* private firms to achieve certain targets but *asked* them to state their own targets. He cites the tenfold increase in assistance to private firms from £80 million a year in 1964–65 to £884 million in 1970–71, the offer of £100 million a year in the form of the Regional Employment Premium to go to the regions of higher unemployment, the 'abject collapse' in December 1975 in the face of Chrysler's threat to close down in Britain, and the 'negotiations' between Crossman and the Building Societies, all there as evidence that Labour Governments or any governments could not impose their will on the private corporation. 'The power of private enterprise – of capitalism in face – remains far greater than Crosland was ever willing to admit, while the power of the state to control capitalism is correspondingly far less than he supposed.' Hence the need to abandon revisionism and return to a full-blooded policy of public ownership.

The problem about this critique is that facts mean different things to different people. The tenfold increase in government aid to industry is cited by Arblaster as evidence of industry's power over government, but it is the power of the drowning man to compel people to dive in to the waves to save him. If he can seriously believe that Upper Clyde Shipbuilders, British Leyland and Rolls Royce engineered their own bankruptcy in order to demonstrate their

---

[2] *The Political Quarterly* (October – December 1977).
[3] *The Socialist Challenge* (Quartet Books, 1975).
[4] See for example Emeff Tyrell, Jnr. (ed.), *The Future that Doesn't Work: Social Democracy's Failures in Britain* (Doubleday, 1977).

resilience and capacity to control British government, then credulity knows no bounds. If he thinks that governments can simply order private firms to invest or to move to certain parts of the country without providing any financial incentives, he is displaying the values and attitudes of Stalinism in what is still a free society. It is one thing to prohibit by law. It is another thing to expect people to engage in positive activities just because a government wants them to do so. By these criteria, Labour and other governments have been defied and defeated by the trade unions far more often and more clearly than they have been defied by the forces of private capital, yet the Marxists are not prepared to accept this point. The whole history of the 1974 social contract and the recent revelations of Mrs Thatcher's inquiry as to whether a Conservative Government could survive a confrontation with the unions shows that British politicians fear union power far more than they fear the power of capitalism.

In reality, this critique is quite misguided. The great weakness of Crosland's position was not that he underestimated the resilience of capitalism but that he over-estimated it. Throughout his book he, like Marxists, classical economists and Keynesians, assumes that the urge driving private people is so strong that they will perform in the economic field whatever the state does to them and whatever the social atmosphere. Crosland did realise that steeply progressive taxation can have an effect on incentives and he wanted to reduce taxes on income and increase taxes on wealth. But he considered that while socialist governments might reduce and circumscribe the private sector, it would still have sufficient internal dynamic and desire to expand, to continue investing and growing. He realised that profits are not evil but are a source of investment and that they must be maintained at a reasonable level. Crosland was writing in the 1950s when the mixed economy was vigorous and it was accepted from extreme Left to extreme Right that all that was needed to achieve certain results was for governments to turn on and off the tap, to ease or restrict the incentives to certain kinds of expansion. In fact, the chief weakness in Crosland's whole position is that the mixed economy has not shown this resilience. The public sector has been demoralised by constant government intervention; and the private sector has lost all confidence because its rewards and reputation have diminished and managers have preferred to play safe, to cut production, to hold back investment, to accept union domination and restrictive practices not as part of a capitalist plot to beat Labour Governments but out of sheer doubt about the future. The one thing academic economists, including Crosland, never appreciated was that when it became clearly

227

pleasanter and more remunerative to be a civil servant, a forecaster, an academic economist or a business consultant than to engage in actual production, then the mixed economy was in jeopardy.

The Right-wing attack mounted by writers such as Samuel Brittan and contributed to in a curious way by alleged Left-wingers such as Peter Jay in his days at *The Times* (he has a chapter in *The Future that Doesn't Work*) concentrates on the weakness of Keynesian methods of controlling the economy and on the impact of trade unions on labour costs. They do not challenge Crosland's ideals in terms of an egalitarian society. They argue that the monopoly power of the unions means that there will be a constant tendency to inflation. This can only be met by devaluation and the result, internally, must be an unacceptable redistribution of wealth from the weak to the strong, and, externally, a progressive decline in British standards of living compared with those of other industrial societies. One or two other critics then go on to say that the kind of public expenditure programmes advocated by Crosland are unsupportable and that the only remedy is a return to private purchase of services in large areas of health, education and housing which have so far been provided by the state.

Some of this criticism is clearly based on events, but it does not adequately consider the difference between British experience and that of other, similar countries. Just at the time when Gaitskell was taking Crosland's philosophy into the central policies of the Labour Party, the German SPD adopted much the same views in the Godesburg Programme. The question is why Germany under SPD leadership managed a 5 per cent growth rate and a relatively low level of inflation when neither were achieved by a Labour Government in Britain. Had there been this level of growth in the UK, the targets of the National Plan would have been met, the reductions in public expenditure enforced in 1966 and thereafter would have been unnecessary, the Labour Government would almost certainly have won the 1970 general election and the criticisms made of social democratic policies would have been mild or non-existent.

If, as Brittan argues, labour monopoly power must be met by monetarist policies or by what Peter Jay calls 'market socialism', this means running a level of unemployment sufficient to reduce the bargaining power of public sector unions and of unions in key industries which would be barely acceptable in societies which believe (rightly) that governments can control the level of unemployment. It was one thing in the nineteenth century to allow the immutable laws of economics to create mass unemployment, it is another to do so deliberately simply to meet right-wing economists' distaste for the laborious and tricky task of negotiating and enforcing sensible wages policies.

Leaving aside the two criticisms from Left and from Right and turning to the history of the period since 1964, why did these governments pursuing Croslandite policies fail? Why have they left no mark on British society comparable to that of the post-war Labour Government or the earlier Liberal Government elected in 1906? One point that must be noticed is that these two governments set out to achieve certain objectives which could be met by legislation. If, in the period before the First World War, a government decided to institute redistributive taxation, to finance old age pensions, sickness and unemployment insurance and to stop certain kinds of exploitation at work, all this could be done by legislation. Similarly, after 1945, the full Beveridge welfare plans, the National Health Service and the public ownership of certain industries were all open to enactment. The political opposition may have been bitter, the pressure groups may have resisted, but once the laws were carried through and complied with, the objective was achieved.

Crosland did not fully appreciate that his programme was different in proposing to alter social attitudes by means of economic and institutional changes when it is by no means clear that the latter will bring about the former. For instance, while a divided education system may intensify or feed class differences, it is not clear that a universal adoption of comprehensive schools will end such differences. Perhaps some comprehensive schools will be regarded as better than others or perhaps a society with such discrimination built into it will then concentrate on differences of occupation or accent. To tax away all inherited wealth may remove the source of 'distance' in Crosland's terms, but this may only lead to a concentration on income differences when he accepts that these must be maintained. Crosland emphasised the value of the social wage, but if taxation has to rise to a level that hits workers with under-average wages, it is possible that providing such a social wage or benefits may exacerbate class feelings and lead to attacks on some groups as 'scroungers'. Putting workers on boards of management may lead to an easier relationship between the two sides in industry. Trade union pressure may produce a reduction in discriminatory work practices. But it is also possible that workers on boards may simply start behaving like managers and that trade union pressure for an end to blue collar-white collar distinctions may only

229

lead to tension between the two sides in industry taking other forms.

A further and much more fundamental weakness of Crosland's policies was his assumption, typical of the 1950s, that growth could and would continue unabated. Significantly, he leaves the problem of running the economy to the last section of his book. He does not favour an incomes policy but thinks that the unions will usually behave with the necessary restraint. He considers the impact of higher taxation on wealth on the propensity to save, but concludes that institutional pressure to save will continue unabated; and also that similar corporate desires for higher output and better performance will keep up activity and investment in the private sector despite heavy taxation and the emphasis any Labour Government must place on public expenditure. In general, he thought that private industry was sufficiently confident and resilient to provide the motor power for innovation and growth; and he saw no great problem about the efficiency of the nationalised industries.

These basic assumptions have been proved wrong. But they also show how unsatisfactory the Left-wing criticism is and why it is driven to argue that capitalism has triumphed by pretending to drop dead. In reality, the building of a social atmosphere which regards profit as sordid and which suspects private enterprise has, over time, weakened and demoralised the private sector to the extent that it no longer provides the necessary growth to keep the whole economy moving. Private capital has preferred to go into property or overseas. The problem in regional and national investment policy was once thought to be a shortage of funds (hence the Development Agencies, IRC, NEB and so on). But this is not the case: it has been a shortage of projects, of industrialists with the confidence to expand. All this has led to a continued flow of talent into administration, academic life, the social services and the media, anywhere but into productive industry. The old theory that men would relentlessly pursue their own economic self-interest may contain some truth; but if society so constrains the private sector that it makes sense to take up salaried posts in local or central government or the professions then these same motives will diminish that area of economic activity.

The real weakness of Crosland was that he did not realise that the balance between the public and the private sectors in a mixed economy cannot be left to natural forces. His whole theoretical position rested on growth and growth is only feasible if there are clear criteria for the distribution of resources within the public sector and incentives for it to operate well; and also if there is some clear legitimacy attached to the private sector so that it feels it is doing a useful job for the nation, that there is some point in the work load and the risks involved. For growth, it is necessary also to produce a proper theory of the relations that should prevail between the public and private sectors and of the role of an incomes policy. Should the state enforce a 'voluntary' policy by refusing discretionary grants and contracts to blacklisted firms? Should nationalised industries be allowed to move into ancillary forms of profitable activity (like the Coal Board going into North Sea Oil) and should private firms be allowed to offer services in competition with the public sector? Crosland did not realise that a theory of socialism must be based on an economic theory capable of producing and maintaining the rate of growth essential if the rest of his programme was to work.

The second major weakness of Crosland's philosophy was his simple assumption that all the changes he wanted would enhance freedom. He was not really interested in political philosophy but he took it for granted that a uniform system of comprehensive schools, by encouraging social contact and reducing class tensions, would do nothing but enhance freedom. He did not accept the need for an incomes policy, so he did not have to face the problem of the freedom to bargain for wages as opposed to the reductions in freedom caused by enhanced, enforced inflation. He assumed that with growth the balance between private and public sectors would remain roughly constant and that no problems would arise over closed shops, the existence in some sectors of a single employer, the state, and of the sort of problems that arise in small, working class towns where there is only one landlord, the local council.

In reality, this is a serious issue and there is a trade-off between some forms of enforced egalitarianism and freedom which those taking Crosland's position have to consider and resolve. For instance, does equality mean that all children from the same area must go to one school, or that they should have a choice of schools but one which does not depend on their parents' wealth? Does equality mean that within one comprehensive school there should be no streaming according to ability or even no examinations? If so, does there come a point where the lack of any indicators of ability or effort militates against the working class child with no connections?

There are many such issues which Crosland did not consider. For instance, some wealth causes inequality; but if there is no inherited wealth and everyone depends on his or her job and if the bulk of well-paid jobs are in the hands of the state or its agencies, does this not produce a patronage state, the clientage system, with consequent reductions in independence and freedom? This whole question of freedom and independence as a positive value in a pluralist society was underplayed in the 1950s when both growth and personal liberty were assumed to be in no need of positive encouragement or preservation.

Does all this mean that Crosland's ideas, now labelled as social democracy, have failed and that they must be abandoned? The interesting fact is that the moral ideas for which he was striving have not been challenged; the argument has been about means of achieving these ends.

The Future of Socialism sets out a programme which was both too deep and too superficial. It was too deep in that it sought to alter aspects of British society which can and are changing but which may be too entrenched to be open to quick political solutions: governments, at least in democratic societies, must not attempt social engineering which is beyond their means, for to set impossible targets only leads to defeat and frustration. It was too superficial in that he did not realise the need for an underpinning of economic theory which justified and maintained a mixed economy nor did he realise that some of his policies could endanger as well as enhance freedom or individual liberty.

The criticisms must be mitigated, however, in that Tony Crosland and Hugh Gaitskell were both men of the 1940s and 1950s. They had seen governments tackle the horrendous problems of war with success, they believed in the sovereignty and efficacy of political action and they had no reason to doubt that the post-war economic expansion of Britain would continue indefinitely. They were chiefly concerned with adapting the inherited Left-wing views of the inter-war period to the realities of the 1950s. So it is perhaps hard to blame them for not foreseeing the full consequences of their policies in the changed circumstances of the 1960s and 1970s – though their policies helped to produce these changes.

So these flaws in their analysis remain. All that can be said is that their passion for social justice and their intellectual honesty still shine through their speeches and writings. If Crosland and Gaitskell were still alive today, they would have been the first to admit that their policies had not been fully successful. They would have struggled to rethink their case, to produce new programmes and to restore an element of idealism to Left-wing politics in Britain.

Part 4

Europe and the world

4.1 'Is Britain a European country?' (Unpublished lecture delivered to Vortrag Deutsch–Englische Gesellschaft, Nov. 1967)

The question of how far Britain is a European power is much more a matter of fact – the European aspect – than of sentiment. We all know that in matters of politics sentiment – especially a kind of backward-looking sentiment – is not difficult to conjure up. People tend in politics to appeal to memories, to old slogans, to situations which, however difficult they were in reality, can be talked about later on as the old glories of the past. This is a familiar trick of politicians of every country and every generation. The real point about Britain is that the European aspects are the factual aspects today. Our task is to build up a sentiment around these facts. For example, it is very interesting that the conversion to a European point of view has occurred to each political party at the time when it was in power. This is significant because it is when they are in power that political leaders have to deal with facts and as the Prime Minister and his colleagues have faced the problems of money, of technology, of foreign policy, they have come to realise how things stand. The reason why the Conservative Party declared officially for Europe before the Labour Party is simply that they were in power before the Labour Party.

What are the facts that have changed? What has altered? In order to give you a fair picture of this I would like to sketch in the old system as it applied to Britain, let us say seventy, eighty, even a hundred years ago. If you look at the old British pattern of politics, the British outlook on the world, it was first of all dependent on the fact that we had acquired – sometimes as the historians said, in a fit of absence of mind, sometimes intentionally – a large Empire, a large number of dominions, the dominions consisting of white settlers that had left Britain to live permanently in Canada, Australia, in parts of South Africa, while others went for periods of their lives to occupied areas, if you like, of India and Asia. Although on occasion this process was disliked by the British Government and at times these areas were annexed even contrary to the orders of the British Government, at other periods when the tide of imperialism was running strong, it was encouraged. One way or the other by the 1870s, '80s, '90s Britain had built up an Empire and we were, as most of you will remember from your history, in rivalry with the French Empire and with the German

Empire at that particular time. If you look at the books and the speeches of British politicians, they comforted themselves with the thought that though Britain was only small – we had only 45 million people while Bismarck's Germany had 70 million and the United States was shooting ahead with over a hundred million, Britain could add to the population of her own small islands the populations of the Empire and be comforted that even if a dozen black men counted as only one white man, we still outnumbered the inhabitants of our immediate European rivals.

British trading and financial relations followed the flag so we built up a world-wide trading connection, and over half of Britain's overseas trade was with areas directly under her political control all over the world. Following this went the financial set-up of sterling as an international trading currency, though sterling as a trading currency and the British banking system went further and penetrated areas not under one direct control. The Bank of London and South America, for instance, penetrated Argentina, Peru and Chile. The Bank of Hong Kong and China moved into China at a time when the European powers merely had concessions in China rather than political domination. In the end 30–40 per cent of the world's trade was being conducted in sterling.

This is a picture, if you like, of a Britain looking overseas to an Empire with a world-wide trading, financial and monetary connection. It is only natural that when such interests are at stake, the country's defensive system was built up to suit these interests and so Britain acquired a string of bases stretching through the Mediterranean, the Suez Canal, through the Indian Ocean into the Pacific and round South Africa. Britain arranged her army and navy to fit this which meant the maintenance of a small army ready to go, not to Europe, but to any part of the overseas Empire that was threatened. But the basic requirement was a large navy capable of keeping what we used to call 'the freedom of the seas' but which to other powers meant that Britain could do what she liked.

As you know, there is a curious way in which every country rationalises in its own national interests and creates an ethos out of them. I always remember shocking my students when they used to tell me, or point out to me, how much Germany spent on her army in the Bismarckian period, the period up to 1914. They would allege that Germany was a militaristic nation by pointing to the amount Germany spent on her army. I had to explain that Britain spent more on armaments every year throughout that period than Germany. In such calculations the old books always carefully forgot to count the expenditure on the navy which was our first line of defence. If anybody said, 'Is Britain a militaristic nation?' the answer was, 'No, we have a tiny army', omitting to notice our sensible – according to us – defensive maxim that the British navy must be stronger than the next two biggest navies in the world put together.

This explains Britain's defensive arrangements, financial and trading arrangements. As you can imagine, Britain's personal connections followed the same pattern and you can see this in every family in Britain. If I go back to my grandmother's and grandfather's house on a small island off the west coast of Scotland, a very small farmhouse, and look at the pictures on the wall of the local football team, all healthy looking boys taken in 1908 or 1909 and say, 'What happened to all the men?' (because the area is derelict now and there is nobody living there), 'Well, Charlie went to Australia, so-and-so went to Canada, so-and-so came back and died in the First World War, while this man drank too much so we gave him a one-way ticket to South Africa.' Not one of them produced a family or lived in Britain – they died in the four corners of the British Empire. This personal connection has been repeated almost up to the last generation. I do not say the present generation because I cannot count myself as this but if you take my own personal history it was not unusual for someone of my age to be born in India and brought up there, that after training in Scotland I should obtain a degree in North America and that I should spend three years of my teaching life in British West Africa. It is also normal, I am afraid, that having spent fifteen years of my life out of Britain, I have never learned to speak a foreign language because all the places I have lived and worked have adopted the English language.

This, then, is the sort of personal pattern. If you add the personal, the defensive, the commercial, the political together and look at the impact this had on Britain's relations with Europe I think you will see why we had the particular relationship that did develop. The attitude of Britain was that her priorities were overseas priorities, this was where all her first interests lay. As a result our interest in Europe was seeing, and again we made a virtue of it as the British so often do, we made a virtue of the idea that Britain believed in a European balance, that is to say that no particular country should be dominant in Europe, the simple explanation being that a dominant country in Europe would then have been able to challenge Britain overseas. Therefore, when France for over a century and a half threatened to dominate Europe we allied with Prussia or with Austria, we put troops on the Elbe, as the Elder Pitt said, to see that we could do what we liked in Canada and India while the French were kept occupied in Europe.

After 1870–80, when the situation was reversed and we were more worried about German predominance in Europe, our chief interest was to prevent German dominance and therefore we allied with whatever power was ready to act as a counter-balance and this is the origin of the so-called special relationship with the United States. For most of the last fifty years, although the United States has never had a central interest in Europe, that country has appreciated that it would be contrary to its interests for one power hostile to the United States to dominate Europe. Britain therefore had an easy partner in seeing that neither Germany nor, in recent years, the Soviet Union dominated Europe in a sense hostile either to Britain or to the United States, hence, as I say, this doctrine that there is a special relationship between these two powers. It is a particularly European relationship because Britain and America have, in some senses, been rivals in the Pacific, in South East Asia over a number of years so it was primarily on Europe that the special relationship was based.

That was the situation up to ten or fifteen years ago. I would now like to go through with you the extent to which the facts have changed this pattern and then to look at the political implications.

In the first place, the Empire or as they were later called, the Dominions, have all either in the period between the wars or since the last war become independent. I do think it important to say this is not a sign of British decadence. It is a simple fact that Britain has to follow through the logic of her own democratic principles. We accept that it is right and proper that people should govern themselves. If we accept this doctrine then we cannot deny it to other nations and on this criterion India, Pakistan, Burma, Ceylon and then all the countries that we controlled in Africa established their independence. I was working in Africa at the time when Nigeria became independent. I think it was evident to anybody that a country that wished to retain its Empire could have done so. After all, whatever you think of Britain, we are a little stronger than Portugal and Portugal has managed to hang on to its Empire in Africa. Had Britain been prepared to use force, it would have been possible to retain imperial control but the logic of the principles for which Britain stood implied self-government in these countries and therefore self-government was achieved, perhaps in some cases faster than was necessary, but the guiding principle again was to go at the pace that the people in the country wanted or that their leaders wanted.

Having granted or permitted self-government to all these territories it was natural that they should formulate their own foreign policy, that they should build up their own connections. Take the old white colonies as an example. It is clear that Canada has her chief links with the United States in a North American context. It is clear that Australia and New Zealand are more interested in the South Pacific than in anything in Europe. Their chief threat, as they see it, is an expansionist China, their chief trade relations are moving to Japan, to the United States, while their particular close attachment with Britain has diminished and declined. It is still real and still important in many ways but it has been a declining connection. In the case of South Africa there has been a political quarrel which has intensified and speeded up the process, the quarrel of over how far Africans should be allowed to have equal political rights. As Britain has been committed to this ideologically over twenty, twenty-five, thirty years, we have been drawn into a quarrel with South Africa which has speeded the separation of that country from Britain.

What was true of the white areas of settlement has, of course, been equally true of India and of the African territories. I have watched this happen myself in the case of India, which I used to call 'home' at one time, and it has not been a question of the rejection of Britain, it has been a normal process of the Indians setting up their own international connections. When I was in Nigeria in 1961, the country had just become independent and I watched politicians saying: 'Up to now everything has gone to Britain, our students have gone to Britain, our trade has gone to Britain, but now that we are independent we do not repudiate this connection but we want other connections with Europe, with the United States, with Japan and with the Soviet Union.' Gradually, quite properly, the uppermost thought in the minds of these countries has been to consider what is in their own best interests. It has not always been to maintain the historic connection with Britain. The result has been that the former British Empire has moved off into various regional groupings, and as a result all the connections that I described to you have been weakened or broken down. For instance, British trade patterns have changed. As recently as 1945 over half our trade was with the Commonwealth; now under a quarter of our trade is with the same countries. On the other hand, looking at the areas of growth, British trade with the EEC countries has increased from 13 per cent in 1945–6 to over 20 per cent in 1966–7. In other ways our position has been changing in Britain as a result of these developments. Our defence patterns have altered to follow. We no longer need to maintain the old sea links and bases as a sole British responsibility; as the various countries have moved off they have undertaken their own defence or, I think more significantly, they have not wanted Britain to undertake their defence for them. As a result Britain has withdrawn her bases. We have given up bases in the Mediterranean, we have now given up the Aden base, we are shortly to give up the Singapore base. We have decided that we will play our part, as I think we should, in any United Nations' action anywhere in the world but it is no longer a special responsibility of Britain to look after the trade routes, the peace and security of these areas unless the people concerned ask us. We want to be in a position to help but it is not a special task of our country.

If you look at the personal patterns you will now find young men and women from Britain not emigrating in the numbers that they used to. If you go to Australia and New Zealand you now find a new generation growing up there who for the first time when they talk about 'home' do not mean Britain, they mean Australia and New Zealand. You find a growing separation of interest and a different attitude in that many young men and women from Britain will now volunteer to do service overseas, as we call it, (unpaid service overseas) but they volunteer to go to anywhere that needs them, be it the old French territories in Africa or the former British territories, be it parts that have never belonged to Europe, they are no longer specifically following a Commonwealth or imperial connection.

Add all this up and you will see how our foreign policy changes as it were, accordingly. We are no longer in Britain a power with a principal interest overseas. We are a power which is becoming once again European in its trade, European in its geography and I would like to suggest to you, European in its connections. Our young people are now travelling much more extensively in Europe, they are coming much more than they used to to European universities rather than going to Canada or the United States. You find that their knowledge of Europe is increasing as our trade, as our connections increase and with all this the idea that the fundamental task of British foreign policy was to keep the European powers balanced or to prevent anybody becoming predominant in Europe has, to some extent, declined. This is part of our problem. We do not want Europe dominated in a hostile sense by the Soviet Union. That remains. But we are no longer particularly concerned to see that Germany or France does not dominate Europe. Indeed we feel a part of Europe and worried by domination by either of the super powers, the United States or the Soviet Union, each of which could threaten our independence.

This is the new pattern that has been developing and before I trace it you may ask, 'Well, what effect has this had on internal British politics? How far has the development I have described been accepted by British politicians?' Here again – and this is very interesting because it cuts across both parties – the conservative members (with a small 'c') in both big parties still tend to look backwards, especially the older men. They have formed their ideas twenty, thirty, forty years ago and it is hard for them to change. So you will find a small minority of people in the Conservative Party who still want Britain to be particularly interested in her Commonwealth responsibilities, who want Britain to maintain an aircraft carrier force so that we can go to help a Commonwealth country in difficulties, who still talk about this. But inside the Conservative Party this is a small minority, a very small minority and a rapidly dwindling one. Inside the Labour Party I should say the minority is a little bigger. Oddly enough this minority consists of people who in their youth fought British imperialism. They are often people who were personal friends of Gandhi and Nehru in India; they are the people who demonstrated when Nkrumah was put into prison; they are the people who regarded the British rulers of the Commonwealth as the same class enemies as they were facing inside Britain and who forged links of sentiment and friendship with African nationalists and with Asian nationalists. They are often connected with the missionary movement in the Church of Scotland and the English Church. They want to do everything they can to build up a viable democracy in Africa and in India and they are frightened that too close association with Europe will diminish this, will take our eyes off these old responsibilities which they still feel and which they want to maintain. Again, this is a minority in the Labour Party and a dwindling one. I was interested, as a result of our efforts, to see at the Labour Party Conference in 1967 that a vast majority of the Labour Party supported the European idea. . . .

If you look at the positive side, who is pro-European in Britain? Who is changing with the times? Again, this is quite interesting. The people who are changing with the times are people who are facing the facts and these are people in charge of Britain's industry, Britain's defence and Britain's foreign affairs. The people who are pro-European are the Foreign Office, the leaders of British industry, the leaders (interestingly enough) of the British trade union movement, barring a few men, most prominently Frank Cousins. The rest of them have come round to the idea that Britain's future now lies with Europe. The press – apart from the Beaverbrook press – is wholeheartedly pro -Europe and, most interesting and significant, so are the youth, the students, the young people who travel for their holidays. These young people are excited by the idea of international understanding, they want to see a federal union built up in Europe because it is an international concept, it suggests an attempt to remove war, to remove bloodshed, to bring people together, and for this younger generation, the old national appeals are not so potent. This is what is happening. There is a change in Britain's trade, in Britain's defence, in Britain's attitude, in Britain's personal connections, realising in every case the country is reverting to what it was until 1750 – a European power of the same status as France, Germany, the Netherlands, existing in a community with which Britain has more in common than with overseas areas with which there were so many connections in the imperial period.

I would like to conclude by taking a trip back to the points I made at the beginning of my lecture because it is interesting and important for people in Britain when they say, 'Is Britain a European Country?', to ask what they actually mean by European? What sort of a Europe would Britain hope to be a part of? Here I think it is important for us and for you to stress that Europe is not just a commercial union in the EEC. This is only a minor part of the whole process and yet I have difficulty in convincing some of my European friends that Britain has not turned to the EEC preponderantly because of a marginal advantage this would confer in selling washing machines in Düsseldorf; this is not the objective of the exercise. It is a far more fundamental change of orientation – political, personal, strategic as well as economic. What is exciting at the moment is that it is not yet absolutely clear what kind of a Europe Britain is intending or hoping to join. Here I think we have an important task as Europeans during the time when Britain and the other EFTA countries come into Europe to work out the future pattern of European connections. What is Europe going to be? You will find at the moment, as I am sure you all appreciate, a lot of changes going on, a lot of very difficult, paradoxical changes.

For instance, it is a primary concern of Germans that Germany is divided and you wish, and I think rightly, to reunite Germany. You wish particularly that the East Germans should be free to express themselves. I think this is not purely a German interest, it is a European interest. It is an interest that any country joining Europe ought to share with you and we should all be thinking collectively about how to solve this and the other major European problems. For instance there is this difficulty that I believe, and I think a lot of Europeans believe with me, that one cannot at this particular juncture ask the United States to leave Europe. Thus in part, Europe's stability depends and has depended since the Cuban crisis on a balance of fear, if you like, a balance of power between the Soviet Union and the United States and the reason why Europe has had a détente has been that these two super powers realise what damage they can do to each other. So we are in the paradoxical situation of wanting to move out of this situation, to create a Europe dependent on neither major power while we have to retain an element of dependence until we have achieved our objective. . . .

These considerations link up with another problem, the problem of détente between East and West. It is clearly very important that we spread freedom into East Europe. Germany has paved the way for this by her commercial treaty, her exchange of representatives with Rumania, with her commercial treaty with Czechoslovakia, with the talks that have gone on with Hungary and Bulgaria. But while it is relatively easy for Germany to re-establish relations with the South-East of Europe it is a much tougher job to spread this view among the countries of North-Eastern Europe which have the traditional fear of Germany, particularly of course Poland. Here I welcome General de Gaulle's idea of a Europe from the Atlantic to the Urals. The only problem I think is that I am not so sure whether anybody other than the General attaches great significance to his powers in this matter and I only hope he is right because I would like to see a Europe free of both alliance systems. My own feeling, again, is that if a Europe includes Britain and is tightly bound up – not just economically, but institutionally – within the EEC it is much easier to convince East Europeans that this kind of a Europe including Britain, France, Germany, Italy and the Netherlands is not interested in a policy of revenge, is not interested in the old 'Drang nach Osten' that we all heard about. Similarly, of course, it is easy to convince certain elements in France that there is no danger of a Rappallo policy – a policy which is always a card open to certain people to play so long as we do not have a united, democratic Western Europe, so long as Central Europe could go to the East as well as remaining with the West.

I hope therefore that I have convinced you that there are a number of problems which are not economic but political, which we want to solve as Europeans, which the British, as members of Europe, can contribute to. And the final of these problems which I want to put to you and which I think in the long-term is the most important is our relations with the United States. I want to be careful here because I am not anti-American and never have been. I am happy to have taught in an American university, I enjoy the company of Americans, I value what they have done for Europe since the Second World War, I value their contribution to NATO *but* I do seriously view with alarm

243

the possibility which is now quite genuine that over the next ten or fifteen years American investments in Western Europe will mean that there will be three major powers in the world – the Soviet Union, the United States and American investment in Europe. . . .

I believe that Europe must have an element of self-control, self-determination in matters of defence, in economic matters, in political matters. If we join together to build aeroplanes, if we join together in electronics and technology there is now no fear that France will dominate Britain or that Britain will dominate Germany. We simply could not dominate each other. It will have to be a partnership, but there is a serious danger that separately we may all, whatever General de Gaulle says, be dominated in the last resort by the United States. Therefore I feel in a certain deep sense that I am a European nationalist in that I want to create an entity in Western Europe which will be capable of running its own politics, of maintaining its own defensive forces, of standing independent of the United States and the Soviet Union. I feel we can do this together if Britain is accepted as a part of Europe. But if it is decided that in some sense Britain is not a European country and if Europe rejects Britain I think it will be a serious set-back for all of us.

4.2 'The battle for entry' (Speech in House of Commons debate on entry into the European Communities, 27 Oct. 1971)

The two most impressive anti-Market speeches that I have heard in the debate – and I refer to them because I feel that it is proper to take on one's opponents – have been, on the Conservative side, that of the Right Hon. Member for Taunton (Mr du Cann) and, on this side, that of my Hon. Friend the Member for Ebbw Vale (Mr Michael Foot).

The interesting thing was that both picked on one major objection, as they thought, to entry to the Common Market, which was, my Hon. Friend said, the derogation of the sovereignty of this Parliament and this country. What is amazing to me is the 19th-century concept of sovereignty being put forward by those two speakers and the many others who agree with them. They have a purely legalistic concept of sovereignty, like an old lady with a basket of apples, who feels that each time she gives a bit of sovereignty in the form of an apple to someone else there is one less in her basket. What a very restricted and oldfashioned concept of sovereignty!

The real point is that no nation has untramelled sovereignty, no nation has complete power to do as it likes, and what matters to the public is not the legal power to act but whether the consequences may mean anything.

I shall give some quick examples, starting with sterling. We in this Parliament have the sovereign power to regulate many things in connection with sterling as a currency, its control and the rates of exchange at which we offer to trade in sterling. If other forces outside the country result in a serious run on our sterling reserves we cannot continue to operate the system; we do not have the sovereignty to carry out economic policies through to the conclusion that our people want. Then the politicians must find the bodies or individuals who have taken that sovereignty away from us, and we turn and blame groups such as the gnomes of Zurich and international speculators. But if instead our legislators deliberately give sovereignty away and share it in an agreement at Basle with a number of other nations so to regulate a reserve currency that Britain's trading objectives can be achieved, then they have conceded some sovereignty to the nations with which they have had to discuss the question. But out of this they can show that they are producing the achievement of solid trading results and stable employment, which was the objective of the sovereignty originally held by this country alone. So the decision to join with the other powers was not in fact a derogation or loss of sovereignty; it was in reality an increase in the effective power of this House.

Another example is the recent successful international negotiation in which we took part, resulting in the agreement on Berlin. That was done by working completely with the other nations involved – America, Germany, and France – in the Committee of Four operating together from Bonn in dealings with the Soviet Union. In that negotiation we pooled our sovereignty with three other nations, producing a result that we could not have achieved by ourselves. These two examples illustrate the correct approach to sovereignty in the modern situation.

When my Hon. Friend the Member for Ebbw Vale says that if we give away power over employment, regional policies, and wages and prices, people will condemn or look down on Parliament, he again has the wrong end of the stick. For years British politicians have told the public, 'We will do this for you and that for you. We will end stop-go. We will have full employment, and even cut prices at a stroke', but they have never delivered the goods. That is why people look down on Parliament. That is why the public are less and less interested – because the politicians cannot achieve what they set out to do.

Why, over a period of time, have successive Governments of both parties failed to achieve their economic objectives? Why have we counted for less in international affairs? Why have we depressed our public by a series of failures? I believe that it is because the context in which Britain is working is not adequate to the present circumstances.

There is something very symbolic and suggestive in the way in which Right Hon. and Hon. Members of the extreme Conservative type oppose entry on the grounds that Britain should remain as it is and always has been, keeping the little sovereignty that it has clutched tightly to its bosom, and the fact that the people with whom they find themselves in closest agreement are those on the Left-wing of the Labour Party. These Left-wing Members dislike Right-wing Conservatives because of their authority and property and power, but want to alter the situation in a traditional fashion, using British sovereignty through the machinery of Parliament, taking things away from an existing class structure which these two groups of Members have both, at different ends of the social scale, known and grown up with. These widely separated elements each want to nurse the class structure and attitudes to their bosom and go on living in the same political relationship with each other that they were familiar with in childhood.

There is, I regret to say, a type of conservative with a small 'c' in the party to which I belong and when we approach change – radical change – in a radical attempt to grapple with the problems of this country, there is a negative response from the Right-wing and Left-wing forces of our society which wish to retain the *status quo*.

We are beginning for the first time to counter these attitudes by attempting a major change in the direction of this country. If one looks at the arguments and reads right through the debate in July and this debate, one finds that speeches of the pro-Marketeers have a background of appreciation that Britain had a Commonwealth and an Empire and that this relationship is declining and disappearing. We had a worldwide defence, trade and currency network but in every case we have begun the retreat and draw back.

We are becoming, without joining, more European in defence and trade interests of all kinds. The act of joining the EEC is a further and major step along the road on which we are already going. It is one which will allow us to turn the corner and look forward to a pattern of politics and economic activity which would give the country a new sense of purpose and an opportunity to tackle problems it has failed to grapple with in the past 20 years. It is more than just signing the Treaty of Rome; it is a broad change of direction.

246

I deeply respect the views of the anti-Marketeers but their speeches have shown no overall philosophy, only a discrete group of fears. They are fearful people, fearful that they cannot adopt a brand of Socialism involving a wide extension of public ownership and physical controls. They fear that the regions will suffer and that it will not be possible to steer the extra growth engendered by a wider market in the right direction towards the regions. They fear contamination with what they regard as a less satisfactory attitude towards the third world, and they fear that British industry will be incapable of taking advantage of the wider opportunities in the Common Market. And as each one of these fears is answered, they fall back on others because the fundamental point is that they are worried about change.

It was summed up for me in a sentence in the *New Statesman* which in a leading article said that the case for entering the Common Market was not proven because one could not prove that all the people in this country would benefit. But if one had to prove that every major change would produce a guaranteed benefit for all sections we should still be running round in the jungle as primitive tribesmen. Now we face a real chance to take a major step forward. I do not take the view that British entry into the Common Market is a panacea, nor of itself a major change, but it is a small sign that we are prepared to change, prepared to move.

I greeted only a few hours ago two friends who had come to hear this debate: an American I knew at Oxford and a German correspondent of the equivalent of the *Financial Times* in Germany. Both said how pleasant it was to return to Britain, because it never changed. In this debate they heard the same arguments; London was the same place with the same atmosphere.

But if one goes to Europe one finds that the startling thing is how much those countries have changed and how much they are moving forward. We want to end our stagnation and move forward, too. If we do not take this step and get the consequential legislation it will not be a disaster, but we shall be stuck in the rut that we have been in for the last 15–20 years. If we make this change we can go purposefully forward along this path more rapidly.

It is as silly to talk about joining a Social Democratic Europe as it is to talk about a totally Conservative Europe. If we go in under Labour leadership we shall try to work for a more egalitarian society in this country, and if we go in under a Conservative leadership we shall go for a more stratified, incentive-conscious society, with higher rewards and greater gaps. But, to whichever party we belong, we shall not get change or an advance unless we turn this corner and join the EEC. It is because I regard this as an important step in the history of our country, an act of symbolic importance as well as one which makes many further changes possible, that I have stayed until 6.30 a.m. to contribute to the debate, and why I shall vote in favour of entry later today. It will be a small act in a small and insignificant public career; yet my affirmative vote will be one of the things that will give me the greatest pleasure in my life.

4.3 'The impotence of ignorance' (From *The Scotsman*, 1 March 1976)

It is hard to know how British politicians can be brought to take an informed and sustained interest in foreign affairs. Perhaps this country has always been insular over these matters. Stanley Baldwin said he did not understand foreign policy and asked a Cabinet colleague to wake him up when this item on the agenda was past.

The lack of informed attention is serious now because 30 years of peace between the major Powers has led many to think this is normal and almost inevitable; that no effort is required to maintain this situation. What emphasises the need for some concern is that for the first time since the war there is a really ineffective President of the United States and even he will be immobilised from now till November by the protracted struggle for nomination and re-election to the Presidency.

Last week's debate on foreign affairs in the House of Commons was a derelict occasion. Active interest seems to be reduced to issues like the cod war and what to do with the Falkland Islands. Part of the trouble is that there has been no steady elaboration of the case for preserving overall political and military balance. In fact, the stability of post-war politics has rested on the maintenance of a clear balance between East and West in central Europe. Is there anything that could disrupt this situation?

Unfortunately, there are several possibilities. The first is that the United States might turn Gaullist in the sense of reaching a direct understanding with the Soviet Union. While such an understanding (or detente) would not contemplate any forward movement of Russia's actual area of occupation in Europe, the reduction of American land forces could so reduce NATO as to expose the countries of Western Europe to much greater Soviet pressure on commercial deals and on tactical political issues such as the future of Berlin.

A second danger is that Left-wing political victories in Italy, Spain or even France could cast such doubt over NATO's southern flank as to make the alliance ineffective, and this in turn might encourage the United States to safeguard its position by direct dealing with Moscow.

A third possibility, particularly relevant in the case of Britain, would be that internal political pressures could so undermine the strength of individual nations' contribution to NATO as to weaken the credibility of the whole alliance. The Defence Sub-Committee of the House of Commons Select Committee on Expenditure has just published a report which does look at the central issue of British defence policy: are the existing forces capable of fulfilling their present obligations?

The answer is only just. A little more trouble in Northern Ireland, and detachment of forces to bolster Rhodesia (if this was thought necessary or desirable), or another of the recent series of 'defence cuts', and the Army would be hopelessly overstretched. Also there is the risk that the fighting edge of the existing troops could be blunted if there were any further economies. It is hard on our soldiers that the best equipment made in Britain is not for them but for sale to Iran and other oil-rich countries.

One of the reasons for the ineffectiveness of recent British policy has been that any worthwhile initiatives or coherent lines of action have to be pursued in common with the other nations of similar size and interest in NATO and in the EEC. This means that British leaders must have an intimate knowledge of relations among these Powers and of the responses likely in view of the domestic politics of these countries.

In fact, many British politicians are puzzled or confused by this requirement; their whole training has been so rooted in British domestic affairs.

To talk with Mr Callaghan about Britain's role in the European Community is to walk into a cloud of boredom and scepticism based on ignorance. But mention a method of defeating some Left-wing trade union candidate standing for election to the National Executive of the Labour Party and his face will light up, and he will plot the path ahead with zeal and animation.

Mrs Thatcher is in the same position. She understands every nuance of middle-class opposition to comprehensive schools and of the value of attacking the menace of international communism, but what line this country should take about direct elections to the European Parliament or the admission of Greece to the Community or what is likely to happen if the Italian Communists join the next coalition in that country, are all puzzling and rather suspect issues; why do they not just go away and leave us alone?

Dr William Wallace in his book on 'The Foreign Policy Process in Britain' tends to blame the Foreign Office for failures in recent years and wants the formation of the main lines of policy research for the Prime Minister and the Cabinet Office. In reality, the very opposite case has more strength. On the whole the Foreign Office has been right in recent policy arguments simply because it does know what is going on abroad and can estimate where British action could produce results. The office was correct about the need for Britain to join the Community; it was rightly opposed to the Suez invasion in 1956, and was also opposed to appeasement in the 1930s.

To bring policy-making back into the hands of officials and Ministers whose main attention is devoted to British domestic affairs would be to intensify the problem. It may, for example, have made sense in terms of English xenophobia and of the need to dish the Scottish Nationalists for Mr Callaghan to have demanded a separate British seat at the world energy conference. But it would have been better if he had consulted his Foreign Office officials and had taken their advice that such a demand would only lead to a humiliating rejection.

What is needed is clarity about Britain's basic objectives. For instance, it may cause difficulties if Rhodesia has increasing trouble with Angolan-based guerrillas, but it is hard to see such activity, even on a large scale, adversely affecting purely British interests in southern Africa. Any threat to the sea route round the Cape is far removed from raids along the Zambesi, and in any case affects many nations besides Britain. On the other hand, the collapse of NATO or the defection of a major Power in southern Europe to pro-Soviet policies would threaten the stability of an area of which we are an integral part.

For these reasons, Britain should devote itself to strengthening, in political terms, the NATO alliance and to the production of a common foreign policy in the European Community. To be able to join Chancellor Schmidt in working along these lines, this country needs to bolster its reduced economic and military strength by building a reputation for consistency, for being a reliable and effective European partner. It is important to capitalise on existing assets. For example, one that has been virtually thrown away was the European view that Britain would bring to the Community a greater knowledge of and belief in democratic practices.

Yet Britain, having voted overwhelmingly to remain a member, is now dragging its feet on direct elections to the European Parliament. It seems mistaken to alienate friends over this point purely because of party fears that European elections on the existing 'first past the post system' will make that system look foolish. The officials in Conservative Central Office and in Transport House have pointed out that if 67 European MPs are chosen in this way, five million Liberal votes could fail to produce a single Liberal European MP. Even worse, the system could mean that all six Scottish MPs in the European Parliament were Nationalists. If this seemed too foolish and proportional representation was introduced, they fear that it might prove to be the thin edge of the wedge leading to proportional representation at Westminster.

Considerations of this kind bulk far larger in the minds of politicians of both major parties than the advantages that might be gained from taking the lead not only in strengthening Community institutions but consequently in carrying the other Powers towards a common position on sharing the costs of American troops in Europe, over negotiations with the Soviet Union on force reductions and in the process of building the weaker nations of Southern Europe into the Community structure.

This country no longer has the sheer political and military weight which enabled us to act on our own, or at least to throw that weight about in international affairs. Much could still be done and needs to be done to look after our own essential interests in East-West stability and in international financial and trade negotiations, but this will only be possible when British leaders can move around in European politics with some of the knowledge and deftness which they show when dealing with the minutiae of British political life.

4.4 'Towards a closer union' (From *The Scotsman*, 17 July 1978)

Politicians, like most of us, judge a gift not only by its intrinsic merits but by the wrapping and the view one takes of the donor's motives. Twice in the last 11 years, Britain has had to go to the International Monetary Fund and ask for a huge loan to stabilise the value of sterling. On both occasions, the officials of the IMF came to Britain, went over the books and said that a loan, paid in instalments, was available provided the British Government would observe certain economic policies. The Chancellor of the Exchequer of the day then sent a 'letter of intent' promising to observe these guidelines and then the loan was paid bit by bit as these policies were applied.

Naturally Opposition politicians made some running on the claim that it required foreign pressure to get the Government to adopt sensible policies but few people said this was a shocking infringement of British sovereignty or that it took power away from Parliament. Moreover, under both the Wilson Government of 1964–70 and the subsequent Heath Government, leaders (notably Harold Lever and Heath himself) complained about the size of the sterling balances and about the fact that a run on sterling due to totally external factors could force this country into unsuitable economic policies simply to prop up the value of the pound.

On July 7, the leaders of the European Community, at their meeting in Bremen, proposed to set up a fund of £26,740 million to provide a reserve larger than that of the IMF, but available only for the nine EEC members. Its objective was to stabilise European currencies in relation to each other and in relation to the dollar, the only requirement being that the EEC countries worked together more closely over monetary policy and over exchange rate policy.

The two countries sponsoring the idea were France and Germany. On the face of it, this was what Britain had been calling for in or out of the Community for over a decade. Here were the richest members of the EEC offering to set up such a fund. As to Britain losing sovereignty by agreeing to work together over monetary and exchange rate policy, this is no more than the conditions imposed on us from time to time by the IMF and this body is far less close to Britain than our fellow members of the European Community.

Why then did Mr Callaghan hesitate, ask for time, complain that he had not been consulted adequately over the formulation of the plan, and so on? Part of the reason may have been political. The Prime Minister is basically an Atlanticist and he has always been sceptical about Europe, which is why the front line posts dealing with the EEC in his Government were given to such staunch anti-Marketeers as Silkin (Agriculture), Shore (Industry) and Benn (Energy). It might be hard for him, at this moment, to take a major step forward in European cooperation without some expressions of caution and anxiety.

But part of the resistance came from the Treasury, who have always been sceptical about the value of the Community and their arguments are more alarming. They pressed caution on the Prime Minister on the grounds that if a big fund stabilised the value of the pound against the mark and the franc and then the competitive capacity of British industry continued to decline, it would not be possible to offset this decline (or a higher rate of inflation or of wages settlements in Britain) by letting the pound slide down a little further. This assumption of a continued fall in our competitive capacity is deeply depressing and one cannot help feel that a monetary agreement that forces British industry to raise its quality of goods, its capacity to deliver on time and its sales methods is highly desirable.

Not only was the basic monthly plan something which Britain and Callaghan himself had called for in the past, but the Prime Minister also won further concessions. He got the members to agree that it was important for all the EEC countries to try to stimulate output and employment, he persuaded them that fixed exchange rates might require some transfer of resources to the weaker countries and he obtained an agreement to review certain aspects of the Common Agricultural Policy.

The lessons of the Bremen meeting are those the Community has had to face time and again. First there is the fact that the EEC was called into existence by the difficulty of a number of economically powerful countries in one small area of the world trying to run different policies. If Japan, Canada, the US and Europe cannot pursue separate and selfish policies without damaging each other, how much more is this true of European nations themselves.

Secondly there is the fact that the Community cannot stand still. Faced by challenges such as the 1973 world energy crisis, the current economic depression, the request for membership from Greece, Spain and Portugal or the need for more democratic authenticity (ie a European Parliament), it can only respond positively and become more integrated and effective or it can refuse to act and slip back into being a kind of customs union of nation states.

On the first point, it is now clear that having tried to speak with one voice in Middle Eastern affairs, there is no chance now of an Arab oil boycott being applied to certain selected members of the EEC. There is an agreement to pool resources and Europe is too important a market for any total boycott to be applied.

As regards the present serious recession, there was always the danger (and such voices are heard in other countries besides Britain) of a return to protectionism. Yet in their relations with each other, the member states have stuck to the free-trade principles on which the Community is based. Enlargement, which sceptics see as weakening the EEC, could well have the opposite effect. The three Mediterranean countries all indicated that a major reason for joining was to underpin their fragile democratic regimes.

A good example of how this could strengthen the Community arose in the case of Portugal. The Portuguese Government went to the IMF for a loan but the terms were so stringent that they threatened to bring about the collapse of the elected Government and a possible return to dictatorship. If the European reserve fund proposed at Bremen had been in existence, it could have helped with a far greater understanding of the importance to Europe of preserving democracy in Portugal.

Again, it has been said that with 12 members instead of nine, the decision-making machinery of the Community will grind to a halt. But it could also lead to a tacit acceptance of majority voting. Faced with the need for rapid action to meet the problems of enlargement, the larger Powers will again have to decide whether to go forward by giving up the unanimity rule or slip back into a loose assemblage of states. So far, in the end, they have always found it in their interests to keep the Community functioning and this means taking the positive step forward.

Now it is agreed that direct elections to the European Parliament will take place in 1979 and this will push the Community forward in two ways. First, the Parliament will say, quite rightly, that it speaks for European voters and it will seek to strengthen the Commission when the latter produces positive proposals and it will provide some counterpoise to the Council of Ministers with the latter's constant emphasis on separate national interests. Secondly, there will be a ground-force of European MPs whose task will be to explain what the Community is doing for their voters and to press for more action when they are in the Parliament.

Each Scottish MP who goes to Europe will represent the equivalent of nine Westminster constituencies and there will be plenty for him to do. For example, in my own constituency alone, the EEC has paid out over half a million pounds in grants to farmers' co-operatives, for building fishing boats and for improving the small industrial estates. The European MPs will have to advise their constituents as to how to make the most use of these funds, they will have to represent them in Brussels and then explain to the voters what has been achieved.

All in all, this recent recession and the Bremen proposals for a common reserve currency and for greater economic cooperation have been further proof of the inter-dependence of the European countries. Chancellor Schmidt is right that trade, output and employment cannot revive if firms do not know the value of the currency they will receive at the time of delivery of the goods. The result must be a measure of monetary union. This, together with the enlargement of the Community and the election of a European Parliament, all show that whatever degree of enthusiasm or caution the various members evince, the logic of events is slowly moving the Community in the direction of a confederation where many of the crucial economic and foreign policy decisions will have to be taken by the member states but acting through EEC institutions and for the benefit of the Community as a whole.

4.5 'The Afrikaner road to disaster' (From *The Times*, 19 June 1978)

Returning to South Africa for the first time since the 1976 riots and repression is a disturbing experience. For many visitors, South Africa is a land of sunshine, great natural beauty and a sense of physical plenty. But if one seeks out the political groups who matter, the Afrikaners who lead the Nationalist Party and what remains of the African leadership, the gulf is frightening.

Many people in the West imagine that the Afrikaners are another, larger, group of settlers who will, in the end, travel down the same road as Mr Smith and the Rhodesian whites. That is to say, it is expected that when the pressure gets strong enough the Afrikaners will ultimately agree to share power with the African majority. But this is not the case. These people believe in their mission in Africa. They trekked inland to set up their own white homeland. They fought the British empire at the zenith of its power and they are determined to stay the dominant force they became when the Nationalist Party won power in 1948.

The Afrikaners are untouched by nineteenth-century liberalism. They are a patriarchal society who believe in authority and in the superiority of their race and culture. One of them said to me: 'If you had seen the way our police shot down these African school kids in Soweto, you would have realized that the white man still has a future in South Africa.'

After Sharpeville, the Nationalist Government had a moment of doubt. But in 1976 when 600 teenagers were killed in Soweto, when similar riots were put down in other townships and the whole African leadership was imprisoned or banned, there was no such doubt or hesitation. A member of the Student Representative Council at the Rand Afrikaans University told me he had joined the paratroops reserve in his spare time. 'It will come to a shoot-out and I feel very positive about the result'.

On the other hand, I have never been looked at with such hatred and bitterness as that which I saw in the faces of the Africans in Soweto and among the students in the segregated blacks-only university.

255

It was no use talking about compromises or reconciliation; they knew the only hope was a transfer of power and realized that any progress in this direction would be at a tremendous cost.

These two groups are so far apart and there is so little contact that wild misunderstanding persists. The Afrikaners, at one level, talk of reforms and concessions. The most liberal are the businessmen and financiers, some of whom even keep cyclostyled lists of changes which they thrust into the hands of visitors. These include the abolition of most forms of social apartheid, job reservation and such distinctions. But when one asks the crucial question, 'Does this include any element of power-sharing?' the ranks close at once. At this point, the Afrikaners not only say 'no', they proclaim their readiness to fight.

There are some attempts to improve the desperate numerical imbalance of 4.3 million whites to 18.6 million blacks. One is to persist with the homelands policy. This was the idea that Africans could be made citizens of tribal areas which would be declared independent, leaving the Africans in white South Africa as merely transient aliens who would, it was hoped, be content to have no political rights.

But few Afrikaners now imagine that the policy will work. First, 18.6 million blacks cannot go back and live in homelands that comprise a mere 13 per cent of the surface area of the country. If the homelands were to be enlarged and consolidated, this would mean either buying out many white farmers at a cost which would be prohibitive or accepting the idea that white minorities could be ruled by black governments – which is unacceptable to the Afrikaner ideology. Meanwhile, all the movement of Africans is still from the underdeveloped homelands in the white industrialized cities.

The core of the problem is what to do with the detribalized urban African – and the heart of African political life is in Soweto, where over a million Africans live in an appalling, overcrowded, miserable ghetto. Even as an amelioration, the homelands policy is not doing what its Afrikaner originators hoped for. For instance, if these are independent territories, are their citizens to be treated as foreigners with exemption from white South Africa's race laws or are they just to be treated in the same way as South African blacks? Will the homeland of Lebowa be allowed to turn the apartheid black University of the North, situated on its land, into a free, open university?

Some of the homelands have behaved themselves so far, accepting Afrikaner civil servants on secondment and maintaining all the necessary subservience to Pretoria. But the way has been pointed – and doubts raised in Afrikaner minds – by the Transkei which, though in no way a liberal state, has severed diplomatic relations with South

Africa. Much more dangerous is the line taken by Chief Gatscha Buthelezi of Kwa Zulu, who shelters behind his position as a homeland premier to call for African political rights. Political parties are banned but he runs a Zulu culture organization which is open to all Africans – its pamphlets are printed in the colours of the banned African National Congress and its appeal is straightforwardly political.

With their doubts about the homeland policy, the Afrikaners have tried to ease their minority position in another way. They have talked of a constitutional reform which would give 'parliaments' to the 2.4 million Coloureds and the 700,000 Indians. These parliaments would link up with the whites in an overall Cabinet of seven whites, four Coloured and three Indian members, under a white president. This is an ingenious but very transparent piece of gerrymandering to ensure, first that the English-speaking minority of whites could never link up with the Coloureds and Indians to outvote the Afrikaners and, second, that the Afrikaner whites would stay in control of the tripartite Cabinet.

Even this clever attempt to boost the number of non-Africans to 7.4 million is unlikely to succeed, for though the better-off Indians and Coloureds are desperate to be received as honorary whites, the poorer, younger and more radical elements in both communities are determined to remain linked to the Africans so long as they are excluded from full and equal political rights – which the Afrikaners will not concede.

And while these improbable attempts to improve the Afrikaners' power base are tried, the sullen, bitter mass of Africans remains a brooding, ever-present force, crushed and largely leaderless, but never out of the whites' minds. Some Afrikaners talk of a moderate African leadership, but no such person could survive in a free election if they did not accept the basic principle of one man–one vote. Even this position is becoming submerged by the call for exclusive black power. The one or two pathetic figures produced by the present regime who talk of other things, of tribal homes and of accepting concessions on petty social regulations in lieu of political rights, count for nothing – and they know it.

So what will happen? The prospect is too awful to contemplate. If South West Africa and Rhodesia can be settled and South Africa dealt with free of international pressures, it will help a little. But the prospect is still one of continued tension, of occasional risings gunned down and an increasingly harsh police state which will continue to brutalize both oppressors and the oppressed.

Bibliography of the political and academic writings of John P. Mackintosh

Compiled by Anne Daltrop and Bernard Crick

1 Books

The British Cabinet (Stevens, London, 1962), pp. 546; 2nd edn, 1968; 2nd edn (paperback) Methuen 1968, pp. 651; 3rd edn Stevens, 1977; 3rd edn (paperback) Stevens, 1977, pp. 656

Nigerian Government and Politics (Allen and Unwin, London, 1966), pp. 651

The Devolution of Power: Local Democracy, Regionalism and Nationalism (Chatto & Windus and Charles Knight, London, 1968), pp. 207; Penguin Special 1968, pp. 207

The Government and Politics of Britain (Hutchinson, London, 1970), pp. 206, hardcover and paperback; 2nd edn, hardcover and paperback, 1971; 3rd edn, hardcover and paperback, 1974, pp. 224; 4th edn, hardcover and paperback, 1977, pp. 244

Editor, *British Prime Ministers*, 2 vols (Weidenfeld and Nicholson, London, 1977), contributing the 'Introduction', pp. 1–22, Vol. I, and 'Harold Wilson', Vol. II, pp. 171–215

2 Contributions to books

'Nigéria', in *Les Constitutions et Institutions des États Nouveaux* (Institut International des Civilisations Différentes, Bruxelles, 1965), pp. 181–206

'The Reform of Parliament', in Ben Whitaker (ed.), *A Radical Future* (Cape, London, 1967), pp. 36–55

'The Reform of the House of Commons: the case for Specialization', in Gerhard Loewenberg (ed.), *Modern Parliaments: Change or Decline?* (Aldine, Atherton, Chicago, 1971), pp. 33–63

Bibliography

'The Role of Parliament in an Open Society', in *Towards an Open Society*, being the proceeding of a seminar organised by the British Humanist Society (Pemberton Books, London, 1971), pp. 104–18

'Introduction' to John Oyinbo, *Nigeria: Crisis and Beyond* (Charles Knight, London, 1971), pp. vii–xxv

'Parliament Now and a Hundred Years Ago', in Dick Leonard and Valentine Herman (eds), *The Backbencher and Parliament* (Macmillan, London, 1972), pp. 244–58

Contributions to *The State of the Nation: Parliament* (Granada Television, London and Manchester, 1973), pp. 102–45 *passim* and 186–8

'The House of Commons and Taxation', in Bernard Crick and William A. Robson (eds), *Taxation Policy* (Penguin, London, 1973), pp. 137–52

'Taming the Barons', in *Reshaping Britain* (PEP Broadsheet No. 548, 1974)

'The Constitutional and Political Implications of the Referendum: In Retrospect', in *The Commonwealth Parliaments* (Lok Sabha Secretariat, New Delhi, 1975), pp. 224–32

'The Declining Respect for the Law', in Antony King (ed.), *Why Britain is Harder to Govern* (BBC Publications, London, 1976)

'The Problems of Devolution – the Scottish Case', in J. A. G. Griffith (ed.), *From Policy to Administration: Essays in Honour of William A. Robson* (Allen & Unwin, London, 1976), pp. 99–114

'Equality and Party Politics', a discussion with Geoffrey Howe, in John Vaizey (ed.), *Whatever Happened to Equality* (BBC Publications, London, 1976), pp. 47–60

'Kann die Sozialdemokratie sich neuen politischen Erfordernissen anpassen?', in *Kritischer Rationalismus und Sozial-demokratie 11* (Dieta, Berlin, 1976), pp. 235–54

'Communication and Politics', *The Art and Business of Communication* (Heriot-Watt University Lectures, 1976), pp. 15–32

'The Politician's View: the Perspective of a Member of the House of Commons in the UK', in W. R. Derrick Sewell and J. T. Coppock (eds), *Public Participation in Planning* (John Wiley, London, 1977), pp. 191–202

'Grossbritannien: Das Unterhaus – "Mutter" der Parliamente', in Claus Schöndube (ed.), *Die Parlamente der neun Eg-Staaten* (Bonn University, 1977), pp. 21–30

'Regions: La Fin du Centralisme', in *Dialogues Franco Britanniques* (Editions Mengès, Paris, 1978), pp. 33–7

Editor, *People and Parliament* (Saxon House and the Hansard Society, 1978), and contributing the Foreword, xi–xiii, pp. 75–83, 113–51, 171–83, 209–14

'Internal Procedure and Organisation', in Donald I. Mackay, *Scotland: the Framework for Change* (Paul Harris, Edinburgh, 1979), pp. 68–79

3 Evidence to Royal Commissions

Royal Commission on Local Government in Scotland, Written Evidence (HMSO, 1967), pp. 3–18, *Minutes of Evidence* (7 Feb. 1967), pp. 3–33

Commission on the Constitution, Written Evidence (HMSO, 1972), pp. 116–30

4 Pamphlets

With David Marquand MP and David Owen MP, 'Change Gear! Towards a Socialist Strategy', Supplement to *Socialist Commentary* (Oct. 1967)

'The Influence of the Backbencher, Now and a Hundred Years Ago' (Manchester Statistical Society, 11 Mar. 1970)

'Specialist Committees in the House of Commons: have they failed?', *Edinburgh University Occasional Papers*, no. 1 (April 1970)

A Parliament for Scotland (Berwick and East Lothian Labour Party, n.d.)

5 Lectures, papers and broadcast talks

'Devolution and the Political Parties: the Labour View', in *Devolution and the Media in the United Kingdom*, a report on a conference organized by The International Press Institute, (Edinburgh, 12 Nov. 1976)

Contributions from the Chair to a panel discussion 'The behaviour of political parties in the United Kingdom and in the Federal Republic of Germany and the development of the respective research and teaching disciplines in this field.' (DAAD-Forum, Bonn-Bad Godesberg 1977), *German Academic Exchange Service: London Office*, 1952-77, no. 9

Britain's Malaise – Political or Economic?, Fawley Foundation Lecture (University of Southampton, 1977)

'Political Pressures on Agriculture', *Report of the Twenty-Fifth Oxford Farming Conference* (Jan. 1971), pp. 39-53 (subsequently reprinted as Unit 14, Open University Course T 27B, Food Production Systems, Open University Press 1978)

'Europe Under Pressure', Opening session speech, *The Königswinter Conference 1974*, pp. 9-11

'The British Parliament', *European Integration and the Future of Parliaments in Europe* (European Parliament, Oct. 1975), pp. 156-68

'Scotland and Europe: Regionalism and Nationalism in the European Community', Lecture to Institut Royal des Relations Internationales (Brussels, 20 Oct. 1975)

'Communications and Politics', lecture to the Heriot-Watt University (18 Nov. 1975)

'The Labour Party and Decolonisation', Anglo-French Colloquium (Paris, 6 May 1976)

'National Perspectives – Britain', paper to Seminar on Direct Elections to European Parliament (LSE University Association for Contemporary European Studies)

Contributions to *Inside British Politics*, Norma Perey (ed.) (Granada Television, June 1977)

'European Law', paper given at Conference of the Law Society of Scotland (Edinburgh, 9 Feb. 1978)

'The Effect of Parliamentary Reform on the Regular Debates on the floor of the House of Commons', broadcast talk (BBC radio 3, 19 June 1978)

'Is there a crisis in British Parliamentary Government?' (no date)

'How far is Britain a democracy?', Earl Grey Memorial Lecture (no date)

6 Journal articles

1957–1959
'The Labour movement in Aberdeen', *Scottish Historical Review*, XXXVI, no. 1, April 1957, pp. 63–5

'The Scottish universities', (problems of Graduate Employment), *Universities and Left Review*, Spring 1957, pp. 60–2

'The early political influence of Queen Victoria 1837–52', *Parliamentary Affairs*, XII, no. 2, Spring 1959, pp. 174–88

1960–1969
'Scotland's development problems', *Scotland*, Jan. 1960, pp. 40–2

'Should there be a fifth university in Scotland?', *University of Edinburgh Journal*, Spring 1961, pp. 67–8

'Role of the Committee of Imperial Defence before 1914', *English Historical Review*, LXXVII, no. ccciv, July 1962, pp. 490–503

'Federalism in Nigeria', *Political Studies*, X, no. 3, Oct. 1962, pp. 223–47

'Electoral trends and the tendency to a one party system in Nigeria', *Journal of Commonwealth Political Studies*, **1**, no. 3, Nov. 1962, pp. 194–210

'Politics in Nigeria: the action group crisis of 1962', *Political Studies*, XI, no. 2, June 1963, pp. 126–55

'The Nigerian Federal Parliament', *Public Law*, Autumn 1963, pp. 333–61

'Devolution, regionalism and the reform of local government: the Scottish case', *Public Law*, Spring 1964, pp. 19–32

Bibliography

'Nigeria since independence', *The World Today*, Aug. 1964, pp. 328–37

'Regional administration: has it worked in Scotland?', *Public Administration*, Autumn 1964, pp. 253–75

'Nigeria's external relations', *Journal of Commonwealth Political Studies*, **11**, no. 3, Nov. 1964, pp. 207–18

'A passion for politics', *Twentieth Century*, second quarter 1967

'Is Britain a European country?', *Deutsch–Englische Gesellschaft E.V.*, Nov. 1967

'Scottish nationalism', *The Political Quarterly*, **38**, no. 4, Oct. – Dec. 1967, pp. 389–402

'Cure for a chronic Scottish malaise', *Scotland*, Nov. 1967, pp. 52–5

'Power of Parliament', *The New Christian*, 2 Nov. 1967, p. 6

'A bed of thistles', *Socialist Commentary*, Dec. 1967, pp. 11–12

'The Prime Minister and the Cabinet', *Parliamentary Affairs*, XXI, no. 1, Winter 1967/8, pp. 53–68

'Forty years on?', *The Political Quarterly*, **39**, no. 1, Jan–Mar. 1968

'What is wrong with British parliamentary democracy?', *Westminster Bank Review*, May 1968

'Britain in Europe: historical perspective and contemporary reality', *International Affairs*, **45**, no. 2, April 1969, pp. 246–58

'Political methods of agricultural development', pts. 1 & 2, *Journal of the Farmers Club*, Nov., Dec. 1969 (with J. E. B. Hill, MP and Prof H. T. Williams)

1970–1973
'The problems of agricultural politics', *Journal of Agricultural Economics*, XXI, no. 1, Jan. 1970, pp. 23–30

'Specialist committees in the House of Commons: have they failed?', Waverly Papers: European Political Studies series, 1, 1970

'The Royal Commission on Local Government in Scotland, 1966–69', *Public Administration*, Spring 1970, pp. 49–56

'Agricultural politics', *Public Affairs*, *Léargus*, Feb. 1970, pp. 5–9

'The House of Commons and taxation', *The Political Quarterly*, **42**, no. 1, Jan. – March 1971, pp. 75–86

'A new Government: the Tories dash for freedom', *The Round Table: The Commonwealth Journal of International Affairs*, Jan. 1971, pp. 161–6

'The Member of Parliament as representative or as delegate', *The Parliamentarian*, Jan. 1971

'Report of the Review Body on Local Government in Northern Ireland 1970: The Macrory Report', *Public Administration*, Spring 1971, pp. 13–24

'It is more dangerous to remain outside . . . the effects of EEC entry on Scottish interests', *Scotland*, June 1971, pp. 18–22

'The problems of the Labour Party', *The Political Quarterly*, **43**, no. 1, Jan. – March 1972, pp. 2–18

'Gemeinsame europäische Aussenpolitike', *Europa Archiv*, June 1972, pp. 365–76

'Socialism or social democracy? The choice for the Labour Party?', *The Political Quarterly*, **43**, no. 4, Oct. – Dec. 1972

'Anybody still for democracy?', *Encounter*, Nov. 1972, pp. 19–27

'The institutions of the Common Market: a British view', *The Round Table: The Commonwealth Journal of International Affairs*, Jan. 1973 pp. 23–38

1974–1975
'The report of the Royal Commission on the constitution', *The Political Quarterly*, **45**, no. 1, Jan.–March 1974, pp. 115–24

'The stark alternatives', *New Outlook*, 1974, nos 7 & 8, pp. 7–22

'Whatever happened to equality? – 3: equality and fairness', *The Listener*, 16 May 1974, pp. 629–31

'Scottish nationalism', *The Listener*, 23 May 1974, p. 657

'The fluidity of British party politics today', review article, *The Parliamentarian*, July 1974, pp. 219–21

'Agricultural politics and European integration', *Economic Journal*, 1974

'The BBC and the General Election', *The Listener*, 25 July 1974, pp. 98–9.

'Do we want a referendum?', *The Listener*, 22 Aug. 1974, pp. 226–7

'How much time is left for parliamentary democracy?', *Encounter*, Aug. 1974, pp. 48–52

'The new appeal of nationalism', *New Statesman*, 27 Sept. 1974, pp. 408–12

'Federalism: central/regional Government relations. Canada and Britain', *University of Edinburgh Centre of Canadian Studies*, Seminar papers no. 1, 1974/75, paper 3

'From the House', *Scottish Farming Leader*, Jan. 1975, pp. 22–3

'The case against a referendum', *The Political Quarterly*, **46** no. 1, Jan.–March 1975, pp. 73–82

'The constitutional and political implications of the referendum: in retrospect', *The Three Banks Review*, Sept. 1975, no. 107

'The pastmasters', review article, *The Listener*, 10 Nov. 1975

1976–1978
'Liberty v. equality', *The Illustrated London News*, Feb. 1976, pp. 25–7

'The role of the Secretary of State', *New Edinburgh Review*, 31, Feb. 1976, pp. 9–16

'Scotland', *The Political Quarterly*, **47**, no. 1, Jan. – March 1976, Commentary, pp. 1–2

'Leadership the Wilson way', *Spectator*, 20 Mar. 1979, p. 5

'A state of almost total confusion: Labour Party politics today', *Encounter*, May 1976, pp. 60–64

'Liberty and equality', *The Political Quarterly*, April – June 1976, Commentary, pp. 125–6

'The British Parliament', *Das Parlament*, 6 July 1976

'Speaker and speakers', review of *Mr Speaker, Sir*, by Selwyn Lloyd, *The Listener*, 18 Nov. 1976, p. 655

'Britain's economic problems – do our institutions help or hinder?', *The Political Quarterly*, **47**, no. 4, Oct. – Dec. 1976, Commentary, pp. 373–6

'Is Labour facing catastrophe?', *Encounter*, Jan. 1977

'A passion for tolerance', a review of *Utopia and Revolution*, by Melvin J. Lasky, *The Listener*, 17 Feb. 1977

'The trouble with Stephen Maxwell', *Question*, 15 April 1977, p. 5: (reply to an article by Maxwell, *Question*, 18 Mar. 1977)

'Krise des Parliamentarismus', *Zeitschrift für Parlamentsfragen*, April 1977, pp. 113–18

'Independence or the status quo – must this be the choice?', *The Political Quarterly*, **48**, no. 2, April – June 1977, Commentary, pp. 125–8

'The national interest', *Blackwood's Magazine*, Aug. 1977, pp. 81–2

'Political Power and Isolation', *Books and Bookmen*, Feb. 1978, pp. 18–19

'Britain's malaise: political or economic?', *The Scottish Banker's Magazine*, May 1978

'The killing of the Scotland Bill', *The Political Quarterly*, **49**, no. 2, April – June 1978, Commentary, pp. 127–32

Review of *The Performers: Politics as Theatre*, Norman Shrapnel, *The Listener*, 1 June 1978, pp. 712–13

'Select Committees and the House', *The Listener*, 6 July 1978

Review of *Conservative Essays*, Maurice Cowling (ed.), *The Listener*, 13 July 1978, p. 59

'Has social democracy failed in Britain?', *The Political Quarterly*, **49**, no. 3, July – Sept. 1978

7   Newspaper articles

The Scotsman
'Lessons of Newham', 21 July 1975

'The Government's first session: an interim report', 4 Aug. 1975

Bibliography

'What's to be done about local government?', 1 Sept. 1975

'The case for candour. A preview of the annual conference of the Labour Party', 29 Sept. 1975

'Liberty and equality: getting the balance right', 13 Oct. 1975

'Making the maximum mess of devolution', 24 Nov. 1975

'Obstacles to an effective Assembly', 8 Dec. 1975

'Chrysler: "a disastrous mistake!"', 22 Dec. 1975

'A decade of depression, and the reasons behind it', 5 Jan. 1976

'Devolution fall-out', 19 Jan. 1976

'Unemployment and Britain's industrial future', 2 Feb. 1976

'What kind of Parliament do we want?', 16 Feb. 1976

'Foreign policy: the impotence of ignorance', 1 Mar. 1976

'A watershed for the Left', 15 Mar. 1976

'Federalism without the faults', 29 Mar. 1976

'What Mr Healey's strategy needs', 12 April 1976

'The case for traditional teaching', 26 April 1976

'Making Scottish Parliament more effective than the Commons', 10 May 1976

'Cautious conservatism: the dominant mood in politics', 24 May 1976

'No clear course through sterling crisis', 7 June 1976

'Scottish Government must reform government', 21 June 1976

'The next General Election and beyond', 5 July 1976

'Checkmate in Rhodesia', 19 July 1976

'Mr Healey's palliatives', 2 Aug. 1976

'A cure for corruption?', 16 Aug. 1976

'The case against a referendum', 30 Aug. 1976

'Has poverty enfeebled the parties?', 13 Sept. 1976

'Israel has the right to live', 27 Sept. 1976

268

'Co-operation for the sake of continuity', 11 Oct. 1976

'What chance of "unity" Government?', 25 Oct. 1976

'Politicians under pressure', 8 Nov. 1976

'Putting country before party', 22 Nov. 1976

'Weaknesses of the Devolution Bill', 6 Dec. 1976

'Pitfalls of extreme Conservatism', 20 Dec. 1976

'1977: a time for decisiveness', 4 Jan. 1977

'Modern "barons" in a reformed House of Lords', 17 Jan. 1977

'The real case for workers' directors', 31 Jan. 1977

'Storm in a Number 10 teacup' [on *The Politics of Power* by Joe Haines], 14 Feb. 1977

'Radical who finally lost his way' [on Anthony Crosland], 16 Feb. 1977

'Distrust of devolution – and of democracy', 28 Feb. 1977

'Long-term possibilities of Labour-Liberal agreement', 28 Mar. 1977

'Two keystones of the Labour-Liberal pact', 11 April 1977

'Learning from the success of British agriculture', 25 April 1977

'Leap in the dark with the Tories', 10 May 1977

'How can bureaucracy be kept in check?', 23 May 1977

'Symptoms of impending demise?', 6 June 1977

'Political weakness and the retreat from commitment', 20 June 1977

'Finding comfort in yesterday's battles', 4 July 1977

'God's laws, man's laws and Parliament's responsibilities', 1 Aug. 1977

'"Overload" and compromises that conceal failure', 15 Aug. 1977

'British foreign policy: influence, not power', 29 Aug. 1977

'Will boredom kill the Devolution Bill?', 12 Sept. 1977

'Conservative insecurity on industrial relations', 26 Sept. 1977

'A possible programme for a minority Government', 10 Oct. 1977

Bibliography

'Some second thoughts about compulsory education', 24 Oct. 1977

'When does liberty of the Press become licence?', 7 Nov. 1977

'What Europe can teach us', 22 Nov. 1977

'A desperate future for the Liberal Party', 5 Dec. 1977

'Glasgow belongs to us', 4 Jan. 1978

'How the dynamic of devolution will work', 16 Jan. 1978

'Will the Government bleed to death in Parliament?', 30 Jan. 1978

'Devolution could end patronage problem', 13 Feb. 1978

'Rhodesia: no margin for error', 27 Feb. 1978

'Do some Scots dread democracy?', 13 Mar. 1978

'What would a Conservative Government do?', 8 May 1978

'Can Commons keep new control over Government?', 22 May 1978

'Will the Tories seek to shelve devolution?', 3 July 1978

'Pressures pushing the EEC into a closer union', 17 July 1978

The Times
'Devolution and the break up of the United Kingdom', 27 Sept. 1976

'A bad time for the political warhorses to get a whiff of gunpowder', 8 Nov. 1976

'IMF loan: Is the Cabinet fiddling while Britain burns?', 13 Dec. 1976

'Economic failure, not ideology, is at the root of our political difficulties', 24 Jan. 1977

'Shifting ground in the centre puts moderation out on a limb', 22 Feb. 1977

'When the manifesto turns into a trap', 28 Feb. 1977

'Britain's defence cuts may be putting the West seriously at risk', 4 April 1977

'Them and us: radical policy to heal divisions in British Society', 9 May 1977

'An ominous moment for the Labour Party', 22 July 1977

'Realignment or simply a hindrance to Labour', 22 July 1977

'The Think Tank should have remembered what foreign policy is for', 22 Aug. 1977

'Why crime should not be an election issue', 27 Mar. 1978

'Now is the time for all good men . . . .', 10 April 1978

'Now what future for the SNP?', 24 April 1978

'Danger signs in the retreat from political commitment', 26 Sept. 1977

'Britain still has the image of a reluctant European', 31 Oct. 1977

'Is Parliament trying to prove it does not adequately represent the people?', 5 Dec. 1977

'The need to put Parliament before party', 23 Jan. 1978

'Why it should be an October election', 1 Mar. 1978

'Government limits', 15 May 1978

'The Afrikaner road to disaster', 19 June 1978

'What chance of the real issues coming out in an election?', 24 July 1978

Other newspapers
'So if you do believe in hanging, why doesn't your MP do as he's told?', *Daily Express*, 19 Feb. 1976

'Head on the right, heart on the left – can anyone follow Wilson?', *Evening Standard*, 17 Mar. 1976

'The three tests a new Leader will have to pass', *Daily Express*, 17 Mar. 1976

Review of *Creative Conflict: The Politics of Welsh Devolution*, John Osmond, *Western Mail*, 19 Jan. 1978

Index

Index

Esso Petroleum Company, 202
Europe
  alignments within, 243
  Britain's position in 235–44
  British attitudes towards, 241–2
  definition of, 242
European Community
  British membership of, 14, 163, 164, 194, 241–2, 244–8, 249
  Britain's role in, 15
  currencies of, 252–3, 254–5
  enlargement of, 253–4
European Parliament, 76, 190, 250–1, 254
Evans, Moss, 198
Expenditure Committee, 12, 75

Fabian tradition, 8–9
Falkender, Lady, 48
Fawley Productivity Agreements, The, 202, 214, 219
Figgures, Sir Frank, 122
Finance Bills, 88
Finer, Professor, 23, 148, 209
Flanders, Allan, 202
Foot, Michael, 12, 13–14, 20, 257, 159, 187, 188, 189, 244
foreign affairs, 248–51
Foreign Office, 250
'Foreign Policy Process in Britain, The', 250
'Forty Years On?' 3, 6, 7, 26, 33–46
France
  and Europe, 243
  socialism in, 156
'free' vote, 142
freedom, *see* liberty
French Economic and Social Council, 127–9
Fulton Report, 66, 70
Future of Socialism, The, 9, 13, 41, 222–5
Future That Doesn't Work, The, 228

Gaitskell, Hugh, 4, 6, 7, 8, 13, 39, 40, 43, 155, 193, 222, 224, 228, 232
Galbraith, Professor, 225
Germany
  economy of, 204, 228
  politicians of, 51, 54
  reunion of, 242
  socialist party of, 155
  within Europe, 243
Gilbert, W.S., 49
Gladstone, W.E., 11, 18, 26, 55, 64, 89
  his view of democracy, 101–3
Glasgow University, 2

government
  and pressure groups, 124–5, 134
  attempts at reform of, 65–7
  balance of power within, 62–3
  future development of, 77
  limitations of, 199–202
  party attitudes towards, 68–76
  policy-making machinery of, 125
  public lack of interest in, 75
Government and Politics of Britain, The, 25, 59–77
government departments
  and pressure groups, 114
'Group of Four', 122, 123
growth rates, 8, 22–3, 43, 121, 203, 207, 209, 228, 230, 231
Grunwick's, 217

Hailsham, Lord, 23, 199, 200, 201
Hansard Society, 5, 211
Hardie, Keir, 199
'Has Social Democracy Failed in Britain?', 7, 21, 222–32
Healey, Denis, 183
Health Services, 37, 70, 100, 101
Heath, Edward, 83, 118, 194, 207
  his government, 204–5
historical change
  'materialist conception', 37–8
Hola camp, 41
Holland, Stuart, 172, 222, 226
House of Commons, 6, 11, 12, 55, 62, 79, 80
  and machinery of government, 80–1
  and possible Upper Chamber, 133
  attendance at, 147–8
  basic purpose of, 145–6
  case for increasing powers of, 86–90
  case for reducing powers of, 85–6
  control over finance of, 88
  cost of, 85
  influence on government of, 82
  other effects of, 85
  reform of, 146, 150
  threat to influence of, 90
  unpopularity of, 77–9, 89–90
House of Lords, 64, 131, 134
housing
  local authority, 170, 171, 186–7, 194
Housing Finance Act, 1972, 17, 164
'How much time left for parliamentary democracy?' 46–54
humour, 54–6

Ibadan University, 2, 42
Immigrants Bill, 84
import controls, 172

274

Index

Index